Research Methods
for Edexcel Psychology
Julia Russell & Cara Flanagan

'All you need to know!'

Published in 2005 by:
Nelson Thornes Ltd
Delta Place
27 Bath Road
CHELTENHAM
GL53 7TH
United Kingdom

05 06 07 08 09 / 10 9 8 7 6 5 4 3 2 1

A catalogue record for this book is available from the British Library

ISBN 0 7487 9433 6

Illustrations by Rupert Besley, IFA Design and Angela Lumley
Page make-up by IFA Design

Printed in Croatia by Zrinski

Acknowledgements

The authors and publishers are grateful to the following for permission to reproduce photographs and other copyright material in this book:

Edexcel examination questions are reproduced with kind permission of Edexcel, when Edexcel exam questions are used in conjunction with model answers, suggested answers etc, Edexcel Ltd, accepts no responsibility whatsoever for the accuracy or method of working in the answers given; Clegg, Simple Statistics: A Course Book for Students, 1983, Cambridge University Press p.105; FACS coding table reproduced by permission of Joseph C. Hager, A Human Face. p.70; Runyon, Fundamentals of Behavioural Statistics, McGraw-Hill, Reproduced by permission of the McGraw-Hill Companies p.106; KaSo 12 graphs reproduced by permission of University Psychiatric Services, Laupenstrasse 49, CH-3010 Bern, Switzerland p.75; Clive Wearing picture, used with kind permission from Deborah Wearing, Forever Today, 2005, Doubleday, p.72; Table 1, p. 579 from Significance Ranking of the Spearman Rank Correlation Coefficient by J.H. Zhar, pp. 578-90, Vol. 67, No. 339, September, 1972. Reprinted with permission from the Journal of the American Statistical Association. Copyright 1972 by the American Statistical Association. All rights reserved p.108.

Photo credits:

Aidan Bell, p.49; Alamy, pp.29, 32; Alamy/Bill Brookes, p.33; Alamy/Flashpoint Pictures, p.13; Alamy/Klovenback' p.27; Alamy/Oote Boe Inc, p.33; Albert Bandura, p.25; © Alexandra Milgram, pp.29, 32; Carol Gilligan, p.48; Corbis/Hulton Getty, p.30; FLPA, p.143; From John Henry and his Mighty Hammer by Rozanne Litzinger. Copyright © 1994 by Troll Communications. Reprinted by permission of Scholastic Inc, p.38; Getty Images/Time & Life Pictures/Lilo Hess, p.31; Kobal/Paramount, p.41; Newcast/Camelot, p.10; Nick Kim, p.51; Powerstock/Age Fotostock, p.4; Retna pictures/Andrew Kent, p.9; Rex Pictures/Sipa Press, p.39; Richard Duszczak Cartoon Studio Limited, p.47; Science Photo Library/John Cole, p.112; Science Photo Library/Michael Donne, p.79; The Far Side, Gary Larsen/Creators Syndicate, p.34; William B. Swann, Jr., University of Texas, Department of Psychology, p.13; www.york.ac.uk/depts/maths/histstat/people/, pp.107,108.

Royalty free:

Corbis Royalty Free p.88; Corel 155 (NT) p.1; Corel 250 (NT) pp.12, 51; Corel 283 (NT) p.1; Corel 291 (NT) p.1; Corel 656 (NT) p.27; Image 100 MRC pp.44, 64; Image 100 SD (NT) p.82; Image 100 EE (NT) pp.35, 66; Photodisc 2 (NT) p.70 (both); Photodisc 6 (NT) p.28; Photodisc 10 (NT) p.52; Photodisc 41(NT) p.10; Photodisc 43 (NT) p.68; Photodisc 44 (NT) p.28 (both); Photodisc 45 (NT) pp.22, 100; Photodisc 46 (NT) p.18; Photodisc 50 (NT) pp.4, 54 (both); Photodisc 56 (NT) p.26; Photodisc 67 (NT) p.57; Photodisc 73 (NT) pp.1, 12; Ruberball WW (NT) p.6; Tom LeGoff/Digital Vision HU (NT) p.14.

Every effort has been made to contact copyright holders, and we apologise if any have been overlooked. Should copyright have been unwittingly infringed in this book, the owners should contact the publishers, who will make corrections at reprint.

Contents

Acknowledgements

First and foremost a huge thanks to Hugh Coolican for answering all of our picky questions with picky answers, and always being ready to help.

Thanks also to so many different people who have contributed ideas, jokes, comments … Adrian Frost, Sara Berman, Beth Black and those unsung others from whom we have stolen ideas and forgotten the source.

Julia and Cara would also like to thank each other for invaluable enthusiasm and support!

And finally the team at Nelson Thornes have provided the enthusiastic backup I have come to expect: Rick Jackman, Nigel Harriss and Tracy Hall who are such a delight to work with.

Dedication

To all my students, past and present, with special thanks to Carly Telford and Laura Evans and all the other girls at The Queen's School who have allowed me to use their work in this text. JR

To my daughter Philippa who kept me company over the hot summer during which I wrote the bulk of this book. And also to the rest of the family: Rob and Jack, and Rosie. CF

Special thanks to the guinea pigs

This book has benefited enormously from the feedback given by the teachers and students of Bristol City College (Tony Willner, Maria Kamba and Lana Crosbie), Claires Court School (Sara Berman) and St Mary Redcliffe & Temple School (Grace Pittman and Rob Endley). They kindly had a go at using the first draft of this book and gave me invaluable feedback.

How to use this book

This book is intended to form the basis of a short course in research methods for covering AS coursework Edexcel and A2 research methods examination questions on Units 5 and 6, which can be based on material in either the AS or the A2 specification content. Both of these are covered in full. It contains many activities, loads of questions and exam questions, with student answers and examiner's comments.

Experience has found that the length of time needed to cover each of the four main chapters is between 4 and 10 hours, depending on how many of the activities you do. Many questions/activities can be set as homework. You may do the course all at once (which may be too much) or spread it out over weeks or even months.

This book does not cover everything there is to know about research methods in psychology but intends to do enough for the Edexcel AS coursework and A2 examination components. If you wish to read more, we recommend a range of books listed in the reference section.

This book aims to provide a thorough understanding of the required concepts. Some users have commented that there is too much depth in some areas, but this has been necessary in order to ensure that students do understand what often appear to be deceptively simple concepts. Students and teachers who have used this book report that the activities made them think a lot, that they felt they really came to understood research methods, and that they found the book interesting and humorous!

So sit back and enjoy yourself.

EXTRAS

There is an Edexcel student workbook to go with this book. Students can use this to record details of all the terms in the book and then use this booklet for revision. You can download this booklet from the Nelson Thornes website (www.nelsonthornes.com/researchmethods).

Also available is a set of answers to all the Qs questions.

In addition, you can obtain from the website a Word file containing templates for certain activities as well as other resources such as graphs, tables, etc., wherever you see this icon .

Introduction

When you were deciding to take psychology at AS, you probably asked yourself the question 'What do psychologists actually do?' Hopefully, you could now give an answer such as 'They try to explain why people do certain things'.

But this begs the question, 'How?' From your AS coursework, and the research methods covered in each of the approaches, you might be able to give the answers below. By the end of this course, you will know for certain.

> One way to conduct research is to ask people why they do what they do, or ask them what they think and feel. This method of conducting research is called an **interview**.
>
> We will look at how to conduct interviews in Chapter 3.

> We can also explore the thoughts, feelings or behaviours of one person in detail. This is called a **case study**.
>
> We will look at this method in Chapter 4

> Or they could write a **questionnaire** containing a variety of questions.
>
> This research method is also looked at in Chapter 3.

> If we want to find out about people through the things they say or write (like reports of their dreams) we can use **content analysis**.
>
> We will learn about this in Chapter 4

> If we want to know what causes people to do certain things, we have to conduct an **experiment**.
>
> There are different kinds of experiment, which are the topic of Chapters 1 and 2.

> Another way to conduct research is to watch what people do. This method of conducting research is called an **observation** or observational study.
>
> We will look at observational studies in Chapter 4.

Qs   **1**

1. Think about how you might conduct your own research.

   The topic is television advertisements. The question is 'What adverts are most effective?'. Suggest **two or more** ways in which you might investigate this research question.

2. What would be the aim of this research?

*Every study has a **research aim** – what it is that the researcher wants to find out, which may include one or more research questions.*

All of these are **research methods** – ways of finding things out in a systematic manner.

Once we have decided on a **method**, we need to **design** the particulars.

Research design is like designing a room – it is the plan of what you are going to do.
Try to bear this in mind – there are research methods and research designs (experimental design, the design of observations, the design of questionnaires, etc.).

These are all bathrooms – but each one has a different **design**.

Symbols used in this book

Qs   **1**

On most spreads, there are questions for you to answer.
Suggested answers can be found at www.nelsonthornes.com/researchmethods

 Activity 1   **A simple experiment:**

Activities are indicated with this symbol and sometimes accompanied by this icon which indicates that the materials can be found on the website if you wish to print extra copies.

The box on the right identifies the terms (key terms and other terms) that you should record notes on in your Edexcel student workbook, which can be found on the Nelson Thornes website. When you have finished this book, you will have a set of revision notes that you have made.

Key terms to record:
(these are terms that you must know)
Aims
Research method

Other terms to record:
(these are terms that are not part of the specification so exam questions will not use these terms, although you will need them when answering questions)

EXPERIMENTS

Contents

Experiments 1

What is an experiment?

An experiment is a way of conducting research where:

One **variable** is made to change (by the experimenter)

(This is called the **independent variable** or **IV**)

The effects of the IV on another variable are observed or measured

(This variable is called the **dependent variable** or **DV**).

*A variable is just a thing – something that can change.
For example, noise is a variable. It can be soft or loud.*

You actually know all about experiments – you conduct them without thinking. For example, when you start a new class with a new teacher, you see how he or she responds to your behaviour – you might make a joke or hand your homework in on time (both IVs) to see whether the teacher responds well (the DV). You are experimenting with cause and effect.

Activity 1

A simple experiment: Does noise affect memory?

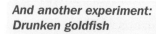

The variable we are going to change (the **IV**) is noise.

The variable we are going to measure (the **DV**) is performance on a memory task.

You will need a radio and two lists of 20 words each. You can use the right-hand wordlist on page 14. There are 40 words in the list.

Divide your class in half: Group N (noise) and Group S (silent).

Group N should have the radio playing very loudly when they are shown the list of words. They have 1 minute to try to remember them and then 1 minute to write them down.

Group S should do the same task, in silence, with the second list of words.

Which group remembered most words?

And another experiment: Is performance affected by expectation?

If you want people to perform better, does it help to lie to them about the quality of materials they are using? Do people perform better if they think the materials they are using are better?

A study by Weick *et al.* (1973) tested this by telling two jazz bands (Band A and Band B) that the piece of music they were rehearsing was either (1) by a composer whose work was well respected or (2) by a composer whose work had been negatively reviewed. Weick *et al.* found that people performed better if they thought they were playing a well-respected work. Participants also remembered the piece better and liked it better.

However, this finding might be because Band A was actually a better band than Band B. To overcome this problem, the experiment was designed so that both bands played both musical pieces: Piece 1 and Piece 2.

Band A were told that Piece 1 was by the superior composer and Piece 2 was by the inferior composer.

Band B were told that Piece 1 was by the inferior composer and Piece 2 was by the superior composer.

Many things that are called experiments are actually investigations. An experiment must have an IV and a DV.

And another experiment: Drunken goldfish

Many early psychology experiments focused on learning in animals. The learning involved simple mazes where the animal was rewarded if it turned in the desired direction at the end of a maze shaped like a Y.

In one experiment, goldfish were trained in a maze and afterwards placed in a water solution high in alcohol. Some of them keeled over.

When the goldfish were retested a week later, those goldfish who had not been exposed to alcohol could remember the maze task perfectly, but those who blacked out in the alcohol solution had no memory for the task. This demonstrates the severe effects of alcohol on learning (Ryback, 1969).

Psychology has been plagued by many foolish experiments – of which this is one. Don't try it at home.

Qs 2

1. Think of some other variables, and for each say how they can vary.
2. *Does noise affect your memory?*
   a. What was the IV?
   b. What was the DV?
   c. What was the aim of this experiment?
3. *Drunken goldfish*
   a. What was the IV?
   b. What was the DV?
4. *Is performance affected by expectation?*
   a. What was the IV?
   b. What was the DV?
   c. What was the aim of this experiment?

KEY TERMS

Aim
Dependent variable
Experiment
Independent variable
Variable

Activity 2 — Reading in colour – the Stroop effect

Students should work in pairs. One person (the participant) reads the word lists while the other person (the experimenter) times how long it takes to read each list (all mobile phones have timers so this should be easy to arrange!).

 Instructions:

1 Participants should read the practice list first so both participant and experimenter can practise what they have to do:

- Cover up lists 1–4.

- Participants should state the colour of the word, not what the word says. For example, for the word 'BLUE' they should say 'red', for the word 'BROWN' they should say 'brown'.

- Participants should take great care to say the colour correctly and not race against the clock. Mistakes should be corrected.

- The experimenter should check that the words are read correctly. In order to do this, a non-colour version is printed below.

- The experimenter says 'start' to signal to the participant to begin reading the first list.

- The participant says 'stop' at the end of the list, so the experimenter can record how long it took to read the list.

2 Participants should now read the remaining lists. Each time, they should cover up the other lists and follow the same instructions as above.

Practice	List 1	List 2	List 3	List 4
green	blue	blue	green	red
blue	red	green	purple	blue
brown	brown	purple	blue	green
red	purple	red	green	red
blue	blue	brown	blue	brown
brown	green	red	brown	blue
green	brown	blue	purple	green
blue	red	green	red	purple
brown	blue	brown	blue	brown
purple	purple	purple	green	red
blue	red	brown	blue	purple
green	green	purple	red	blue
purple	brown	red	brown	purple
green	green	blue	purple	brown
purple	brown	red	green	purple
red	purple	green	brown	blue
blue	red	blue	purple	green
purple	blue	brown	red	brown
red	brown	purple	brown	blue
green	green	green	red	brown
purple	blue	purple	blue	red
blue	purple	red	purple	green
red	red	green	brown	red
green	green	blue	green	brown
red	brown	red	purple	green
brown	green	brown	blue	purple
blue	purple	blue	red	red
green	red	green	brown	blue
brown	blue	brown	green	purple
blue	purple	purple	red	green
stop	stop	stop	stop	stop

Practice	List 1	List 2	List 3	List 4
brown	red	blue	green	brown
green	blue	green	purple	red
red	green	purple	blue	brown
purple	brown	red	green	purple
red	purple	brown	blue	green
brown	blue	red	brown	purple
green	red	blue	purple	brown
blue	brown	green	red	brown
red	green	brown	blue	red
blue	red	purple	green	purple
purple	purple	brown	blue	green
red	red	purple	red	brown
purple	blue	red	brown	green
green	brown	blue	purple	red
purple	purple	red	green	blue
red	red	green	brown	purple
green	green	blue	purple	red
red	purple	brown	red	green
purple	blue	purple	brown	red
green	purple	green	red	blue
purple	brown	purple	blue	green
blue	green	red	purple	brown
green	brown	green	brown	blue
brown	red	blue	green	purple
blue	green	red	purple	blue
purple	purple	brown	blue	red
blue	brown	blue	red	green
green	blue	green	brown	purple
brown	purple	brown	green	blue
purple	blue	purple	red	brown
stop	stop	stop	stop	stop

When you have finished, turn the page for the next step …

A debriefing

You no doubt realized that in lists 1 and 4, the colour words were written in conflicting colours, which made these lists take longer to read than lists 2 and 3. This is called *The Stroop effect* after a study first conducted by J. Ridley Stroop in 1935. You can read his original article at http://psychclassics.yorku.ca/Stroop/.

Qs   **3**

1. What was the IV?
2. What was the DV?
3. What were the aims of this experiment?
4. Did you guess what the aims of the experiment were?
5. Draw a bar chart to show your class findings.

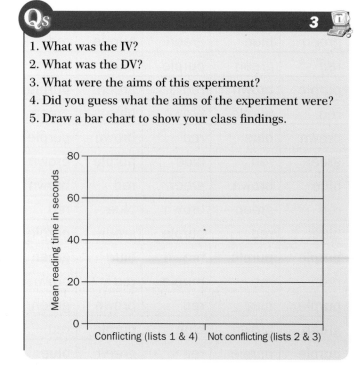

People who take part in an experiment are called **participants**. *Psychologists used to use the term 'subjects'.*

Explanation of the Stroop effect

The interference between the different information (what the words say and the colour of the words) that your brain receives causes a problem. One way to explain this is in terms of automatic processing – we read words automatically so when trying to name the colours, we cannot help but read the words, and this causes interference.

A way to test this is to see if children who are only just learning to read have as much difficulty with the task. They can read the words, but reading is not yet an automatic activity and therefore they are not as affected by the conflict. Try this out on some small children who know their colours but cannot yet read! We would imagine that the children would not get confused by this puzzle because the words would not be read automatically. Research studies support this expectation.

The Stroop effect is not just an interesting phenomenon, it is also useful. It is used to identify people with brain-damage because they find the task more difficult than non-brain damaged people.

Stroop's findings

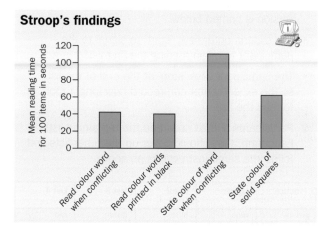

Pilot studies

If you tried one or more of the experiments, you were probably aware that there were flaws. Did you realize beforehand that there would be flaws? Or did some of the flaws become apparent after conducting the experiment? If you did not try these experiments, can you think what flaws there might be?

It is always a good idea to conduct a **pilot study** before the experiment proper. A pilot study is a small-scale trial of a research design run before doing the real thing. It is done in order to find out whether certain things do not work. For example, participants may not understand the instructions or they may guess what the experiment is about, or they may get very bored because there are too many tasks or too many questions.

OTHER TERMS

Pilot study

Qs   **4**

Consider that the experiments you have conducted were pilot studies.

Suggest one thing you might change about each of the experiments so they worked better.

Hypotheses

A **hypothesis** states what you believe to be true. It is a precise and testable statement of the relationship between two variables.

The hypothesis for Stroop's experiment is:

'People take longer to state the colour of a word when it is written in a conflicting colour than when the word and the colour it is written in are the same.'

OR *'It takes longer to read a list of conflicting words than non-conflicting words.'*

The hypothesis is sometimes called the **experimental hypothesis** (H_1) or the **alternative hypothesis** (alternative to the null hypothesis H_0).

A hypothesis is not the same as the research aims.

When writing your own hypothesis it is essential that you say how the variables were measured or manipulated. This is called operationalisation -see page 11.

Qs 5

1. Write a hypothesis for the experiment on noise and performance on a memory task. 1+1+1
2. State whether your hypothesis is directional or non-directional and explain why you choose this kind of hypothesis. 1+1
3. What were the aims of this experiment? 1
4. For each of the following, decide whether it is a directional or a non-directional hypothesis:
   a. Boys score differently on aggressiveness tests from girls. N
   b. Students who have a computer at home do better in exams than those who do not. D
   c. People remember the words that appear early in a list better than the words that appear later. D
   d. People given a list of emotionally charged words recall less than participants given a list of emotionally neutral words. D
   e. Hamsters are better pets than budgies. D
   f. Words presented in a written form are recalled differently from those presented in a pictorial form. N
5. Now write your own. For each of the following experiments, write a directional and a non-directional hypothesis, and a null hypothesis:
   a. A study to find out whether girls watch more television than boys.
   b. A study to see whether teachers give more attractive students higher marks on essays than students who are less attractive.
   c. A study to investigate whether lack of sleep affects schoolwork.

3+3+3

Directional and non-directional hypotheses

A **directional hypothesis** states the kind of difference or relationship between two conditions or two groups of participants.

A **non-directional hypothesis** simply predicts that there will be a difference or relationship between two conditions or two groups of participants.

Directional	People take *longer* to state the colour of a word when it is written in a conflicting colour than when the word and the colour it is written in are the same.
Non-directional	Performance speeds are *different* when people state the colour of a word when it is written in a conflicting colour than when the word and the colour it is written in are the same.
Directional	People who do homework *without* the TV on produce *better* results than those who do homework with the TV on.
Non-directional	There is a *difference* between work produced in noisy or silent conditions.

One-tailed and two-tailed
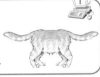
Some people say 'one-tailed' instead of 'directional' and 'two-tailed' instead of 'non-directional'. When you look at a one-tailed cat you know which way it is going.

The null hypothesis (H_0)

In some circumstances (that you don't need to bother about), there is a need to state a null hypothesis – this is a statement of *no difference* or *no relationship* between the variables.

For example:

• There is no difference between work produced in noisy or silent conditions.

• There is no relationship between age and intelligence.

NOTE: *A hypothesis should concern populations and not samples. These concepts are explained on page 10.*

Why have directions?
Justifying the use of directional and non-directional hypotheses

Why do psychologists sometimes use a directional hypothesis instead of a non-directional one?

Psychologists use a directional hypothesis when past research (theory or study) suggests that the findings will go in a particular direction.

Psychologists use a non-directional hypothesis when past research is unclear or contradictory.

KEY TERMS
Directional hypothesis
Experimental/alternative hypothesis
Hypothesis
Non-directional hypothesis
Null hypothesis
One-tailed hypothesis
Two-tailed hypothesis

EXPERIMENTS

Repeated measures and independent groups design

The experiment on noise and memory is an example of an **independent groups design.**

Each participant was tested in only one condition (noise or no noise).

There were two separate (independent) groups of participants.

We could redesign this as a **repeated measures design**.

Each participant would be tested in both conditions. They would be tested in the noise condition and retested in the no noise condition.

	Noise condition			No noise condition		
Independent groups	Sara	Rob	Mike	Linda	Pip	Janet
	Paul	Sue	Sam	Chris	Rosie	Jack
Repeated measures	Sara	Rob	Mike	Sara	Rob	Mike
	Paul	Sue	Sam	Paul	Sue	Sam

Qs 6

Noise and memory

1. Write a suitable hypothesis for the new version of the experiment that uses a repeated measures design.

2. Explain why you think that the repeated measures design would not be as good as the independent groups design.

Stroop effect

3. How could you do this study as an independent groups design?

4. What might be the disadvantage of using an independent groups design for this experiment?

Alcohol and goldfish

5. Was this an independent groups design or a repeated measures design?

Is performance affected by expectation?

6. Was this an independent groups design or a repeated measures design?

7. What do you think was the advantage of choosing this design?

For each of the following experiments, state whether it is a repeated measures or an independent groups design.

To do this, ask yourself, 'Would the findings be analysed by comparing the scores from the same person or by comparing the scores of two (or more) groups of people?' (Write your answer down.)

8. Boys and girls are compared on their IQ test scores. *I*

9. Hamsters are tested to see if one genetic strain is better at finding food in a maze than another group. *I*

10. Reaction time is tested before and after a reaction time training activity to see if test scores improve after training. *R*

11. Participants are tested on a memory task in the morning and in the afternoon. *R*

12. Three groups of participants are each asked to remember different word lists (one with nouns, one with verbs and one with adjectives) to see which is easier to recall. *I*

13. Participants are asked to give ratings for attractive and unattractive photographs. *R*

[6]

Repeated measures
Same participants in each condition (noise or no noise).

Independent groups
Two (or more) groups of participants, one for each condition.

*These are called **participant** (or **experimental**) **designs.***

The experiment on the Stroop effect was an example of a **repeated measures design**.

Each participant was tested on both conditions (i.e. variations of the IV) – words that were either conflicting or not conflicting.

Learning about research methods is a bit like learning a foreign language. When you learn a foreign language, you have to learn a new set of words and more especially what they mean. One of the best ways to do this is to speak the language – the same is true for research methods. Don't hold back, start using the words.

Try this one

In Stroop's original study, the participants had two word lists: one of colour words in a conflicting colour, the other was of colour words printed in black. There were two groups of participants:

- Group 1 read conflicting colour and then black words.

- Group 2 read black and then conflicting colour words.

This was done to control for practice and fatigue (called **order effects**, as you will see on the next page).

Is this now an independent groups design, or is it still a repeated measures?

It is still repeated measures because the analysis still involves comparing the same individual's performance on two conditions (conflicting colour and black words).

Repeated measures

Disadvantages

1. One of the memory tests may be more difficult than the other and this is why the participants do better in one condition (the noise condition) than the other (no noise condition).
2. When the participants do the second memory test, they may guess the purpose of the experiment, which may affect their behaviour. For example, some participants may purposely do worse on the second test because they want it to seem as if they work better in noisy conditions.
3. The order of the conditions may affect performance (an **order effect**). Participants may do better on the second test because of a **practice effect** OR participants may do worse on the second test because of being bored with doing the same test again (**boredom** or **fatigue effect**).

Advantages

You can work out the advantages by looking at the disadvantages of independent groups design.

Independent groups

Disadvantages

- No control of **participant variables** (i.e. the different abilities of each participant). For example, participants in Group 1 might be more able than those in Group 2.
- You need twice as many participants.

Advantages

You can work out the advantages by looking at the disadvantages of repeated measures design.

Matched participants design

This is a third kind of experimental design. It involves the use of independent groups, but each participant in Group A is paired with one in Group B. This is done by pairing participants on key variables (e.g. IQ, memory ability, gender – any characteristic that might affect the findings) and then placing one member of each pair into each group.

Disadvantages

- Very time-consuming to match the participants.
- May not control all the participant variables.

Advantages

- Controls some participant variables.
- Participants won't guess study's aims.

Dealing with the problems created by repeated measures design

Dealing with point 1.

You can make sure the tests are equivalent. Create a list of 40 words and **randomly allocate** these to two lists so both lists are equivalent.

Dealing with point 2.

You can lie to the participants about the purpose of the test to try to prevent them guessing what it is about. This is called a **single blind** design (the participant is blind to the aim of the study).

Dealing with point 3.

You can use **counterbalancing** (see right).

Dealing with the problems created by independent groups design

1. Randomly allocate participants to conditions to ensure that the groups are equivalent (see 'randomness' on page 10).

2. Match participants in each group on key variables (see below).

Counterbalancing

Counterbalancing ensures that each condition is tested first or second in equal amounts, as we did for the Stroop effect (see page 5). If participants read a conflicting list first and then a non-conflicting list, we might expect them to read the second list more quickly because they had had more practice.

There are two ways to counterbalance order effects:

Way 1. Counterbalancing

Group 1: the participants do the conflicting list first and then the non-conflicting words.

Group 2: participants do the non-conflicting list first and then the conflicting list.

This is still a repeated measures design even though there are two groups of participants because a comparison will be made for each participant on their performance on the two conditions (conflict and no conflict).

Way 2. ABBA

Condition A: conflicting lists.

Condition B: non-conflicting list.

Each participant takes part in every trial.

Trial 1: Conflicting list A

Trial 2: Non-conflicting list (B)

Trial 3: Non-conflicting list (B)

Trial 4: Conflicting list A

Counterbalancing literally means achieving balance by having an equal weight at both ends.

*A **participant variable** is a factor that could affect the DV that is caused by differences between participants (e.g. in mood or ability) - apart, of course, from the IV.*

Qs 7

1. Which of the two forms of counterbalancing (1 or 2) did we use in the experiment on the Stroop effect on page 5?
2. What participant variables might have affected the findings of the Stroop effect study?
3. To what extent were these participant variables controlled?
4. Look back to the experiment 'Is performance affected by expectation?' on page 4. Counterbalancing has been used here, although not for order effects. Explain in what way this design is counterbalanced.
5. *A psychologist conducted a study to see whether visual imagery helps memory. To do this, there were two lists to be recalled – one had words only, the other had images instead of words.*
   a. Describe how you could conduct this study using (a) a repeated measures design, (b) an independent groups design and (c) a matched pairs design.
   b. Which design would be best? Explain your answer.
   c. For which kind of design would counterbalancing be necessary?
   d. Explain how you would design the counterbalancing.

KEY TERMS

Counterbalancing
Participant variables
Advantages ☺ and disadvantages ☹ of
Independent groups design
Matched participants design
Repeated measures design

OTHER TERMS

Boredom effect
Fatigue effect
Order effect
Practice effect
Random allocation
Single blind design

Selection of participants

When conducting any research study you need to find some participants!

Participants are drawn from **'the target population'**: the group of people that the researcher is interested in.

This is a selection or **sample** of the target population.

Researchers make generalisations about the target population from the sample as long as the sample is *representative of the target population* (i.e. represents the target population).

*All sampling methods aim to produce a **representative** sample but are inevitably **biased**.*

Opportunity sample

How? Ask people walking by you in the street, i.e. select those who are available.

☺ The easiest method because you just use the first participants you can find.

☹ Inevitably biased because the sample is drawn from a small part of the target population. For example, if you do an experiment using people in the street, the sample is selected from people walking around the centre of a town – not those who work, or those living in rural areas.

A sampling method is about how participants are identified NOT about who eventually takes part. For example, in an opportunity or random sample, some potential participants may refuse to take part. The remaining participants are 'volunteers'.

This is not true for all opportunity/random samples as in a field experiment described in chapter 2, where participants cannot refuse.

Volunteer sample

How? Advertise in a newspaper or on a noticeboard.

☺ Access to a variety of participants.

☹ The sample is biased because the participants are likely to be more highly motivated and/or have extra time on their hands (= **volunteer bias**).

Random sample

How? Put the names of the target population into a hat and draw out the required number.

☺ Unbiased: all members of the target population have an equal chance of selection.

☹ You usually end up with a biased sample (e.g. more boys than girls) because the sample is usually too small (see Activity 3).

Quota sample

How? Subgroups within a population are identified (eg boys and girls or age groups: 10-12, 13-14 etc.). Then an opportunity sample (quota) is taken from each subgroup

☺ More representative than an opportunity sample because equal representation of subgroups.

☹ Although the sample represents the subgroups, each quota taken may be biased in other ways.

Systematic sample

How? Selecting every nth person from a list of the target population.

☺ Sample is spread evenly across the population, avoiding bias.

☹ The sample may be unrepresentative if the systematic basis does not allow for all subgroups within the population to be captured e.g. if every 10th person is always sitting at the front of the class.

Many students mistake a **systematic sample** for a random sample – selecting every 10th person is not random, it is a systematic method of selection. However, if you select a number using a random method and start with this person and then you select every 10th person, this would be a random sample.

If you want equal numbers of girls and boys (or 10 and 11th years, etc.), one way to do this is to put all the boys' names in hat and draw out 5, and do same for the girls' names. This is called a **stratified sample**.

Randomness

The most obvious way to obtain a random selection is to draw numbers or names *'out of a hat'*. It is sometimes called the 'lottery method'.

Random selection is used to obtain a **random sample** of participants (as described above) or for the **random allocation** of participants to conditions when using an independent measures design (as described on the previous page). For random allocation, for example, you put all the participants' names into a hat and draw out half of the names for group 1 and place the remaining names in group 2.

Random means that each member of the population has an equal chance of being selected.

Activity 3 — How random is random?

Take 40 pieces of paper and write 20 boys' names and 20 girls' names.

Put them in a hat and draw out 10 slips of paper. If the selection is unbiased, you should ideally get five boys and five girls.

Put the slips of paper back and draw 10 out again. Repeat this a total of four times and then try it with a larger sample. Each time, record how many boys' and girls' names were drawn. You can record your results in the table below.

	Sample size 10				Sample size 20				Total
Trial no:	1	2	3	4	1	2	3	4	
Boys									
Girls									

The point is that, in principle, random selection results in an unbiased and representative sample, but only if the sample is large enough.

Is this what you found? What happens if you put 40 boys' names and 40 girls' names in the hat?

Key terms

Advantages ☺ and disadvantages ☹, and how to do:

Opportunity sample
Quota sample
Systematic sample
Random sample
Volunteer sample
Sampling technique

Other terms

Random allocation
Stratified sample
Target population
Volunteer bias
Research prediction

Operationalisation

Qs 8

1. Look back to page 7, Question 5. You were asked to write a hypothesis for three studies. Now write an aim and a research prediction for each of these three studies.

2. *A psychologist conducted a study to look at whether watching certain films made children more helpful (one film was about being helpful, the other was neutral). He advertised for participants in the local newspaper. A large number of children volunteered, and a sample of 30 was selected for the actual experiment.*

   a. What is the IV in this experiment? *1 (IV) 1 (levels)*

   b. What is the DV? *1*

   c. How could you operationalise the DV? *max 2*

   d. State a suitable hypothesis and/or research prediction for this study. *1 + 1 op.*

   e. Is your prediction directional or non-directional? *1*

   f. Explain your choice of direction. *1*

   g. What kind of experimental design would you use in this study? *1*

   h. Describe **one** disadvantage of this experimental design.

   i. How could you deal with this problem?

   j. Describe the target population.

   k. What kind of sample was obtained?

   l. Suggest how the experimenter might select the sub-sample from all those who applied.

3. *A psychology experiment aims to investigate how preschool children differ from those already at school in terms of their ability to remember symbols that look like letters.*

   a. If the experimenter wanted to obtain a random sample of each of the two age groups, how might this have been done?

   b. Explain the purpose of using a random sample.

   c. What is the IV in the experiment?

   d. What is the DV?

   e. The children were shown 20 different symbols. Why was it better to use 20 symbols rather than just two?

   f. Why might it be better to use two rather than 20 symbols?

4. *Mary Smith organises a project to enable her psychology class to have a go at using a matched pairs design. The class is divided into two groups; one will receive word list A (nouns) and the other word list B (verbs). They will be tested on recall.*

   a. Suggest **two** participant variables that could be used to match the classmates.

   b. Explain why each of the variables you chose would be important to control in this study.

   c. What are the two conditions in the experiment?

   d. If Mary decided to use an independent measures design, suggest **two** ways in which participants could have been allocated to the conditions.

   e. The teacher used words that were all of two syllables and of similar length. Give **one** reason why.

   f. The teacher decided to repeat the study using all the pupils in the school. She selected every fifth pupil on the register. Why is this not a random sample?

A 'good' hypothesis should be written in a testable form, i.e. in a way that makes it clear how you are going to design an experiment to test the hypothesis.

Think back to the Stroop effect. Stroop's research aim was to investigate the effects of interference on performance speeds. To turn this aim into an experiment, he needed to state his belief:

Hypothesis *People take longer to perform a task when word and colour conflict with each other than when they do not.*

The concept of 'interference' has been **operationalised** in order to produce a testable hypothesis ('interference' = 'word and colour conflict'). 'Operationalisation' means specifying a set of operations or behaviours that can be measured or manipulated. For example:

Hypothesis *People work better in quiet rather than noisy conditions.*

What precisely do we mean by 'work better' and 'quiet' and 'noisy'? We need to define the operations:

'work better' = obtain a higher score on a memory test
'quiet' = no sound
'noisy' = radio playing.

Operationalised hypothesis *People obtain a higher score on a memory test when tested in quiet (no sounds) rather than noisy (radio playing) conditions.*

Hypothesis *People are happier if they work.*

'happier' = higher score on happiness questionnaire
'work' = have a full-time job (over 40 hours per week).

Operationalised hypothesis *People obtain a higher score on a happiness questionnaire if they work full time (over 40 hours per week) than if they work part time (less than 20 hours per week).*

Don't make the mistake of confusing the terms hypothesis and research prediction. There is an important difference. A hypothesis is a general claim about the world. In order to test a hypothesis, we need a prediction about how the participants in a study will behave.

The **hypothesis** is about **populations** (people). It states our expectation about the world. It can be operationalised.

The **research prediction** is about **samples** (participants). It predicts what we expect to find in a study. It is stated in the future tense and must be operationalised.

Qs 9

1. *Do older people sleep more or less than younger people?*

   a. Identify the IV and DV in this experiment.

   b. How could you operationalise the IV and DV?

   c. Write a fully operationalised directional hypothesis.

   d. Write a fully operationalised non-directional hypothesis.

2. *People rate food as looking more attractive when they are hungry.* Answer questions a–d above.

3. *A teacher wishes to find out whether one maths test is harder than another maths test.* Answer questions a–d above.

Experimental control

EXPERIMENTS

There are DVs and IVs, and then there are extraneous variables . . .

Order effects are an **extraneous variable**.

For example, in the noise and memory experiment (*repeated measures design*), noise (IV) should affect recall (DV).

1. Participants do the memory test with noise.

2. Participants do the memory test without noise.

They do better on the second test.

Is this because they do better when tested without noise? (Noise/no noise is the IV.)

Or because they have *practised* doing the test? (Practice/no practice has become an alternative and unintentional IV.)

Practice/no practice is an extraneous variable.

The experimenter 'controls' the IV in an experiment – making it change to see what happens. The experimenter also has to control other variables (**extraneous variables**) to make sure they do not change – otherwise this may spoil the experiment.

*An **extraneous variable** is a variable other than the IV that may affect the DV and should thus be controlled. The term is used interchangeably with the term **uncontrolled variable**.*

*Extraneous variables include **participant variables** and **situational variables**. A situational variable ia a factor in the environment that could affect the DV, so should be controlled.*

*A **confounding variable** is a variable other than the IV that has affected the DV and has thus confounded the findings of the study.*

Qs 10

1. In the repeated measures study described above, how could you control the extraneous variable?

2. In the independent groups study described on the right, how could you control the extraneous variable?

3. Look at the examples in 'Still more extraneous variables'. Which are participant and which are situational variables?

4. A researcher conducts a study on memory for words. During the study she identifies various extraneous variables which are listed below. Which are participant and which are situational variables?

   P a. Some of the sample are tested just before lunch and are hungry so do not concentrate on the task.

   S b. Other participants are tested early in the morning before the lab heating has come on so it is very cold.

   P c. One person has travelled by train but it was delayed and they arrive very flustered.

   S d. There are posters on one wall of the lab with words on that act as cues to help the participants with the memory task.

another extraneous variable . . .

Noise and memory experiment (*independent groups design*)

Group 1 do the noisy test in the morning.

Group 2 do the test without noise in the afternoon.

Group 2 do better on the test.

Is this because people do better when tested without noise? (Noise/no noise is the IV.)

Or because people do better on memory tests when tested in the afternoon?

Time of day has become a substitute IV – it is an extraneous variable.

still more extraneous variables . . .

Consider the Stroop effect study. Imagine that each participant is tested individually. In this situation, there may be both **situational** and **participant extraneous variables**.

S • Some participants are tested in a noisy classroom, whereas others are tested in a quiet one-to-one situation.

P • One participant is wearing tinted glasses.

P/S • Some participants are uncertain so the experimenter offers to help them fill in the answer sheet.

S • In later test sessions the sun is setting and making the test room glow orange.

All of these variations may affect participant performance and may affect the DV.

*Standardised procedures include **standardised instructions** – the instructions given to participants about what to do*

and a final extraneous variable . . .

Finally, we can consider **investigator effects.** The behaviour of an investigator/experimenter may affect the participants and thus affect the DV.

For example, the way in which the investigator asks a question may *lead* the participant to give the answer the investigator 'wants'.

Or the way in which the investigator responds may encourage certain kinds of response. For example, the investigator may smile as if to say 'Yes, that's the right answer'.

How to deal with this extraneous variable

Experimenters use **standardised procedures** to ensure that all participants receive the same instructions and to prevent the experimenter affecting participants' behaviour, for example by using leading questions.

Standardised procedures are like a recipe – if different procedures are used, the different outcomes may be due to the procedures and not the IV.

How to deal with investigator effects

Investigators use **standardised instructions** to prevent using leading questions.

Or you can use a **double blind** design – neither the participant nor the person conducting the experiment (who has not designed it) knows the aims of the experiment; therefore, the experimenter cannot affect the participants' performance.

The way in which an investigator asks a question (the words used, the tone of voice, the facial expression) may affect the responses that are given.

Confederates

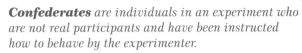

The IV in an experiment is sometimes a person.

For example, you might want to find out if people respond differently to orders from someone wearing a suit or dressed in causal clothes. In this experiment, the IV would be the clothing worn by a 'friend' of the experimenter. The experimenter would arrange for a person to give orders either dressed in a suit or dressed casually. This person is called a **confederate**.

Confederates are not always an IV; they may simply help to guide the experiment.

Confederates are individuals in an experiment who are not real participants and have been instructed how to behave by the experimenter.

The woman on the left in the photograph (a confederate) talks 'blirtatiously' (loudly and effusively) to see what this effect this has on the person who is studying.

Ethics

In your study of psychology, you will be aware of ethical criticisms. Many studies are criticised for lack of ethics. It is not acceptable for participants to be harmed during the course of any experiment.

What, however, constitutes 'harm'? Is it harmful for a person to experience mild discomfort or mild stress?

Is it acceptable to lie to participants about what an experiment is about? Such deception may be necessary so that participants' behaviour is not affected by knowing the aim of the experiment.

One way to deal with deception is to **debrief** participants afterwards. At the start of an experiment, participants are briefed about what the task will involve. At the end, they are debriefed.

This debriefing has two functions:

1. *Ethical*: It is an opportunity to reassure the participant about their performance. If any deception took place, participants are told the true aims of the study and offered the opportunity to discuss any concerns they may have. They may be offered the opportunity to withhold their data from the study.
2. *Practical*: The debrief allows the researcher to thank individuals for participating. The experimenter may ask for further information about the research topic. For example, he or she may ask why the participant found one condition more difficult, or may ask whether the participant believed the set-up.

The **brief** is given to each participant prior to the study and serves to explain to them what they will be required to do. It should contain sufficient detail about the study for the participant to give informed consent – they have to know what they are letting themselves in for.

A **debrief** is conducted after the experiment for ethical and practical reasons.

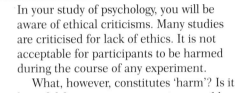

This experiment may damage your health

Briefing for an experiment

This experiment is concerned with reading coloured print. Some people find it harder to identify certain colours. You will be shown five word lists and asked to identify the colours of the written words.

Qs   11

1. Who was the confederate in Milgram's study of obedience (if you are not familiar with this study, see outline on page 29)?
2. Why do you need to 'brief' participants?
3. Why is it necessary to debrief participants?
4. Why would it be necessary to deceive participants in the study described on the left?
5. Imagine you were given the briefing and debriefing shown here. What answers would you give to Questions 3 and 4?

Debriefing

Thank you for taking part in the experiment. The true purpose of the study was to find out if it takes longer to identify the word colour when the word and colour are conflicting. This is called the Stroop effect.

1. Would you like to know the overall findings from the study?   YES/NO

2. Did you feel distressed by any aspect of the study?   YES/NO

3. What did you think the purpose of the study was?

4. Did you think that some of the lists were harder to read than others?   YES/NO
   If yes, which lists?

5. Do you think this might have affected your performance?   YES/NO
   If yes, in what way?

DIY: Design it yourself

Two possible activities are suggested on this page. They enable you to try to design and conduct your own experiment. Questions 12 will guide you in designing and conducting your experiment.

Activity 4 — Memory and organisation

A favourite experiment for students is one that concerns organisation and memory. If words are presented to a participant in categories (as shown on the near right), they are more easily memorised than if they are presented in a random order (list on the far right).

Qs — 12

Design decisions to make – answer these questions for either Activity 4 or Activity 5 (whether or not you are actually doing the activities).

1. What is the IV and what is the DV?

2. How should the IV be operationalised?

3. How will the DV be operationalised (i.e. how will you measure it?)?

4. Should you use repeated measures or independent groups? Write down the relative advantages/disadvantages of each.

5. Write a suitable aim and hypothesis for your study and a research prediction.

6. How many participants will you need?

7. How will you select these participants? (For ethical reasons, you should only use participants over the age of 16.)

8. Are there any extraneous (situational or participant) variables that need to be controlled?

9. How will you control these?

10. After you have conducted the study, record the findings for each participant in a table.

11. What do you conclude from your findings?

Activity 5 — Emotion

One theory of emotion proposes that we experience general levels of physiological arousal and label these as love, attraction, fear, stress, etc. according to the cues that are available. For example, if you are physiologically aroused (e.g. from watching a scary movie) and at the same time are in the presence of an attractive man or woman, you might feel the arousal is because that person is attractive to you.

One experiment that tested this arranged for participants to run on the spot for one minute (creating physiological arousal) and then rate a set of photographs for attractiveness. Those people who did not run on the spot gave lower ratings than those who did (White *et al.*, 1981).

Does this photograph look more attractive to someone who has been running on the spot for a minute?

Organised list	Random list
Dogs	Pear
Labrador	Beagle
Beagle	Clarinet
Boxer	Hail
Spaniel	Rain
Fruit	Drinks
Apple	Rose
Pear	Squash
Plum	Hand
Orange	Boxer
Weather	Iron
Snow	Coke
Rain	Gold
Sleet	Harp
Hail	Piano
Flowers	Metal
Daffodil	Apple
Rose	Body
Pansy	Fruit
Tulip	Instruments
Instruments	Daffodil
Harp	Plum
Piano	Nose
Flute	Weather
Clarinet	Copper
Drinks	Labrador
Water	Water
Milk	Flowers
Squash	Brass
Coke	Foot
Body	Tulips
Nose	Pansy
Foot	Dogs
Toe	Sleet
Hand	Milk
Metal	Orange
Brass	Toe
Gold	Snow
Copper	Flute
Iron	Spaniel

*A **conclusion** is the statement(s) you make about human behaviour (populations) on the basis of your research study with a small set of participants (a sample). Conclusions should be written in the present tense and be about 'people' rather than 'participants'.*

Selection of materials

In any study, the researchers need some materials, such as visual stimuli, stories or questionnaires. The validity of the experiment relies in part on how well selected these materials are. If the choice is representative of the participant's day-to-day experiences then the study is more likely to have **mundane realism** (which is explained in the next chapter). For example, if you were testing memory for words, as in activity 1, a list of psychological terms might have relevance for a group of psychology students but be completely irrelevant for a group of geographers. Furthermore, aspects of the materials may cue the participants to guess the purpose of the study, that is, they provide **demand characteristics** (another concept that will be explained more fully in the next chapter). In Activity 5 above, if some of the photos are obviously attractive and others obviously not, the aim might be more apparent than if there was an even spread of differing attractiveness. It is therefore important to choose wisely.

Descriptive statistics: how to represent your data

*There are three ways to **describe** the data that you found from your research: Measures of central tendency; Graphical representation; Measures of dispersion.*

Measures of central tendency

Measures of central tendency inform us about central (or middle) values of a set of data. There are three different 'averages' – ways of calculating a typical value for a set of data.

The **mean** is calculated by adding up all the numbers and dividing by the number of numbers.

☺ It makes use of the *values* of all the data.

☹ It can be misrepresentative of the numbers if there is an extreme value.

☹ It can only be used with **interval** or **ratio** data (see page 95).

The **median** is the *middle* value in an *ordered* list.

☺ It is not affected by extreme scores.

☺ It can be used with **ordinal data**.

☹ It is not as 'sensitive' as the mean because not all values are reflected in the median.

The **mode** is the value that is *most* common.

☺ It is useful when the data are in categories (such as number of people who like pink), i.e. **nominal data**.

☹ It is not a useful way of describing data when there are several modes.

Graphical representation

A picture is worth a thousand words! Graphs provide a means of 'eyeballing' your data and seeing the findings at a glance.

Bar chart: The height of the bar represents frequency. Unlike a histogram, you can exclude empty categories. There is no true zero, and data on the horizontal axis are not continuous. Suitable for words and numbers.

Histogram: Essentially a bar chart except that the area within the bars must be proportional to the frequencies represented and the horizontal axis must be continuous. *There should be no gaps between bars.*

*There are three ways to **describe** the data that you found from your research.*

Measures of dispersion

A set of data can also be described in terms of how dispersed, or spread out, the numbers are.

The easiest way to do this is to use the **range**. Consider the data sets below:

3, 5, 8, 8, 9, 10, 12, 12, 13, 15

mean = 9.5   range = 12 (3 to 15)

1, 5, 8, 8, 9, 10, 12, 12, 13, 17

mean = 9.5   range = 16 (1 to 17)

The two sets of numbers have the same mean but a different range, so the range can help us to describe the data. If we just used the mean, the data sets would appear to be the same.

The **range** is the difference between the highest and lowest numbers.

There are more informative methods of expressing dispersion, called the **variance** and the **standard deviation**. These measure the spread of the data around the mean. This can be calculated using a mathematical calculator.

The variance is the average variation around the mean (the average difference from the mean of each score). The standard deviation is the square root of this figure. Both of these tell us about the spread of the scores. When two groups of data (e.g. levels of the IV) have a similar dispersion of scores they will have similar variances (and similar standard deviations). So why have two different measures? The calculation of variance involves squaring the difference between each score and the mean, as a consequence it is a big number. The standard deviation, being the square root of the variance, returns the value to the same numerical domain as the initial data set so standard deviations are easier to compare to the original scores.

The standard deviation for the two sets of numbers above is 3.69 and 4.45 respectively. Which data set looks more varied and which has the greater standard deviation?

	Advantages	Disadvantages
Range	Provides you with direct information Easy to calculate	Affected by extreme values Does not take into account the number of observations in the data set
Standard deviation	More precise measure of dispersion because all values are taken into account	May hide some of the characteristics of the data set (e.g. extreme values)

Qs 13

1. For each of the data sets below, calculate the (a) mean, and (b) median and (c) mode, (d) state which of these would be most suitable to use and why.

Data set	
1.	2, 3, 5, 6, 6, 8, 9, 12, 15, 21, 22
2.	2, 3, 8, 10, 11, 13, 13, 14, 14, 29
3.	2, 2, 4, 5, 5, 5, 7, 7, 8, 8, 8, 10
4.	cat, cat, dog, budgie, snake, gerbil

2. Why is it better to know about the mean and range of a data set rather than just the mean?

3. Explain why it might be better to know the standard deviation of a data set rather than the range.

4. Standard deviation tells us on average how close each of the numbers is to the mean – it tells us how a set of numbers are distributed around the mean. Look at the following data sets. Which one do you think would have the *smaller* standard deviation?

Data set A: 2 2 3 4 5   9 11 14 18 20 21 22 25

Data set B: 2 5 8 9 9 10 11 12 14 15 16 20 25

KEY TERMS

Measures of central tendency
Range
Standard deviation
Variance
Nominal data
Ordinal data
Interval data
Ratio data

NOIR (see page 98 for an explanation)
Bar chart
Histogram
Measures of dispersion

More on graphs

A graph should be simple. It should clearly show the findings from a study.

There should be a short title.

The *x* axis must be labelled (the *x* axis goes across the page; it is usually the IV).

The *y* axis must be labelled (the *y* axis goes up vertically; it is usually the DV or 'frequency').

Always use squared paper if you are hand-drawing graphs.

Aims, procedures, findings and conclusions

When psychologists conduct research, they write a report of their study that contains the following information: **aims** (the intended area of study), **procedures** (a description of the **standardised procedures** so that the study can be repeated), **findings** (the data or results produced by the study) and **conclusions** (an interpretation of the findings).

This is an example of a finding:

> Participants obtained a higher score when tested in the no noise condition.

This is an example of a conclusion:

> The findings suggest that people work better on memory tasks when there is little noise.

The distinction is subtle but important. One is a fact about the *participants*, the other is a generalisation made about what *people* do. Like the distinction between a hypothesis and a research prediction, findings are about *samples*, conclusions are about *populations*.

Qs 14

1. Why is Graph A meaningless?
2. Write a title that would be suitable for all three graphs.
3. Describe the *y* axis of all three graphs.
4. A class of psychology students studies the Stroop effect and produces the following data showing the time taken (in seconds) to read each kind of word list:

Student	1	2	3	4	5	6	7	8	9	10	11	12	
Colour conflict	29	25	20	26	22	31	28	28	26	28	21	29	27
No conflict	20	16	14	20	18	21	20	17	20	19	15	16	18.5

  (a) Calculate the mean, median, mode and range for each data set.
  (b) What measure of central tendency would be most suitable to use to describe this data?
  (c) The standard deviations were as follows: colour conflict (3.48) and no conflict (2.34). What does this tell you about the data sets?
  (d) Draw both a bar chart and a histogram to represent the data from this study.

Each of the graphs below presents the data collected in an experiment on organisation and memory.

Only one of these graphs is useful; two of them are a 'waste of time' – which one is the useful one?

Graph A

Participant number 1 in the organised word group is placed next to participant number 1 in the random word group. Students like to draw 'participant charts' BUT THEY ARE TOTALLY MEANINGLESS.

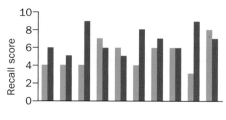

■ Organised word list ■ Random word list

Graph B

The findings from each participant are shown in this graph. They are grouped together so that you can see all the scores from participants in the organised word group and all the scores from the participants in the random word group.

This is *slightly better* than Graph A because we can just about tell that the random word list led to better recall – but a glance at the means (as in Graph C) shows this effortlessly.

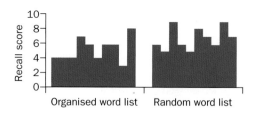

Graph C

This graph shows the mean scores for each group. The findings are clear, which is the point of using a graph.

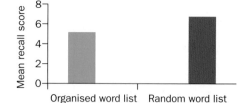

Note: *the horizontal axis of a graph is called the x axis, and the vertical axis is called the y axis.*

OTHER TERMS
Procedures
Findings

Multiple choice questions

1. The independent variable in a study is
   a. The one that is excluded.
   b. The one that is manipulated by the experimenter.
   c. The one that is observed or measured.
   d. Not of interest to the experimenter.

2. A pilot study is
   a. The first study conducted by a research team.
   b. A preliminary investigation.
   c. A small-scale trial run of a research design.
   d. A research project on efficient flying of aeroplanes.

3. Which of the following hypotheses is a non-directional hypothesis?
   a. Participants in the no noise condition do better on the memory test than those in the noise condition.
   b. Participants who drink alcohol have a slower reaction time than those who have no alcohol.
   c. Participants like words that are familiar more than those that are not familiar.
   d. Participants who expect to perform better perform differently from those given lower expectations.

4. One reason for using a directional hypothesis is because
   a. Past research suggests that participants will do better on one condition than another.
   b. Past research is uncertain about how participants will perform.
   c. There is no past research.
   d. The researcher wants to make a strong statement.

5. An extraneous variable is a variable that
   a. Has been controlled by the experimenter.
   b. Confounds the findings of the study.
   c. May influence the dependent variable.
   d. The experimenter wants to find out more about.

6. A student plans to investigate the effects of practice on IQ test performance. Some participants are given two practice tests prior to the IQ test, whereas others do no test beforehand. The dependent variable in this study is
   a. The participants.
   b. The effects of practice.
   c. The IQ test performance before the study.
   d. The IQ test performance at the end of the study.

7. The study described in question 6 is
   a. A repeated measures design.
   b. An independent groups design.
   c. A matched pairs design.
   d. A careful design.

8. In an independent groups design
   a. There are two or more separate groups of participants.
   b. The analysis involves comparing measures from two or more separate groups of people.
   c. The analysis involves comparing two measures from the same person.
   d. Both a and b.

9. One advantage of doing a matched pairs design is
   a. You need fewer participants than for repeated measures.
   b. You can control some participant variables.
   c. Order effects are not a problem.
   d. Both b and c.

10. The letters 'ABBA' refer to a research design
    a. Created by a Swedish rock band.
    b. To control participant variables.
    c. To counterbalance for order effects.
    d. To control extraneous variables.

11. All sampling methods are
    a. Representative of the target population.
    b. Biased.
    c. Random.
    d. Difficult to conduct.

12. Selecting participants who just happen to be available is called
    a. Opportunity sampling.
    b. Volunteer sampling.
    c. Random sampling.
    d. Quota sampling.

13. Which of the following could not be an extraneous variable in a study
    a. An investigator effect.
    b. A confederate.
    c. An order effect.
    d. A lack of standardised procedures.

14. One way to improve the design of a study is to:
    a. Conduct a pilot study beforehand to see if some things do not work.
    b. Have lots of variables.
    c. Use a repeated measures design.
    d. Use a confederate.

15. Which of the following is a disadvantage of using a repeated measures design?
    a. It does not control participant variables.
    b. You have to use more participants than for an independent groups design.
    c. There are more likely to be investigator effects than for an independent groups design.
    d. There may be order effects.

16. In an experiment, half the participants do Condition A first followed by Condition B, whereas the other participants do the conditions in the reverse order. This procedure is called
    a. Countercontrol.
    b. Countercalling.
    c. Counterbalancing.
    d. Counteracting.

17. An individual who is instructed about how to behave by the researcher, often acting as the IV, is called
    a. An extraneous variable.
    b. A dependent variable.
    c. The investigator.
    d. A confederate.

18. Which of the following is a random sample?
    a. Names drawn from a hat.
    b. Asking people if they would like to take part.
    c. Using every 10th name on a register.
    d. Taking whoever happens to be there.

19. Which of the following is a measure of central tendency?
    a. Range.
    b. Bar chart.
    c. Mode.
    d. Interval.

20. Debriefing involves
    a. Telling a participant the true aims of a study.
    b. Giving participants a chance to discuss any psychological harm they may have experienced.
    c. Asking participants for feedback about the experiment.
    d. All of the above.

Answers are on page 21

Exam-style question for chapter 1

1. SOURCE MATERIAL

One area of psychological research concerns prejudice – people make biased judgements of another person's abilities based on ethnic group, age, gender, etc.

Many studies have looked at the effects of gender. For example, in one experiment participants were asked to mark students' essays. Those essays supposedly written by boys were given higher marks, on average, than girls' essays.

A group of psychology students decided to repeat this research to see if students today were still prejudiced about gender. The researchers selected four essays (Essay 1, Essay 2, Essay 3, Essay 4). All the essays had been given a C grade by their teacher.

The participants were divided into two groups. For Group 1, Essays 1 and 2 were given girls' names and Essays 3 and 4 were given boys' names. For Group 2, this was reversed.

Participants were asked to give a mark out of 10 to the essays, where 10 was excellent. The mean scores for boys and girls essays are shown in the graph below.

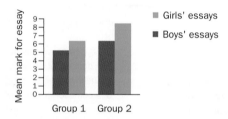

(a) (i) Write a suitable experimental hypothesis for this study. *[2]*

   (ii) Identify whether your hypothesis is directional or non directional (one-tailed or two-tailed) and explain why you chose such a hypothesis. *[2]*

(b) Which participant (experimental) design is being used in this study? *[2]*

(c) Identify **one** method of selecting participants for this study and describe **one** advantage and **one** disadvantage of using this method. *[1 + 2 + 2]*

(d) Various factors, apart from the IV, could influence the marks allocated by the participants.

   (i) Identify **two** such factors that the students should have considered. *[2]*

   (ii) Suggest how **one** of these could have affected the findings from the experiment if the essays were not selected carefully. *[2]*

(e) Explain why the experiment was designed so that half the participants had girls' names for essays 1 and 2 and the other half had girls' names for Essays 3 and 4. *[2]*

(f) (i) What measure of central tendency was used to describe the findings? *[1]*

   (ii) Explain why this measure was used to give the average for this data. *[2]*

(g) Describe **one** finding and **one** conclusion that can be drawn from the bar chart. *[2]*

[Total 25 marks]

In your answers to this question you should include relevant information from the whole of your course, where appropriate.

2. A researcher devises an experiment to measure activity during dreaming by recording rapid eye movements (REM) of participants during different states of sleep. She records the number of REMs per minute.

(a) Identify a suitable method for selecting participants and justify why you use it in this situation. *[2]*

(b) (i) What is meant by a 'measure of dispersion'? *[1]*

   (ii) Name **two** measures of dispersion. *[1]*

   (iii) Which measure of dispersion would you use in the situation above and why? *[1]*

(c) (i) Define the term 'operationalisation'. *[1]*

   (ii) How has activity during dreams been operationlised? (1 mark)

(d) (i) The researcher would need to brief the participants before the experiment. Why is this necessary? *[2]*

   (ii) Write a suitable brief for participants in this study. *[1]*

   (iii) Participants would also need to be debriefed at the end of the study. Explain **two** functions of the debrief. *[2]*

[Total 11 marks]

TOTAL FOR SECTION: 36 MARKS

Examiner's tips

Question 1

The number of marks available for each part of the question indicates the amount of detail required. When there are 2 marks available, you should ensure that you give more than a brief answer – you need to provide further details, such as saying more than 'measure recall' if asked to describe the dependent variable in an experiment or more than saying 'it is easy' as an advantage of opportunity sampling.

(a) (i) Remember that the hypothesis should be about populations and not samples. And it should be in the present and not the future – it is not a research prediction. However note that this is 'should' and not 'must'. You will still receive credit for a hypothesis about samples and in the future tense.

(a) (ii) This is effectively one mark for identifying whether the hypothesis is directional or non-directional (one- or two-tailed) and a further two for the justification.

(b) Note that to gain the mark you do not have to justify your choice on this question.

(c) If you are asked to provide 'one' of anything, for example 'one method' as in this question, and you provide more than one answer, there is a risk that only your first answer will be considered by the examiner OR none of your answers will be considered. This is because with one word answers you could simply list every word you can think of and one of them might be right.

(d) (i) Here you are being asked for two ideas. There aren't any 'right answers' although some ideas, such as handwriting, are more obviously important than others. Don't try to make your answer 'special' and risk losing easy marks.

(d) (ii) Again there are no 'right answers' but there are sensible ways to earn marks. Will the factor you have chosen make people's judgments more or less accurate, or just more random? Make sure that you explain why.

(e) This is a case of having to use your knowledge – the answer is related to counterbalancing.

(f) (i) Remember that your answer must be either mean, median or mode.

(f) (ii) Note that the question is referring to this study, it is not asking for general reasons – you must apply your answer to the data collected here.

(g) Students find it difficult to distinguish between findings and conclusions. Conclusions are about people (rather than participants) and are stated in the present tense (rather than the past tense). They are statements made about the target population on the basis of what was found with the selected participants. There are two marks for the findings and two for conclusions.

Question 2

(a) Make sure that your justification is appropriate to this study (i.e. the answer does have to be contextualised).

(b) (i) This requires a definition – you need to learn these.

(b) (ii) You should know at least three possible answers to this so shouldn't find this difficult – but read part (iii) first before deciding which two to write about.

(b) (iii) To answer this question correctly you must identify the level of measurement.

(c) (i) Again you need to have learned this definition – it is one of your key terms.

(c) (ii) You can find this answer in the source text about the sleep experiment.

(d) (i) This answer needs to explain the function of briefing. The answer does not have to relate to the question, although this might help – though you want to avoid using material that would be relevant to (d)(ii).

(d) (iii) Again, this question is asking for an explanation of function as in (d)(i) and, similarly, does not have to relate to the question, although this may make answering the question easier.

Model answer* for exam-style question

Question 1

1. (a) (i) Write a suitable hypothesis for this study.   [2]

Essays that appear to be written by boys get higher marks than essays written by girls.

   (ii) Identify whether your hypothesis is directional or non-directional and explain why you chose such a hypothesis.   [3]

The hypothesis is directional. I chose this because past research suggests that boys will do better.

(b) Which participant (experimental) design is being used in this study?
                                                                        [1]

Repeated measures.

(c) Identify **one** method of selecting participants for this study and describe **one** advantage and **one** disadvantage of using this method.   [5]

One method would be to use an opportunity sample.

One advantage is that it is easy because you just use the first participants you can find and this saves time.

One disadvantage is that the sample is biased because it is drawn from a small part of the target population.

(d) Various factors could influence the marks allocated by the participants.
   (i) Identify **two** such factors that the students should have considered.   [2]

Handwriting and essay length.

   (ii) Suggest how **one** of these could have affected the findings from the experiment if the essays were not selected carefully.   [2]

Some handwriting looks more 'girlie' than others and this effect might have been more important than the effect of telling the participants which essays were written by boys and by girls so, although stereotypes about gender could have been important, these might not have shown up in the results.

(e) Explain why the experiment was designed so that half the participants had girls' names for Essays 1 and 2 and the other half had girls' names for Essays 3 and 4.   [3]

This design would counterbalance any order effects. For example, if everyone had the same essays with girls' names, it might be that those essays were slightly worse and this would act as an extraneous variable.

(f) (i) What measure of central tendency was used to describe the findings?   [1]

The mean.

   (ii) Explain why this measure was used to give the average for this data.   [2]

The mean takes all the values of the scores into account, and it can be used with these numerical data.

(g) Describe **one** finding and **one** conclusion that can be taken from the bar chart.   [4]

The participants in both groups gave lower ratings to the girls, lower by 1 mark of 10 in group 1 and lower by 2 marks out of 10 in group 2. These findings suggest that people do have gender biases against women and they were consistently given lower marks for their essays.

Examiner's comments

(a) (i) 1 mark would be given for 'Essays that appear to be written by boys get higher marks' because this alternative hypothesis is incomplete.

(a) (ii) If your answer to the first part of this question is wrong, you will get no marks for the second part. You would get no marks for saying 'because I said that boys would do better than girls' as this explains the direction but does not justify it. You would get 1 mark for saying 'I chose this because past research suggests it'.'

(b) If you used an alternative term for repeated measures, such as 'within groups', you would still gain the mark.

(c) You would get only 1 mark for an advantage that said 'it is easy'. Easier than what? Why is it easy?

   For the disadvantage, you again need to provide detail. An answer that said 'because the sample is biased' would only get 1 mark because the same is true for all sampling methods.

(d) (i) The factors don't have to be justified.

   (ii) This answer makes two points, that handwriting styles differ, and also explains how this could affect the results.

(e) This is the only question worth 3 marks so you have to be sure to squeeze out some extra material for those extra marks. Just saying 'counterbalance' would only receive 1 mark. You need to explain this concept and make sure you place it in the context of this study (in other words, if you just describe the principle of counterbalancing, you will not get full marks).

(f) (i) A short answer is all that is needed.

(f) (ii) This is just about OK but does rely rather heavily on defining the term rather than explaining *why* it was used. Two answers have been given here, which is fine because no number was specified in the question (if the question was 'Give **one** advantage of using this measure of central tendency' then only one advantage would be credited).

(g) Note that in both cases there is considerable detail provided. Basically you need *at least* one idea per available mark.

*A model answer is an answer that would get full marks. However, it is not the only possible answer that would get full marks, it is simply one possible answer.

Question 2

(a) Identify a suitable method for selecting participants and justify why you would use it in this situation. *[2]*

A volunteer sample could be used because it would make finding participants easier than random sampling as not everyone who was selected in a random sample would be willing to sleep in a lab.

(b) (i) What is meant by a 'measure of dispersion'? *[1]*

A way to judge how spread out or clumped together the points are around the middle of the data.

(ii) Name **two** measures of dispersion. *[1]*

The range and standard deviation.

(iii) Which measure of dispersion would you use in the situation above and why? *[1]*

The standard deviation because REMs per minute is an interval scale so this is the best one to use.

(c) (i) Define the term 'operationalisation'. *[1]*

It means saying exactly what to do to manipulate or measure a variable consistently.

(ii) How has activity during dreams been operationlised? *[1]*

Recording rapid eye movements (REM) per minute of participants.

(d) (i) The researcher would need to brief the participants before the experiment. Why is this necessary? *[2]*

To ensure that they knew what to expect in the study so that they could give their informed consent.

(ii) Write a suitable brief for participants in this study. *[1]*

You will need to spend the night asleep in a lab with recording electrodes stuck to your eyes. They cannot harm you and you will still be able to open your eyes. The electrodes will record the movements of your eyes while you are asleep and this information will be stored in a computer. No one will be able to link your name to your data. Are you happy to participate?

(iii) Participants would also need to be debriefed at the end of the study. Explain **two** functions of the debrief. *[2]*

To explain the true purpose of the study if the participants were deceived and ask participants if they agree for their results to be included. Also to ask the participants questions about what they thought or felt that might help the experimenter to understand the results.

Examiner's comments

(a) This identifies a suitable method although other answers could have earned marks, such as opportunity or random sampling. It also justifies the choice in the context of this experiment by making a contrast with another sampling method, which is a good way to do this. This justification would be different for other choices of sampling method.

(b) (i) The phrase 'clumped together' isn't very technical, but the point is clear.

(b) (ii) Variance would have been a third choice.

(b) (iii) This is just enough for two marks, ideally 'best' could have been expanded – best because it is more informative than the range.

(c) (i) This answer makes the point that it's about specifying variables.

(c) (ii) This would not have earned the mark if 'per minute' had been missed out.

(d) (i) This answer contains the two key ideas in one sentence: giving sufficient information and getting real (i.e. informed) consent.

(d) (ii) This is a good answer, with more detail than necessary. It would have been sufficient to explain the purpose of the electrodes and ask participants if they would participate.

(d) (iii) This explains the two essential reasons: ethical and practical reasons.

Answers to MCQs from page 17

1b	2c	3d	4a	5c	6d	7b	8d	9d	10c
11b	12a	13b	14a	15d	16c	17d	18a	19c	20d

Contents

More about experiments

field experiments and natural experiments

Field experiments

In Chapter 1, we considered experiments. All experiments have an independent variable and a dependent variable.

There are different kinds of experiment:

Laboratory experiment
An experiment conducted in a *special environment* where variables can be *carefully controlled*. Participants are aware that they are taking part in an experiment, although they may not know the true aims of the study.

Field experiment
An experiment conducted in a more *natural environment*, i.e. 'in the field'. As with the laboratory experiment, the independent variable is still *deliberately manipulated* by the researcher. Participants are *often not aware* that they are participating in an experiment.

Field study
Any study that is conducted in a natural environment. Note that not all studies conducted in a laboratory are experiments. There are controlled observations that are conducted in a laboratory (which we will look at in Chapter 4).

*An experiment permits us to study **cause and effect.** It differs from non-experimental methods in that it involves the manipulation of one variable (the independent variable – IV), while trying to keep all other variables constant. If the IV is the only thing that is changed, then it must be responsible for any change in the dependent variable (DV).*

Qs 15

1. What are the research aims of the experiment on the left?

2. How do you know it is an experiment?

3. How do you know it is a field experiment?

4. Write a suitable hypothesis for this experiment.

5. Why should the same person dress in the two different outfits (instead of using two confederates)?

6. What is a 'confederate'?

7. What method did you use to select your participants?

8. Give **one** advantage and **one** disadvantage of using this method of selecting participants.

9. What was the experimental design that you used?

10. Can you think of **one** ethical issue raised in this study (i.e. something that may harm participants)?

11. Name a suitable measure of central tendency to use with your data and explain why.

12. Present your data in a table like the one below.

	Smartly dressed	Casually dressed
Passer-by said 'yes'		
Passer-by said 'no'		

13. Draw a graph to illustrate your findings.

14. What do you conclude?

Activity 6 — A field experiment

A number of studies have investigated the effects of appearance on behaviour, for example:

Bickman (1974) left a dime in a telephone box. If the experimenter was dressed in a suit, he got the dime back 77% of the time; if he was wearing unkempt work clothes, there was a 38% return rate.

Bickman also found that New York pedestrians were more likely to obey someone dressed as a guard than someone in a milkman's uniform or casually dressed. The confederates issued orders to passers-by to 'Pick up this bag for me', 'This fellow is overparked at the meter but doesn't have any change; give him a dime' , or 'Don't you know you have to stand on the other side of the pole?'.

In these field experiments, the IV is appearance and the DV is helping behaviour.

For Activity 6, students may work in pairs. One member of the pair is the observer and the other is the confederate who wears one of two outfits:

1. Smartly dressed.
2. Casual.

The task is to ask people if they would be prepared to stop and answer some questions for a school project.

If the passer-by says 'no', then thank them.

If the passer-by says 'yes' then explain that this was an experiment for your school work and all you wished to know was whether they were prepared to help or not.

The observer should record :

1. How many passers-by said yes or no for each condition (smart or casual).
2. Any other comments made by passers-by.

Lab versus field experiments

It may help you to understand the difference between lab and field experiments by looking at the examples on this page.

A Helping behaviour was investigated in a study on the New York subway. A confederate collapsed on a subway train and investigators noted whether help was offered. The confederate was either holding a black cane or carrying a paper bag with a bottle of alcohol and smelled of alcohol (thus appearing drunk). Piliavin *et al.* (1969) found that when the victim carried a cane, 95% of bystanders helped within 10 seconds; if he appeared drunk, help came in only 50% of the trials.

B Participants were asked to wait in a room before the experiment began. There was a radio playing either good or bad news, and a stranger was present. When participants were asked to rate the stranger, the degree of liking was related to the kind of news they had been listening to, showing that people are attracted to others who are associated with positive experiences (Veitch and Griffitt, 1976).

C The participants were children aged 3–5 years old. Each child was taken on their own to a special room where there were lots of toys including, in one corner, a 5-foot inflatable Bobo doll and a mallet. The experimenter invited the 'model' to join them and then left the room for about 10 minutes. Half of the children watched the model playing aggressively with a life-sized Bobo doll while the others watched the model play non-aggressively with the doll. Later they were given an opportunity to play with toys, including the Bobo doll, and were observed through a one-way mirror. The children who saw the aggressive behaviour were more likely to behave aggressively (Bandura *et al.*, 1961; see right).

D One group of school pupils were given information about how their peers had performed on a maths task. They were either told that their peers had done well or that they had done poorly on the test. The children were later given a maths test in class. Those who expected to do well did better than those led to expect they would do poorly (Schunk, 1983).

E The Hawthorne Electric factory in Chicago asked researchers to study what factors led to increased worker productivity. The study found that increased lighting led to increased productivity – but then also found that decreased lighting led to increased activity (Roethlisberger and Dickson, 1939).

The conclusion was that the participants knew they were being studied and this interest in their work was what explained their increased output, masking the real IV. This has been called the **Hawthorne effect**.

F Participants were tested in their teaching room, given nonsense trigrams (e.g. SXT) and then asked to count backwards until told to stop. The participants were then asked to recall the trigram. The counting interval was used to prevent the trigram being rehearsed. When the counting interval was 3 seconds, participants could recall most trigrams; when it was 18 seconds, they could not recall many trigrams (Peterson and Peterson, 1959).

Lab experiments are artificial or 'contrived'

- Participants know they are being studied, and this is likely to affect their behaviour.

- The setting is often not like real life. This is described as being low in **mundane realism**. People behave more like they 'normally' do when a study is high in mundane realism.

- The IV or DV may be operationalised in such a way that it does not represent real-life experiences, e.g. using trigrams to test how memory works.

For all these reasons, participants in a laboratory experiment are less likely to behave as they would in real life.

The same problems may also arise in field experiments; so that field experiments are not necessarily more like real life then laboratory experiments.

Mundane realism refers to how an experiment mirrors the real-word. 'Mundane' means 'of the world', commonplace, ordinary.

Qs 16

For each of the examples on the left (A–F), answer the following questions:

1. Identify the IV and DV.
2. Was the task required of participants artificial?
3. Was the study conducted in a natural setting?
4. Was the setting high or low in mundane realism?
5. Did the participants know they were being studied?
6. Were the participants brought into a special (contrived) situation, or did the experimenter go to them?
7. What relevant variables might not have been controlled?
8. Do you think this was a lab or a field experiment?

Field experiments are not all good

Field experiments may be more natural but it is more difficult to control extraneous variables in the 'field'.

There is also a major ethical issue – if participants do not know they are being studied, is it right to manipulate and record their behaviour?

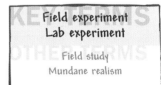
KEY TERMS
Field experiment
Lab experiment
OTHER TERMS
Field study
Mundane realism

Validity: internal validity

Losing sight of the wood for the trees

Does it matter whether an experiment is classified as a field experiment or a lab experiment? No. What matters is an understanding of the bigger picture:

- *Participant awareness.* Awareness factors are threats to **internal validity**.

- *Experimental control.* Lack of experimental control is a threat to **internal validity**.

- *Artificiality (low mundane realism)* is a threat to **external validity** (which we will look at on pages 28 and 29).

*The term **'validity'** refers to how true or legitimate something is.*

The dog hates Maths homework

Every time you start to do your Maths homework your dog starts to howl. You think it's because he doesn't like you doing your maths homework – but this is an invalid effect. Actually it's because the neighbours have a she-dog round every Wednesday evening and as it happens Maths homework is also set on a Wednesday. The same thing happens in psychology experiments!

Internal validity is the degree to which an observed effect is due to the experimental manipulation rather than other factors such as extraneous variables.

If internal validity is low, the results have little value.

Internal validity in an experiment is concerned with the following questions:

- Did the IV produce the change in the DV?

- Or was the change in the DV caused by something else?

High internal validity means that the differences that were found between groups on the DV in an experiment were directly related to what the researcher did to the IV and not due to some other unintended variable (confounding variable). Internal validity is also an issue in questionnaire or observational studies, see chapter 4.

Participant effects

Why don't we want participants to be aware that they are participating in a study? Knowing that you are being studied (increased attention) may act as an alternative IV (a **confounding variable**), as it did in the Hawthorne study. This is known as the **Hawthorne effect** (see page 25).

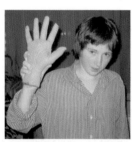

Participants want to offer a helping hand. If they know they are in an experiment, they usually want to please the experimenter and be helpful; otherwise, why are they there? This sometimes results in them being over-cooperative – and behaving artificially.

The opposite effect is also possible when a participant deliberately behaves in such a way as to spoil an experiment. This is sometimes called the '**screw you effect**.'

Social desirability bias is a form of participant reactivity. Participants wish to present themselves in the best possible way and therefore may not behave according to personal preference but behave in the most socially acceptable way for the purposes of a research study.

Demand characteristics create participant effects

We always seek cues about how to behave, particularly in a new environment such as being in an experiment and particularly if a person knows they are in an experiment. Participants actively look for clues as to how they should behave. The result is that they do not behave as they usually would.

Thus, demand characteristics may act as a substitute IV (confounding variable) because they explain the change in the DV.

Participant effects occur because of cues in an experimental situation that may bias a participant's behaviour, e.g. because they know they are being studied or because of demand characteristics.

Demand characteristics are cues in an experimental situation that may unconsciously affect a participant's behaviour.

Dealing with participant effects

Single blind design
The participant does not know the true aims of the experiment or does not know that they are involved in an experiment.

Or the person conducting the experiment (who has not designed it) does not know the aims of the experiment and therefore cannot produce cues about what he or she expects.

Double blind design
Both the participant and the person conducting the experiment (who has not designed it) are 'blind' to the aims.

Experimental realism
If you make the experimental task sufficiently engaging, participants pay attention to the task and not to the fact that they are being observed.

Paying homage to formal terms*

As we have already said, learning about research methods is a bit like learning a foreign language. You have to learn to use a whole new vocabulary, and you have to learn the meaning of this vocabulary. The problem with the vocabulary is that the meaning of the terms is not always black and white. You have to learn to look for the 'general drift' and not be fazed when you find that there are slightly different meanings as your understanding increases.

*An excellent phrase 'invented' by Hugh Coolican (2004a) to explain this problem.

Qs 17

1. *In a study, participants' memory was tested in the morning and in the afternoon to see if there was any difference in their ability to recall numbers.*

   a. Give an example of **one** possible uncontrolled variable that could arise from the investigator's behaviour effect in this study.

   b. Describe how you might deal with this uncontrolled variable.

   c. Give an example of how the participant's understanding of the study might affect the findings of this experiment.

   d. Describe how you might deal with this problem of participant reactivity.

   e. Give an example of a possible demand characteristic in this study.

   f. Describe how you might deal with this problem.

2. *A study looked at whether first impressions matter. Participants were given a list of adjectives describing Mr. Smith. One group had positive adjectives first, followed by negative adjectives. The other group had the adjectives in reverse order. They were all then asked to describe Mr Smith.*

   a. Give an example of a possible demand characteristic in this study.

   b. Describe how you might deal with this problem.

Investigator effects

Investigator effects, like participant effects, may reduce the internal validity of an experiment.

Direct effects

An investigator may directly affect a participants' behaviour. This was described in chapter 1. An investigator might design a study AND conduct it, however, in many experiments the person who designs the experiment is not the same as the minion who actually deals with the participants. To distinguish these roles we talk of investigators and **experimenters**.

It is the person who interacts directly with participants who will be the source of direct investigator effects.

Indirect effects

An investigator may indirectly affect a participant in a number of ways, such as:

- *Investigator experimental design effect:* The investigator may operationalise the measurement of variables in such a way that the desired result is more likely or may limit the duration of the study for the same reason.

- *Investigator loose procedure effect:* The investigator may not clearly specify the standardised instructions and/or procedures which leaves room for the results to be influenced by the experimenter.

Some people take a narrower view and define investigator effects only as the direct effects of an investigator/experimenter on the behaviour of participants rather than the effects of the investigator on the overall design of the experiment.

Investigator effects: investigator affects participant directly or indirectly (through the design of the study).

Experimenter effects: those effects due to direct interaction with the participant.

Participant reactivity: participant responds to unconscious cues from the investigator.

Validity

Demand characteristics
Internal validity
Investigator effects
Participant effects
Experimental realism
Experimenter
Experimenter bias
Hawthorne effect
Investigator
Participant reactivity
Social desirability bias

The bottom line ...
Investigator effects are any cues (other than the IV) from an investigator/ experimenter that encourage certain behaviours in the participant, leading to a fulfilment of the investigator's expectations. Such cues act as a confounding variable.

Experimenter bias

This is the term used to describe the effects of an experimenter's expectations on a participant's behaviour. A classic experiment by Rosenthal and Fode (1963) showed that even rats are effected by an experimenter's expectations – psychology students were asked to train rats to learn their way around a maze. they were told that there were two groups of rats: one group were 'fast learners' having been bred for this characteristic, whilst the other group were 'slow learners'. In fact there were no differences between the rats. Despite this, the findings of the study showed that the supposedly brighter rats actually did better. The only explanation can be that the student's expectations affected the rats performance.

Ethical issues

In Chapter 1, we considered ethics. There is, however, considerably more to ethics than what was discussed there.

*An **ethical issue** is a conflict between what the researcher wants and the rights of participants. It is a conflict about what is acceptable.*

For example, an experimenter might want to study the effects of tattooing on self-esteem. But you cannot tattoo someone without their permission. And even if you did have their permission, there would have to be a very good reason for doing this study in order to justify the procedures used.

I want to find out important things about human behaviour, which means I need to design my experiment in this way.

I have rights.

Ethical issues are like a see-saw.

Deception

Is it acceptable to deceive a participant about the true aims of a study?

From the researcher's point of view, deception is sometimes necessary because otherwise participants might alter their behaviour to fit the experimenter's expectations.

From the participant's point of view, deception is unethical – you should not deceive anyone without good cause. Perhaps more importantly, deception prevents participants being able to give informed consent. They may agree to participate without really knowing what they have let themselves in for, and they might be quite distressed by the experience.

Deception also leads people to see psychologists as untrustworthy. It means that a participant may not want to take part in psychological research in the future.

Informed consent

From the researcher's point of view, informed consent means you have to reveal the true aims of the study – or at least you have to tell participants what is actually going to happen, and then participants are likely to guess the aims.

From the participant's point of view, you should be told what you will be required to do in the study so that you can make an informed decision about whether you wish to participate. This is a basic human right (established during the Nuremburg war trials – Nazi doctors had conducted various experiments on prisoners without their consent).

Protection from physical and psychological harm

From the researcher's point of view, some of the more important questions in psychology involve a degree of distress to participants.

From the participant's point of view, nothing should happen to you during an experiment that will make you less happy, lower your self-esteem or feel embarrassed about your behaviour – i.e. have negative feelings.

Research participants should be protected from undue risk during an investigation. There are many ways in which you can cause harm to participants, some physical (e.g. getting them to smoke, drink alcohol or drink coffee excessively), some psychological (e.g. making them feel inadequate, embarrassing them, etc.).

Normally, the risk of harm must be no greater than in ordinary life.

Participants should be in the same state after an experiment as they were before *unless they have given their informed consent otherwise*.

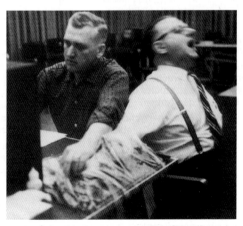

This is a photograph of one of Milgram's studies of obedience. The confederate (on the right) is screaming because he is supposedly receiving an electric shock as the participant presses the confederate's hand on the shock plate.

Do you think that the participant would be unduly distressed by the experience of thinking that he was causing such harm to another? If so, is this 'acceptable' psychological harm?

Confidentiality

From the researcher's point of view, it may be difficult to protect confidentiality because the researcher wishes to publish the findings. A researcher may guarantee *anonymity* (withholding your name), but even then it may be obvious who has been involved in a study. For example, knowing that a study was conducted in St Helena permits some people to be able to identify participants.

From the participant's point of view, the Data Protection Act makes confidentiality a legal right. It is acceptable for personal data to be recorded if the data are not made available in a form that identifies the participants (i.e. confidentiality through anonymity).

Confidentiality and privacy – what's the difference?

The words confidentiality and privacy are sometimes used interchangeably, but there is a distinction between the two.

__Confidentiality__ concerns the communication of personal information from one person to another, and the trust that this information will then be protected.

__Privacy__ refers to a zone of inaccessibility of mind or body, and the trust that this will not be 'invaded'.

In other words, we have a right of privacy. If this is invaded, confidentiality should be respected.

The right to withdraw

From the researcher's point of view, it may not be possible to offer participants this right, e.g. when conducting a field experiment and participants are not aware they are being studied.

From the participant's point of view, if you have been deceived about the aims of the study you still ought to have the option to quit if you find that you do not like what is going on. This compensates for the fact that you did not give informed consent. Even with informed consent, you may not fully understand what is involved.

Privacy

From the researcher's point of view, it may be difficult to avoid invasion of privacy in a field experiment.

From the participant's point of view, people do not expect to be observed by others in certain situations. We have a right to privacy.

In one study, psychologists investigated invasion of personal space by conducting a field experiment in a urinal. There were three conditions: a confederate stood either immediately next to a participant or one urinal away, or was absent. The experimenter recorded micturation times (how long they took to pee) as an indication of how comfortable the participant felt (Middlemist *et al.*, 1976).
Is it unacceptable to observe people in such a place?

 Qs   **22**

1. Do you think that participants in Milgram's study would have been unduly distressed by taking part?
2. If they were distressed, do you think that this is acceptable?
3. Do you think it is unacceptable to observe people in a public urinal?
4. In Milgram's experiment, do think it was acceptable to deceive his participants?
5. Did Milgram obtain informed consent from his participants? Explain your answer.
6. Did Milgram give participants the right to withdraw from his experiment? Explain your answer.

More on Milgram

The participants in Milgram's study were told that it concerned the effect of punishment on learning. They were asked for their consent to take part and told they would be paid $4.50 for taking part. Furthermore, they were told that they could withdraw from the experiment at any time and would still be paid for having taken part.

During the experiment, if a participant asked to stop, the experimenter had been instructed to deliver a set of 'prods' such as saying, 'It is absolutely essential that you continue' or 'You have no other choice; you must go on.'

Does this count as informed consent?

Does this count as the right to withdraw?

> **KEY TERMS**
>
> Consent
> Ethics
> Ethical issues
> Confidentiality
> Right to withdraw
> Deception
> Informed consent
> Privacy
> Protection from psychological harm

How to deal with ethical issues

There are many ways to deal with ethical issues. We will consider a few of them and, for each one, offer some evaluation.

Ethical guidelines

Psychologists are a group of professionals (like solicitors, doctors, etc.). They have a professional organisation consisting of fellow professionals that monitors their behaviour – in the UK, it is the Bristish Psychological Society (BPS); in the US, it is the American Psychological Association (APA). These associations draw up a set of guidelines or principles, or a code of conduct, that tells psychologists what behaviours are not acceptable and tells them how to deal with ethical dilemmas.

BUT

The existence of guidelines means that each individual researcher can say 'I have followed the guidelines and therefore my study is ethically acceptable'. A researcher is, in a way, absolved of responsibility for thinking or making any decisions. Guidelines close off discussions about what is right and wrong.

***Ethical guidelines** are concrete, quasi-legal documents that help to guide conduct within psychology by establishing principles for standard practice and competence.*

Issues versus guidelines

This is another case of 'homage to formal terms'. Issues are not the same as guidelines even though informed consent is both an issue and a guideline. An issue is a conflict; a guideline is a means of resolving this conflict.

*Note that **debriefing** is a not an issue.*

Debriefing

A way to compensate for deception is to inform participants of the true nature of the study, after the research has taken place. In general, the aim of debriefing is to restore the participant to the state he or she was in at the start of the experiment. (A debriefing may also be used to collect useful extra information from participants.)

BUT

You cannot put the clock back. If a participant was distressed by taking part in the experiment, this is difficult to undo. Participants may say they did not mind and enjoyed the experience even if this was not the case.

THE FAR SIDE® BY GARY LARSON

Sorry, your highness, but you're really not the dictator of Ithuvania, a small European republic. In fact, there is no Ithuvania. The hordes of admirers, the military parades, this office -- we faked it all as an experiment in human psychology. In fact your highness, your real name is Edward Belcher, you're from Long Island, New York and it's Time to go home, Eddie.

Presumptive consent

There are situations in which it is not possible to obtain informed consent (such as field experiments or where informed consent would invalidate the study). An alternative to gaining informed consent from participants is to gain informed consent from others. This can be done, for example, by asking a group of people whether they feel that the study is acceptable. We then *presume* that the participants themselves would have felt the same had they been given the opportunity to say so.

Ethical committees

All institutions where research takes place have an ethical committee, and the committee must approve any study before it begins. They look at all possible ethical issues and at how they have been dealt with, weighing up the value of the research against the possible costs in ethical terms. In some cases, the balance is seen to be reasonable; in other cases, it is decided that the costs are simply too great or the research is simply not of sufficient value.

The BPS guidelines contain the following comments:

On deception:
Intentional deception of the participants over the purpose and general nature of the investigation should be avoided whenever possible. Participants should never be deliberately misled without extremely strong scientific or medical justification. Even then there should be strict controls and the disinterested approval of independent advisors.

On informed consent:
Wherever possible, the investigator should inform all participants of the objectives of the investigation. The investigator should inform the participants of all aspects of the research or intervention that might reasonably be expected to influence their willingness to participate. The investigator should, normally, explain all other aspects of the research or intervention about which the participants enquire. Failure to make full disclosure prior to obtaining informed consent requires additional safeguards to protect the welfare and dignity of the participants.

On children:
Research with children or with participants who have impairments that limit understanding and/or communication such that they are unable to give their consent requires special safe-guarding procedures.

On protection from harm:
Investigators have a primary responsibility to protect participants from physical and mental harm during the investigation. Normally the risk of harm must be no greater than in ordinary life i.e. participants should not be exposed to risks greater than or additional to those encountered in their normal life styles.

If harm, unusual discomfort, or other negative consequences for the individual's future life might occur, the investigator must obtain the disinterested approval of independent advisors, inform the participants, and obtain real, informed consent from each of them.

Activity 8 — Ethical committee

Divide your class into groups. Each group should devise a study that raises one of the ethical issues listed in the table below – but not a wild idea! Something that might be just acceptable. Look through your psychology textbook for ideas.

Write a research proposal that identifies the ethical issues and how you intend to deal with them. You should also be clear about the aim of the research and why it is important.

Then present your proposal to an ethical committee. This committee should be composed of people who represent the different interests: for example, university psychology department, researchers, participants.

How to deal with particular ethical issues

Ethical issue	How to deal with it	Limitations
Deception	The need for deception should be approved by an ethical committee, weighing up benefits (of the study) against costs (to participants)	Cost–benefit decisions are flawed because both are subjective judgements. And the costs are not always apparent until after the study
	Participants should be fully debriefed after the study and offered the opportunity to withhold their data	Debriefing cannot turn the clock back – a participant may still feel embarrassed or have lowered self-esteem
Informed consent	Participants are asked to formally indicate their agreement to participate, and this should be based on comprehensive information concerning the nature and purpose of the research and their role in it	If a participant knows such information, this may invalidate the purpose of the study
	An alternative is to gain **presumptive consent**	Even if researchers have sought and obtained informed consent, that does not guarantee that participants really do understand what they have let themselves in for
	You could also offer the right to withdraw	The problem with presumptive consent is that what people say they would or would not mind is different from actually experiencing it
The right to withdraw	Participants should be informed at the beginning of a study that they have the right to withdraw	Participants may feel they should not withdraw because it will spoil the study
Protection from harm	Avoid any situation that may cause a participant to experience psychological (e.g. negative feelings) or physical damage	In many studies, participation is a requirement of an undergraduate psychology course so students would not feel that they could withdraw
Confidentiality	Researchers should not record the real names of any participants; they should use numbers or false names instead	Researchers are not always able to accurately predict the risks of taking part in a study
Privacy	Do not observe anyone without their informed consent unless it is in a public place	It is sometimes possible to work out who the participants were on the basis of the information that has been provided, e.g. the geographical location of a school
	Participants may be asked to give their retrospective consent or withhold their data	There is no universal agreement about what constitutes a public place
		Not everyone feels this is acceptable, e.g. lovers on a park bench.

Qs 23

Study A

In order to study the effects of sleep deprivation, students are asked to limit their sleep to 5 hours for three nights and then sleep normally for the next three nights. Each day, the students' cognitive abilities are assessed using a memory test.

Study B

Participants volunteer to take part in a study. They are told that the study is about public speaking, but the real aim is to see how people respond to encouragement by others. Some participants speak in front of a group of people who smile at them, whereas others talk to a group who appear disinterested.

Study C

Marathon runners are assessed on how much sleep they have the night before and the night after a race to see what the effects of exercise are on sleep.

Study D

A teacher is doing a psychology course and decides to try a little experiment with her class of 8-year-olds. She gives half the class a test in the morning, whereas half of them do the same test in the afternoon to see if time of day affects performance.

For each study, answer the following questions:

1. Identify the IV and DV.
2. How could you operationalise the DV?
3. Identify **one** possible extraneous (uncontrolled) variable.
4. In what way is this study high or low in external validity?
5. What kind of experiment do you think this is? (Explain your answer.)
6. Identify at least **two** possible ethical issues.
7. Describe how you would deal with each ethical issue.
8. Describe **one** limitation for each of your methods of dealing with the ethical issues.

KEY TERMS

Debriefing
Ethical guidelines
Ethical committee
Presumptive consent

The use of non-human animals in psychological research

The American Psychological Association (APA) estimates that about 8% of psychological research uses non-human animals (NHA). There are several issues to consider:

1. **What studies** use NHA?
2. How valuable is research with NHA in terms of what it can tell us about human functioning and behaviour i.e. the **scientific arguments**?
3. How ethical is it to use NHA, i.e. the **ethical arguments**?
4. What **constraints** exist to control the use of NHA in psychological research?

When considering the use of NHA in psychological research, remember
- *It is important to be logical and not emotional.*
- *This is not research on cosmetics, i.e. it is not trivial.*
- *This is not medical research, i.e. it is not life-saving.*
- *Some of the studies that you may be familiar with would not be allowed to take place today because of more stringent constraints.*

What studies?

On page 31 we looked at some animal learning studies. These are not the only kind of psychological research that uses NHA:

- NHA studies have been the major contributor to our knowledge of learning and motivational systems (research on operant conditioning).

- NHA studies are needed to license any new drug such as those used to treat schizophrenia or depression.

- NHA studies have investigated connections between stress and disease, and helped understanding of drug abuse and physical dependence, Alzheimer's disease and the effects of ageing.

Some specific studies

Rechtschaffen et al. (1983) tested the effect of sleep deprivation on rats. Pairs of rats (one experimental, one control) were placed on a turntable over water. If the experimental animal fell asleep the turntable was rotated in order to wake it up and this meant both animals had to keep walking to avoid the water. In between, when the turntable was still the control animal could sleep. None of the experimental animals lived for more than 33 days, some were so ill they had to be killed.

Morgan (1995) demonstrated that the supra-chiasmatic nucleus (SCN) is the biological pacemaker in the brain by transplanting the SCN from a mutant' hamster to another. The mutant hamster was bred to have an abnormal circadian rhythm of 20 instead of 24 hours. The other hamster developed the same rhythm.

Harlow (1959) raised infant rhesus monkeys with a wire 'mother' which had a feeding bottle attached. The monkeys preferred to cling to a cloth-covered-wire mother, showing that contact comfort rather than food was the key to attachment. These young monkeys become maladjusted adults, being reluctant to mate and rejecting any offspring. This research has had important consequences for understanding maternal deprivation.

Dian Fossey spent many years observing and recording the behaviour of gorillas in the natural habitat, increasing our understanding of the social lives of these animals.

What constraints?

Laws

The Animals (Scientific Procedures) Act (1986) requires that that any study using NHA must be licensed by the Home Office to ensure that no animal suffers more than is necessary.

- Researchers – must be experienced e.g. they must be able to administer anaesthesia if prolonged pain is a possibility.

- Premises – the facilities must provide the animals with adequate care in terms of cleanliness and temperature.

- Projects – must fulfill criteria of worth and aim to limit distress.

- Species – research should use species that suffer less. If using rewards consider animal's natural requirements.

British law also requires that any new drug must be tested on at least two different species of live mammal. One must be a large non-rodent.

Guidelines

Professional organisations like the APA and BPS advise on ethical considerations to assist psychologists to work within the law. Guidelines include recommendations about:

- Confinement, restraint, stress and harm – these should be minimised to reduce trauma to the animal.

- Numbers of animals used in laboratory studies – the smallest number possible should be used by optimising design and choice of statistical test.

- Deprivation (of food and water) – should be considered in the light of the needs of the species and the individual.

- Wild animals – disturbance (e.g. to breeding or feeding) should be minimised and endangered species should only be used in conservation research.

Alternatives to NHA research

Recently the House of Lords (2002) pledged commitment to the three R's: Reduction, refinement, replacement – using alternatives such as human research or computer simulation.

The scientific arguments

There are many reasons for using NHA in experiments, for example:

- They are similar to people but simpler, many physiological systems are the same. Behaviourists believe that behavioural building blocks are the same (the idea of evolutionary continuity), their behaviour should therefore be easier to explain so they offer a way to understand more complex human behaviours, such as decision making.

- It is possible to use NHA in experiments when it would be impossible to use humans for ethical reasons, for example, experiments involving isolation, deprivation or surgery.

- The NHA species used in laboratories have shorter natural lifespans than humans so developmental processes may be easier to observe.

- They are interesting in their own right, for instance to find out about breeding patterns or feeding behaviour that might help in conservation.

- Research can have greater control and objectivity. NHA are less likely to respond to demand characteristics than humans.

The ethical arguments

1. Pain and distress

Do NHA experience pain? One study (Sneddon *et al.*, 2003) injected rainbow trout with bee venom and found that the fish started rocking from side to side, indicating distress and pain. However, just responding to a noxious stimuli may not mean NHA feel pain.

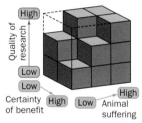

Do NHA have feelings (i.e. are they sentient beings)? They do form lasting relationships and they do demonstrate psychological capacities such as self-awareness. For example, Epstein *et al.* (1981) attached paper dots to pigeons feathers and found they could remove them by looking in the mirror. However, is this truly self-awareness or just self-recognition?

We might nevertheless remember that some human beings (e.g. those with brain damage) lack sentience.

2. Speciesism

Peter Singer (1975) suggested that it was speciesist to discriminate between humans and other animals merely on the basis of the species that an animal belongs to. It is no different to racist arguments that black people do not deserve the same rights, or sexist arguments about women's rights.

Jeffrey Gray (1991) argued that we have a special duty of care to human beings. He asked 'If you see two creatures fighting and you have a gun, who would you shoot if (1) it was your son and a stranger, (2) both are strangers, (3) it was your son and a lion, (4) it was a stranger and a lion?' He predicted that most people would first say 'save my son' and then say 'save the stranger' rather than the lion because we have a special duty of care to humans.

- Important research has been conducted, such as the studies described on the left.

However,

1. Physiology and behaviour may be similar but not the same.

For example NHA may not be good models for human circadian rhythms. Many species used, such as hamsters, are nocturnal whereas we are diurnal and, whereas our infradian cycle remains fairly constant (our sleep patterns do not vary much over the year), some animals naturally hibernate in winter.

In addition, human behaviour is affected by emotion, social context and cognition.

2. The stress that animals endure in labs can affect experiments, making the results meaningless.

Singer's response was that there is a difference between questions about life and about inflicting pain. He also pointed out that human behaviour is not always determined by principles of natural selection (the duty of care to your own species). For example we overcome natural instincts of aggression in some situations.

3. Rights

Singer argues that, nevertheless, animals should be sacrificed for 'greater good' (a utilitarian argument), whereas Tom Regan (1984), claims that NHA should never be used in research. 'We don't want fewer cages, we want empty cages'. Regan claims that NHA have the right to be treated with respect.

However, humans have rights because they have responsibilities.

We can distinguish between rights and obligations. Obligations are owed by humans to animals (e.g. acting humanely, being aware of animals sentience, no gratuitous imposition of pain and suffering, etc.), but it does not follow from that fact that animals have rights.

 Qs   **24**

1. Give one reason why NHA are good models for human behaviour, and one reason why they aren't.
2. Describe two Home Office requirements for conducting scientific research with animals.
3. Describe four guidelines which the BPS recommends for the conduct of animal research.
4. Identify one study that uses non-human animals and describe two ways in which it is ethically sound and two ways in which it could be challenged ethically.
5. Choose two approaches from AS and explain whether animal research in this area can be justified.

Making up your mind

Costs

- Pain and distress.

- Lasting harm to NHA participants.

Benefits

- To humans and to animals.

- Includes costs of not doing the research

Experimental and control groups

A researcher might want to investigate the effect that rewards have on performance. To do this, children are asked to collect rubbish from a playground and offered a chocolate bar as a reward. They collect several bags of rubbish.

We cannot conclude anything about the effects of the reward because all the children were told that they would receive a reward. We need to have a control group so that we can make a comparison.

We need two groups: an **experimental group** (offered a reward) and a **control group** (offered no reward). This allows us to compare the effects of the reward (IV) on collecting rubbish (the DV).

Or we need to have two conditions: an **experimental condition** (children offered a reward on one occasion) and a **control condition** (offered no reward on another occasion).

Threats to internal validity

If there is an experimental group and a control group, it is possible that the experimental group will perform differently for reasons other than the IV (experimental treatment).

Consider a study on the effectiveness of a new teaching programme. One class are taught using the new programme (experimental group) and compared with another class taught using the 'old' programme (control group).

- The experimental group might improve simply because the teaching programme is new.
- The classes may have had different teachers.
- Or the control group might try extra hard to show that the old way is just as good or better than the new approach. This is called the **John Henry effect**.

John Henry is an American legend. He worked on building the railroads, drilling holes by hitting thick steel spikes into rocks. There was no one who could match him, although many tried.

Then one day someone tried to sell a steam-powered drill to the railroad company, claiming that it could out-drill any man. They set up a contest between John Henry and that drill. The foreman ran the newfangled steam-drill. John Henry pulled out two 20 pound hammers, one in each hand. They drilled and drilled, dust rising everywhere. The men were howling and cheering. At the end of 35 minutes, John Henry had drilled two 7-foot holes – a total of 14 feet, whereas the steam drill had only drilled one 9-foot hole.

Thinking back to Milgram and Hofling

After Milgram's research, another study found real-life support for the findings. Dicks (1972) interviewed former German soldiers and found that they displayed the same psychological mechanisms of obedience shown by participants in laboratory-based obedience research. However, one event of the Second World War found the opposite (Mandel, 1998). In an encounter between German troops and civilians, the commander, Major Trapp, had orders to kill all the Jews in a small town – but Trapp told his men that if they did not wish to obey orders, he would assign them to other duties. Nevertheless, most of the men did obey – despite the fact that, according to Milgram, the task involved many of the factors that should lead to reduced obedience (face-to-face contact, some disobedient peers, absence of pressure from an authority figure).

This challenges our original conclusion because now it appears that Milgram's findings have not been replicated in other settings.

The moral of the story: Don't assume that any study has **ecological validity** – search for confirming evidence. All research conducted in the real world is not automatically ecologically valid, and all laboratory studies are not automatically ecologically *invalid*. Every study has some ecological validity – some are just more ecologically valid than others.

OTHER TERMS
Control group/condition
Experimental group/condition
John Henry effect

Qs 25

A playgroup wishes to investigate whether children play differently if an adult is present or not.

1. Describe how you might design a study to investigate this using an independent groups design.
2. Which is the experimental group and which is the control group?
3. Identify **one or more** ethical issues and suggest how you would deal with these.
4. To what extent would the findings of your study have representativeness?
5. To what extent would the findings of your study have generalisability?
6. How could you conduct a study with the same aims using a repeated measures design?
7. Identify the experimental and control conditions in this new study.
8. Describe **one** advantage and **one** disadvantage of using a repeated measures design in this study.

 Activity 9   **What is validity all about?**

Using what you have learned in this chapter, create something to represent the various aspects of validity. It could be a PowerPoint presentation, a mobile, a poster for your classroom, a leaflet, a cartoon strip, a poem, a rap song – anything that is entertaining AND forces you to process the material (as processing leads to deeper understanding and long-term memories).

Multiple choice questions

1. Which of the following is *not* a characteristic of a field experiment?
   a. It is conducted in a natural environment.
   b. The IV is directly manipulated by the experimenter.
   c. Extraneous variables can be well controlled.
   d. Participants are often not aware that they are being studied.

2. Which of the following is *not* a characteristic of a lab experiment?
   a. It is conducted in a natural environment.
   b. The IV is directly manipulated by the experimenter.
   c. Extraneous variables can be well controlled.
   d. Participants are often aware that they are being studied.

3. Mundane realism refers to
   a. Using video film to capture participants' behaviour.
   b. An experiment being boring and therefore not holding the participant's interest.
   c. The extent to which an experiment mirrors the real world.
   d. A Spanish football team.

4. Variables in an experiment are operationalised, which means they are
   a. Understandable to participants.
   b. Used in a medical experiment.
   c. Described in a way that can be easily measured or manipulated.
   d. Turned into numbers.

5. Lab experiments are sometimes artificial because
   a. Participants know they are being studied and this may affect their behaviour.
   b. The setting may lack mundane realism.
   c. The IV may be operationalised in such a way that it does not represent real-life experiences.
   d. All of the above.

6. Internal validity is concerned with
   a. The generalisability of research findings.
   b. The consistency of measurement.
   c. Whether an observed effect can be attributed to the IV.
   d. Whether the findings are what the experimenter expected.

7. External validity refers to
   a. The generalisability of research findings.
   b. Whether the findings are what the experimenter expected.
   c. Whether an observed effect can be attributed to the IV.
   d. All of the above.

8. Deception is sometimes necessary in experiments. Why? Because psychologists:
   a. Do things that they ought to be ashamed of.
   b. Want to hide the true purpose of the experiment from participants.
   c. Deception is easier than getting informed consent.
   d. Need to reduce situational variables.

9. Demand characteristics are
   a. Features of an experiment that cannot be controlled.
   b. Threats to external validity.
   c. Problem behaviours.
   d. Cues in an experimental situation that unconsciously affect a participant's behaviour.

10. Which of the following would *not* be a threat to internal validity?
    a. Experimenter bias.
    b. Participant reactivity.
    c. Social desirability bias.
    d. Single-blind design.

11. The person who designs an experiment is called the
    a. Investigator.
    b. Experimenter.
    c. Participant.
    d. Designer.

12. Confidentiality refers to
    a. Maintaining the privacy of individuals.
    b. Keeping the identity of participants a secret.
    c. Whether the experimenter appears confident enough.
    d. All of the above.

13. Ecological validity concerns
    a. Representativeness.
    b. Generalisability.
    c. Representativeness and reliability.
    d. Representativeness and generalisability.

14. Which of the following is the best definition of ecological validity?
    a. Ecological validity is the degree to which behaviour in the laboratory reflects real life.

b. Ecological validity is the extent to which findings can be generalised from the lab to the real world.
    c. Ecological validity is the extent to which findings can be generalised from the experimental setting to other settings.
    d. Ecological validity is the degree to which findings can be generalised from one group of people to the target population.

15. Offering participants the right to withdraw:
    a. Can be an alternative to obtaining informed consent in some situations.
    b. Is not possible in all experiments.
    c. Is an ethical issue.
    d. All of the above.

16. In a natural experiment
    a. The IV is controlled by an experimenter.
    b. The IV varies naturally.
    c. The DV is controlled by an experimenter.
    d. The DV varies naturally.

17. Natural experiments are not 'true' experiments because
    a. Participants are not randomly allocated to conditions.
    b. The sample studied may have unique characteristics.
    c. The IV is not directly manipulated by the experimenter.
    d. All of the above.

18. Validity is best defined as:
    a. The extent to which findings are true or legitimate.
    b. Value for money – whether paid participants finish the experiment or withdraw.
    c. A measure of whether participants understand what is expected in an experiment.
    d. Whether or not something is consistent.

19. Debriefing is
    a. An ethical issue.
    b. An ethical guideline.
    c. An ethical issue and an ethical guideline.
    d. A folder for research notes.

20. If informed consent is not possible, a possible alternative is to
    a. Give participants the right to withdraw.
    b. Debrief participants.
    c. Obtain presumptive consent.
    d. All of the above.

Answers are on page 41

Model answer for exam style question

Question 1

(a) (i) What was the experimental design in this study? *[1]*

Independent groups.

(ii) Describe **one** advantage of using this design. *[2]*

One advantage is that you won't suffer from order effects such as guessing what the study was about if each participant had to watch all three films. You'd also have to wait until the effects of each film wore off, so each participant would have to come back again.

(b) (i) Identify a suitable sampling method for this study. *[1]*

Volunteer sampling.

(ii) Explain how you would carry this out. *[2]*

You would advertise in certain places, like a newspaper, asking for people who would be willing to take part in a psychology experiment.

(c) (i) Explain why this study could be considered to be a field experiment. *[2]*

The study involves the use of real-life materials (a film) and takes place in a natural environment (a cinema).

(ii) Describe **one** advantage and **one** disadvantage of doing a field experiment. *[4]*

One advantage is that participants behave more like they usually would, and this means that you can generalise to real life better.

One disadvantage is that it is more difficult to control extraneous variables such as noise.

(d) (i) Explain what is meant by demand characteristics. *[2]*

They are features of an experiment that lead participants to unconsciously respond in predictable ways.

(ii) Describe a way that demand characteristics might have been a problem in this study. *[2]*

It might be that other aspects of the romantic film led people to be relaxed, like the music that is used in such films.

(e) Identify **one** ethical issue and say how you would deal with it. *[3]*

One issue would be psychological harm if a participant didn't want to watch The Godfather. You could deal with it by asking participants for their informed consent before the experiment began, which would involve telling them everything they would be required to do.

(f) Explain why the third group watched a documentary on the Amazon rainforest. *[2]*

This was a control condition to ensure that the effects were due to the different kinds of film.

(g) (i) Define the term validity. *[2]*

Validity is the ability to make a correct decision based on research findings, so that we conclude that a hypothesis is true when it is true, or conclude a hypothesis is false when it is false.

(ii) Describe **one** reason why this study might lack validity. *[2]*

The sample of participants might be unrepresentative of the wider population, and thus the study would lack population validity.

(h) Describe **one or more** conclusion(s) that could be drawn from this study. *[3]*

The findings suggest that hormones lead to the responses we recognise when watching certain sorts of film. This is true for romantic films, but it seems that only men are affected by exciting films, which could explain why women find such films boring.

(i) (i) Identify a suitable graph that could be used to show the findings from this study. *[1]*

Bar chart.

(ii) What labels would you put on the x and y axes (horizontal and vertical axes) of this graph? *[2]*

The x axis would be labelled 'Romantic film, exciting film and Amazon rain forest'. The y axis would be labelled with increase in levels of hormones.

Examiner's comments

(a) (i) Perhaps a bit of a tricky question because each participant was tested twice and therefore it might appear to be a repeated measures design – but the final analysis was a comparison between the three groups.

(a) (ii) Here is an example of a candidate giving two answers when only one is required. Fortunately, both answers are worth 2 marks. Just saying 'order effects' would be worth 1 mark.

(b) (i) Random sampling might not be very suitable; volunteer or opportunity sampling would be the most likely.

(b) (ii) For 2 marks, your answer does not need to be very detailed, but just saying 'I would advertise' would be worth 1 mark.

(c) (i) Two answers have been given, but they are both creditworthy as there is no requirement for only one answer. Each answer would be worth one mark seperately, though just saying 'natural experiment' on its own would get no marks because it is not related to the study.

(c) (ii) It might appear that two answers have been given for the advantage, but 'and' has been used to link two related points so it is all creditworthy.

(d) (i) This is probably a definition you know or do not know. An answer that said 'unconscious cues' might receive 1 mark.

(d) (ii) This is a difficult question that requires you to think on your feet. You would get a mark for saying anything that suggests you have tried to apply the concept appropriately, i.e. found something in the study that would elicit certain behaviour from the participants – aside from the IV – but you cannot just repeat the definition again.

(e) Simply saying 'informed consent' would only gain 1 mark. The remaining two marks are given to a detailed description of how you would deal with the named issue.

(f) The term used is 'explain', which means that just saying a 'control condition' would not count as a sufficient answer because it does not really explain why.

(g) (i) An excellent definition and more detail than would be required.

(g) (ii) It is acceptable to describe any of the types of validity – such as population, ecological or even historical validity; even though this might not affect responses to a film, it could affect them.

(h) It is useful to start your answer in this way to ensure that you are giving a conclusion and not a finding. The second sentence starts with a finding but does end with a second conclusion. There was no requirement to give two conclusions but this is a good way to write enough for 3 marks.

(i) (i) The answer 'histogram' would be incorrect.

(i) (ii) The answer 'the IV' would be true, but not sufficient for 2 marks; the names of the films would be an appropriate alternative answer.

Question 2

(a) Explain **two** ethical considerations that are important in conducting research with non-human participants and indicate how these issues may be overcome. [6]

One issue is pain, this should only arise if there is no alternative but to use animals and when the experiment is justified by it's potential outcome. One solution is to use other techniques such as simulation so that animals do not suffer. An alternative is to anaesthetise the animal so that it doesn't feel pain.

Another issue is caging and conditions; animals should not be kept in social and physical surroundings that are inappropriate to their species. Researchers should be aware of the needs of the species they are using and chose the species that will be least affected by the conditions required by their study.

Examiner's comments

(a) The candidate has suggested two ways of dealing with the first ethical consideration, either of these would have been sufficient.

Similarly, the second consideration/issue has two solutions and, with a little more detail, either point for the second issue could have stood alone.

There were other issues that would have been acceptable, such as the source of animals, or risk of disturbing animals in their natural habitat, or numbers of animals used. Some are easier than others to expand for the second part of the question. For example, limiting the numbers of animals used might be acheived by using a repeated measures design or by using statistical tests that allow for small group sizes.

SELF-REPORT MEASURES

Contents

Self-report measures

questionnaires, interviews and studies using correlational analysis

Questionnaires

A **questionnaire** (or questionnaire survey) is a set of questions.

It is designed to collect information about a topic or even more than one topic.

The two great strengths of questionnaires are:

1. You can collect the same information from a large number of people relatively easily (once you have designed the questionnaire, which is not so easy).

2. You can access what people think – experiments rely on 'guessing' what people think on the basis of how they behave. With a questionnaire, you ask people – whether they give you valid answers is another matter.

Writing good questions

When writing questions, there are three guiding principles:

- *Clarity*. Questions need to be written so that the reader (respondent) understands what is being asked. One way to do this is to **operationalise** certain terms. There should be no ambiguity.

- *Bias*. Any bias in a question might lead the respondent to be more likely to give a particular answer (as in a **leading question**). The greatest problem is probably **social desirability bias**. Respondents prefer to select answers that portray them in a positive light rather than reflect the truth.

- *Analysis*. Questions need to be written so that the answers provided are easy to analyse. If you ask 'What kind of job do you do?' or 'What makes you feel stressed at work?', you may get 50 different answers from 50 people. These are called **open questions**. Alternatively, one can ask **closed questions**, where a limited range of answers are provided, such as listing 10 job categories or 10 sources of stress. Such closed questions are easier to analyse.

Examples of open questions

What factors contribute to making work stressful?

When do you feel most stressed?

Advantages of open questions

- Allows the researcher to collect detailed, qualitative data.
- Allow respondents to express themselves.
- Mean that unexpected information can be collected.

Advantages of closed questions

- Tend to produce quantitative data.
- Easier to analyse the data.
- Easier for respondents to fill in.

BUT the respondents' answers may not be represented so that they are forced to be untruthful.

Quantitative and qualitative data

Questionnaires may collect:

- **Quantitative data**: numerical information for example, about your age, how many hours you work in a week, how highly you rate different TV programmes.

- **Qualitative data**: information that cannot be counted for example, about how you think or feel.

Quantitative data are data that represent how much, how long or how many, etc. there are of something; i.e. behaviour is measured in numbers or quantities.

Qualitative data are a more complex account of what people think or feel. Qualitative data cannot be counted but they can be summarised. They may be converted to quantitative data and then counted.

Qualitative data typically come from asking open questions to which the answers are not limited by a set of choices or a scale, whereas closed questions generate quantitative data directly.

Examples of closed questions

1. Which of the following factors at work makes you feel stressed? (You may tick as many answers as you like.)

☐ Noise at work ☐ Lack of control
☐ Too much to do ☐ Workmates ☐ No job satisfaction

Note that these questions do concern what people think and feel, but such questions would not produce qualitative data because respondents' choices have been limited.

2. How many hours a week do you work?

☐ 0 hours ☐ Between 20 and 30 hours
☐ Less than 10 hours ☐ More than 30 hours
☐ Between 10 and 20 hours

Forced choice question

3. A. The worst social sin is to be rude
   B. The worst social sin is to be a bore

Likert scale

4. Work is stressful.

☐ Strongly agree ☐ Agree ☐ Not sure
☐ Disagree ☐ Strongly disagree

5. How much stress do you feel in the following situations? (Circle the number that best describes how you feel.)

At work	A lot of stress	5 4 3 2 1	No stress at all
At home	A lot of stress	5 4 3 2 1	No stress at all
Travelling to work	A lot of stress	5 4 3 2 1	No stress at all

Semantic differential technique (Place a tick to show your feelings.)

6. People who are bosses are usually:

Hard _ _ _ _ _ _ _ Kind   Small _ _ _ _ _ _ _ Large
Passive _ _ _ _ _ _ _ Active   Beautiful _ _ _ _ _ _ _ Ugly

Designing good questionnaires

A good questionnaire should (obviously) contain good questions. Some other things to consider when designing a good questionnaire:

- *Filler questions*: It may help to include some irrelevant questions to mislead the respondent from the main purpose of the survey. This may reduce **demand characteristics**.

- *Sequence for the questions*. It is best to start with easy ones, saving questions that might make someone feel anxious or defensive until the respondent has relaxed.

- *Pilot study*: The questions can be tested on a small group of people. This means that you can refine the questions in response to any difficulties encountered.

Sometimes people don't know what they think.

 Qs 26

A psychology student designed a questionnaire about attitudes to eating. Below are three questions from this questionnaire:

i. *Do you diet?*
ALWAYS / SOMETIMES / NEVER
(circle your answer)

ii. *Do you think that dieting is a bad idea?*

iii. *Explain your answer to (ii).*

1. For each question:
   a. State whether it is an open or closed question.
   b. State whether the question would produce quantitative or qualitative data.
   c. Give **one** criticism of the question.
   d. Suggest how you could improve the question in order to deal with your criticism.
   e. Suggest **one** strength of the question.

2. *You have been asked to write a questionnaire about people's attitudes about ghosts and other paranormal phenomena.*
   a. Write **one** closed question that would collect quantitative data.
   b. Write **one** open question that would collect qualitative data.
   c. Write an example of a leading question for this questionnaire.
   d. Explain how social desirability bias might affect the validity of the responses to your questionnaire.
   e. Describe **one** advantage of using questionnaires to collect data in this study.
   f. Describe **one** disadvantage of using questionnaires to collect data in this study.
   g. Explain the difference between qualitative and quantitative data.
   h. Why might it be preferable to collect quantitative data?
   i. Why might it be preferable to collect qualitative data?

A questionnaire can be a research method or a research technique.

*The aims of a study may be to find out about smoking habits in young people. The researcher would design a questionnaire to collect data about what people do and why. In this case, the questionnaire is the **research method**.*

*The aims of a study might be to see if children who are exposed to an anti-smoking educational programme have different attitudes towards smoking than children not exposed to such a programme. The researcher would use a questionnaire to collect data about attitudes, but the analysis would involve a comparison between the two groups of children – an experimental study using a questionnaire as a **research technique**.*

 Activity 10   **Design and use your own questionnaire**

Select a suitable topic, for example 'Methods of studying and exam revision', 'Why people choose to study psychology' or you could choose a topic related to your studies, such as a questionnaire on flashbulb memories, sleep or dreams.

Steps in questionnaire design

- Write the questions. (Keep the questionnaire short, somewhere between 5 and 10 questions. Include a mixture of open and closed questions.)
- Construct the questionnaire.
- Write standarised instructions.
- Pilot the questionnaire.
- Decide on a sampling technique.

Conduct the questionnaire

- Collect data.
- Analyse the data. (Just select a few questions for analysis. For quantitative data, you can use a bar chart. For qualitative data, you can identify some trends in the answers and summarise these.)
- Write the report.

KEY TERMS

Qualitative data
Quantitative data
Questionnaires
Survey

OTHER TERMS

Closed questions
Forced choice questions
Leading questions
Likert scale
Open questions
Semantic differential technique

Interviews

A questionnaire can be given in a written form or it can be delivered in real-time (face to face or over the telephone) by an interviewer. There are advantages and disadvantages:

☺ The interviewer can adapt questions according to the interviewee's answers, taking advantage of on-the-spot flexibility. This is sometimes called the **clinical** or **unstructured interview**.

☹ An interviewer may unconsciously lead respondents to provide certain answers by verbal or visual cues.

☹ People may feel less comfortable about revealing personal information.

Quantitative and qualitative data

Questions in an interview, as in a questionnaire, may produce **quantitative** or **qualitative** data. An unstructured interview is more likely to produce qualitative data because the questions that develop are likely to ask respondents to elaborate their answers (e.g. 'Why do you feel that?').

Questions may be quantitative (e.g. 'How often do you feel like that?'), but they are still less predictable than questionnaires.

Advantages and disadvantages

Quantitative data

☺ Easier to analyse because the data are in numbers.

☹ Reduces information about people to over-simplified statistics (statistically significant but humanly insignificant).

Qualitative data

☺ Represents the true complexities of human behaviour and gains access to thoughts and feelings that cannot be assessed using other methods.

☹ More difficult to analyse so that conclusions are difficult to draw.

Activity 11 — Try your own interview

Try out the moral interviews on the right with a partner in class. Take turns being the interviewer and interviewee as you try out both kinds of interview.

Discuss:

- What you found out.
- The differences in the information obtained.
- Which questions worked best and why.
- How truthful the answers were and why.

Qs 27

1. Would you describe Kohlberg's and Gilligan's interviews as structured, unstructured or semi-structured (somewhere in between)? Explain your answer.

2. In the questions on the right, find an example of a closed question, an open question, a question that would produce quantitative data and a question that would produce qualitative data.

Structured and unstructured interviews

An **interview** consists of questions asked to a participant (the interviewee) in real time either face to face or over the telephone.

A **structured interview** has predetermined questions; i.e. a questionnaire that is delivered face to face.

An **unstructured interview** has less structure! New questions are developed as you go along, similar to the way in which your GP might interview you. He or she starts with some predetermined questions, but further questions are developed as a response to your answers. For this reason the unstructured or semi-structured approach is called the **clinical method**.

Examples of structured and unstructured interviews

Lawrence Kohlberg (1978) interviewed boys about their moral views. Interviewers gave the boys an imaginary situation (such as the one below) and then asked a set of questions.

Lawrence Kohlberg

In Europe, a woman was near death from a special type of cancer. There was one drug that the doctors thought might save her. It was a form of radium that a druggist in the same town had recently discovered. The drug was expensive to make but the druggist was charging 10 times what the drug cost him to make. He paid $400 for the radium and charged $4000 for a small dose of it. The sick woman's husband, Heinz, went to everyone he knew to borrow the money, but he could only get together about $2000, which is half of what it cost. He told the druggist that his wife was dying and asked him to sell it cheaper or let him pay later. But the druggist said 'No. I discovered the drug and I'm going to make money from it.' Heinz got desperate and broke into the man's store to steal the drug for his wife.

- Should Heinz steal the drug?
- Why or why not?
- (If the subject originally favours stealing, ask: 'If Heinz doesn't love his wife, should he steal the drug for her?')
- (If the subject originally favours not stealing, ask: 'Does it make a difference whether or not he loves his wife?')
- Why or why not?
- Suppose that the person dying is not his wife but a stranger. Should Heinz steal the drug for the stranger?
- Why or why not?

Carol Gilligan also investigated moral principles (Gilligan and Attanucci, 1988). Participants were asked a set of questions about moral conflict and choice:

Carol Gilligan

- Have you ever been in a situation of moral conflict where you had to make a decision but weren't sure what was the right thing to do?
- Could you describe the situation?
- What were the conflicts for you in that situation?
- What did you do?
- Do you think it was the right thing to do?
- How do you know?

The interviewer asked other questions to encourage the participants to elaborate and clarify their responses, such as saying 'Anything else?'. Special focus was on asking participants to explain the meaning of key terms such as 'responsibility', 'fair' and 'obligation'.

A comparison of questionnaires and interviews

	Advantages ☺	Disadvantages ☹
Questionnaires *Respondents record their own answers*	• Can be easily repeated so that data can be collected from a large number of people relatively cheaply and quickly (once the questionnaire has been designed) • Questionnaires do not require specialist administrators • Respondents may feel more willing to reveal personal/confidential information than in an interview	• Answers may not be truthful, e.g. because of **leading questions** and **social desirability bias** • The sample may be biased because only certain kinds of people fill in questionnaires – literate individuals who are willing to spend time filling them in
Structured interview *Questions predetermined*	• Can be easily repeated • Requires less skill than unstructured interviews • More easy to analyse than unstructured interviews because the answers are more predictable	• The interviewer's expectations may influence the answers the interviewee gives (this is called **interviewer bias**). This may especially be true because people do not always know what they think. They may also want to present themselves in a 'good light' and therefore give 'socially desirable' answers (**social desirability bias**) • In comparison with unstructured interviews, the data collected will be restricted by a predetermined set of questions
Unstructured or semi-structured interviews *Interviewer develops questions in response to respondent's answers*	• Generally more detailed information can be obtained from each respondent than in a structured interview • Can access information that may not be revealed by predetermined questions	• More affected by interviewer bias than structured interviews • Interviews may not be comparable because different interviewers ask different questions (low **inter-interviewer reliability**). **Reliability** may also be affected by the same interviewer behaving differently on different occasions • The answers from unstructured interviews are less easy to analyse because they are unpredictable.

Special tip

Students often write something like 'The advantage of a questionnaire is that you can collect lots of data.' The problem with this is that it is not clear what 'lots of data' means. Compared with what? You can collect lots of data in an experiment or interview.

• You need to provide clear detail. (What is 'lots of data'? Why is there 'lots of data'?)

• You need to offer a comparison. (Compared with what?, e.g. compared with an interview.)

A good answer would say, 'The advantage of a questionnaire is that you can collect data from more people than you would if using the interview methods, which results in lots more data.'

KEY TERMS

Interview
Advantages ☺ and disadvantages ☹ of questionnaires and interviews qualitative and quantitative data

OTHER TERMS
Clinical interview
Inter-interviewer reliability
Interviewer bias
Structured interview
Unstructured interview

Interviewing an elephant for Australian TV.

Qs 28

1. Explain the difference between a structured and an unstructured interview.
2. Explain the difference between a questionnaire and an interview.
3. If you wanted to find out about attitudes towards dieting, why would it be preferable to conduct an interview rather than use a questionnaire?
4. Why might it be better to use a questionnaire than conduct an interview?
5. How can 'leading questions' be a problem in interviews or questionnaires?
6. What is the 'social desirability bias'?
7. What kind of data are produced in interviews? Explain your answer.

Ethical issues for questionnaires and interviews

• **Deception** may be necessary.

• Questions may be related to sensitive and personal issues (**psychological harm**). Respondents may feel that they have to present themselves in a good light.

• **Confidentiality** and **privacy** must be respected.

Correlational design

A **correlation** is a relationship between two variables. Age and beauty co-vary. As people get older, they become more beautiful. This is a **positive correlation** because the two variables increase together.

You may disagree and think that as people get older they become less attractive. You think that age and beauty are correlated but that it is a **negative correlation**: as one variable increases, the other one decreases.

Or you may simply feel that there is no relationship between age and beauty. This is called a **zero correlation**.

A scattergraph is a graph that shows the correlation between two sets of data (or co-variables) by plotting dots to represent each pair of scores.

The scatter of the dots indicates the degree of correlation between the co-variables. A statistical test is used to calculate the correlation coefficient, a measure of the extent of correlation that exists.

Notice that all correlation coefficients are no greater than 1. Some correlation coefficients are written as –0.52, whereas others are +0.52. The plus or minus sign shows whether it is a positive or a negative correlation. The coefficient (number) tells us how closely the co-variables are related. –0.52 is just as closely correlated as +0.52; it's just that –0.52 means that as one variable increases, the other decreases (negative correlation), and +0.52 means that both variables increase together (positive correlation).

Scattergraphs

A correlation can be illustrated using a **scattergraph**.

For each individual, we obtain a score for each co-variable – in our case, the co-variables are age and beauty.

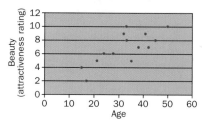
A scattergraph showing the relationship between age and beauty

The top graph illustrates a positive correlation.

The middle graph shows a negative correlation.

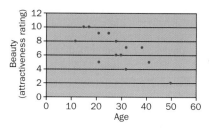

The bottom graph is a zero correlation.

The extent of this correlation is described using a **correlation coefficient** – this is a number between +1 and –1 that is calculated using a statistical test. +1 is a perfect positive correlation, and –1 is a perfect negative correlation.

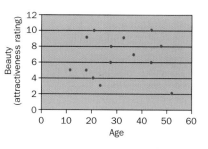

The correlation coefficients for the three graphs are:
(1) 0.76
(2) – 0.76
(3) 0.002

Qs 29

1. Think of two variables that are likely to be positively correlated (such as height and weight).
2. Think of two variables that are likely to be negatively correlated.
3. What does a correlation coefficient tell you about a set of data?
4. Give an example of a positive correlation coefficient and a negative correlation coefficient.
5. Explain what the following correlation coefficients mean:

   +1.00 –1.00 0.00
   –0.60 +0.40 +0.10

Activity 12 — Playing with correlation: the Excel method

Using **Excel**, you can enter and alter pairs of numbers to see how this affects a scattergraph and correlation coefficient. Both are produced automatically by Excel if you follow these steps:

1. Open a new document (select <file> <new> <blank workbook>).
2. Select <insert> <chart> <XY (scatter)> and press <next>.
3. Place the cursor at the very top left of the page; click and drag across 2 rows and then down 16 rows. Press <next> <next> <finish>.
4. Now enter pairs of scores in rows 2–16 (these can be invented or you could try entering a real set of numbers to see if they are correlated – such as height and shoe size). Do not enter data in the top row.
5. To calculate the correlation coefficient: Place the cursor in any empty box. Select <insert> <function>. In the top box, type 'correl' and press 'go' and then <OK>.
6. The screen now says 'array1' and 'array2'. Click in 'array1' and then move the cursor to the top of the first column of your numbers; then click and drag to the bottom of the column. Do the same for array2.
7. Try changing some of the numbers and see how this alters your scattergraph and correlation coefficient.

(See the list of websites (page 148) for sites where you can plot correlations.)

KEY TERMS
Correlational design
Significance

OTHER TERMS
Co-variables
Negative correlation
Positive correlation
Single blind
Zero correlation
Correlation coefficient
Scattergraph

Significance

Significance is the extent to which something is particularly unusual.

When we look at a correlation coefficient, we need to know whether it is strong or weak. In order to do this, we use tables of significance, which tell us how big the coefficient needs to be in order for the correlation to be significant (unusual).

The table below gives an approximate idea of the values needed. The more pairs of scores you have, the smaller the coefficient can be.

A coefficient of either –0.45 or +0.45 would be significant if there were 16 pairs of data but not if there were 14 pairs.

The *magnitude* of the number informs us about significance; the *sign* tells us which direction the correlation is in (positive or negative).

Investigations using a correlational analysis

A correlation is not a research method. Therefore we do not talk about a correlational investigation but about an investigation using a correlational analysis.

	Advantages ☺	Disadvantages ☹
Experiments (lab and field)	• Cause can be determined because we observe the effect of an IV on a DV	• May not be possible to manipulate variables because of ethical problems
Investigations using correlational analysis	• Can be used when an experiment would be unethical or impractical • If correlation is significant then further investigation is justified • If correlation is not significant then you can rule out a casual relationship	• People often misinterpret correlations and assume that a cause and effect relationship has been found, but this is not possible • There may be other, unknown (**intervening**) variable(s) that can explain why the co-variables being studied are linked
Both	• The procedures can be repeated which means that the findings are confirmed	• May lack **internal/external validity**.

Significance table

N =	One-tailed test
4	1.000
6	0.829
8	0.643
10	0.564
12	0.503
14	0.464
16	0.429
18	0.401
20	0.380
22	0.361
24	0.344
26	0.331
28	0.317
30	0.306

These values are for Spearman's test of correlation. The full table is given on page 108.

Qs   30

1. Consider the number +0.36. Identify the magnitude and sign of this number.
2. If this value (+0.36) were obtained after testing 20 people, would it be significant?
3. Sketch a scattergraph to illustrate this correlation.
4. If you conducted a study with 30 participants, would a correlation of +0.30 be significant?
5. Would –0.40 be significant?
6. *A study investigates whether there is a negative correlation between age and liking for spicy foods. Participants are asked to rate their liking for spicy foods on a scale of 1 to 10 where 10 means they liked it a lot.*
   a. What is meant by the term 'negative correlation' in this context?
   b. Why might you expect to find a negative correlation?
   c. Suggest **three** suitable descriptive statistics that could be used in this study.
   d. Describe **one** advantage and **one** disadvantage of this study.
7. *Guiseppe Gelato always liked statistics at school, and now that he has his own ice cream business he keeps various records. To his surprise, he has found an interesting correlation between his ice cream sales and aggressive crimes. He has started to worry that he may be irresponsible in selling ice cream because it appears to cause people to behave more aggressively. The table below shows his data.*

All data rounded to 1000s	Jan	Feb	Mar	Apr	May	Jun	Jul	Aug	Sep	Oct	Nov	Dec
Ice cream sales	10	8	7	21	32	56	130	141	84	32	11	6
Aggressive crimes	21	32	29	35	44	55	111	129	99	36	22	25

   a. Draw a scattergraph to display Guiseppe's data.
   b. What can you conclude from the data and the scattergraph?
   c. What intervening variable might explain the relationship between ice cream and aggression?
   d. Describe how you would design a study to show Guiseppe that ice cream does (or does not) cause aggressive behaviour. (You need to operationalise your variables, decide on a suitable research design and sampling method, etc.)

> Remember that conclusions are an *interpretation* of the findings.

Reliability

Reliability refers to whether something is consistent.

If you use a ruler to measure the height of a chair today and check the measurement tomorrow, you expect the ruler to be reliable (consistent) and provide the same measurement. You would assume that any fluctuation was because the chair had changed.

Any tool used to measure something must be reliable, such as a psychological test assessing personality or an interview about drinking habits.

If the 'tool' is measuring the same thing, it should produce the same result on every occasion. If the result is different, we know that the thing (chair or personality) has changed.

This means that we can feel confident that any difference between objects/people is due to variation in the objects and not the measuring device.

Different archers produce the following patterns of arrows.

Being reliable is being consistent; being valid is being on target (related to what you are aiming to do)

Reliable, but not valid   Not reliable, not valid   Reliable and valid

Assessing reliability of questionnaires and interviews

Internal reliability is a measure of the extent to which something is consistent within itself. For example, all the questions on a psychological test should be measuring the same thing.

External reliability is a measure of the extent to which one measure of an object (like a chair) varies from another measure of the same object. Two rulers should give the same measure even if there is a month between measurements.

If the same interview were conducted one day and then one week later, the outcome should be the same – otherwise the interview is not reliable.

Two interviewers should produce the same outcome. This is called **inter-interviewer reliability**.

Internal reliability

e.g. a psychological test (a type of questionnaire)

External reliability

e.g. a psychological test or in an interview

e.g. an experiment

Split-half method: A single group of participants all take the test once. Each person's scores are then divided into two sets (such as odd and even numbered test items). These sets of data should correlate strongly. This shows that the items within the test are measuring the same phenomenon as each individual's scores are consistent.

The split-half method can be difficult to achieve as it is essential that the two halves are closely matched (eg in difficulty or the particular aspect of a phenomenon that they are testing).

Equivalent forms method: Two versions of the test are produced. These should consist of similar questions, such as you find in 'Find your own IQ' books that have lots of almost identical questions in each IQ test. Each participant takes both tests and their scores are correlated. As with test-retest a strong correlation means that the test is reliable – ie the measure is consistent between the two forms.

This method has the advantage of avoiding problems with practice. However, not all techniques lend themselves to the production of equivalent tests.

Test-retest method: One group of participants is given a test or interview once, and then again sometime later (when they have had a chance to forget it). Their scores from the first and second time are correlated. If the correlation is strong then the measure is reliable – it was consistent across the two occasions.

However, this method is not useful if the test is easy to remember – the effect of practice may interfere with participants' responses.

Replication: An experiment is repeated using the same standardised procedures to see if the findings are the same.

Qs   31

In a study on self-esteem, the researcher constructs a scale to measure a person's self-esteem. The scale consists of 30 questions.

1. How could the researcher assess the reliability of the self-esteem scale?
2. Why would it matter if the reliability of the scale were poor?
3. How could the researcher improve the reliability of the scale?
4. How could the researcher assess the validity of the self-esteem scale?
5. Why would it matter if the validity of the scale were poor?
6. How could the researcher improve the validity of the scale?

Activity 13   Split-half method and test-retest method

Try these methods of assessing reliability yourself. At the end of this chapter (page 60), there is a psychological test – a scale that measures a person's belief in the paranormal.

Split-half method. Construct two smaller versions of this scale to see if it is internally reliable. There are 25 items on this scale so you cannot divide it exactly in half.
Get everyone in your class to do the test and then calculate their score for Form A and Form B. Use the Excel method described on page 50 to calculate the correlation. Is it positive? Is it significant?

Test-retest method. Do the same questionnaire again (after a few days). Compare the second score for each person with their first score. Use the Excel method to calculate the correlation. Is it positive? Is it significant?

Assessing validity of questionnaires and interviews

When conducting questionnaires (including psychological tests and scales) and interviews, we are also concerned with validity.

The **external validity** concerns the extent to which the findings can be generalised (as we studied before on page 28, chapter 2).

But the **internal validity** is now a different matter because there is no IV and DV – therefore, we cannot be concerned with the extent to which the IV solely caused the changes in the DV.

The internal validity of a questionnaire/interview is related to the question of whether the questionnaire or interview or psychological test really measures what you intended to measure.

There are several ways to do this, the most common being:

- **Face validity**. Does the test look like it is measuring what you intended to measure? For example, are the questions obviously related to the topic?

- **Concurrent validity**. This can be established by comparing the current test with a previously established test on the same topic. Participants take both tests and you then compare their scores on the two tests.

Improving reliability

To improve reliability, you first need to assess the reliability of the questionnaire or interview!

Internal reliability: Select the test items that produce the greatest similarity. You can do this by removing certain items and seeing if there is a stronger correlation with the remaining items.

External reliability: This should be improved by greater internal reliability or increased validity.

Improving validity

Validity is also improved first of all by assessing the validity of a questionnaire or interview. If such measures of validity are low:

Internal validity: If one or more measures of internal validity are low, the items on the questionnaire/interview/test need to be revised, e.g. to produce a better match between scores on the new test and an established one.

External validity: Use a different sampling method to improve population validity.

Activity 14 — Validity and reliability of a questionnaire

You can use the quiz on the right or obtain your own questionnaire from a teenage magazine such as *Go Girl* or *Sugar*.

You could try one or all of the following activities:

- Measure the internal reliability of the quiz.
- Measure the external reliability of the quiz.
- Assess the face validity of the quiz.
- Assess the concurrent validity of the quiz by comparing the outcome with an established psychological test that measures the same variable. For example, psychologists may measure sensation seeking using Zuckerman's (1994) Sensation Seeking Scale (You can take the test and get your score at: www.bbc.co.uk/science/humanbody/mind/surveys/sensation/)
- Rewrite the quiz to improve reliability and validity.
- Rewrite the quiz using the knowledge you have gained in this chapter. For example, where tests are presented in 'flowchart'

form (as in the example), these could be rewritten as closed, forced choice questions to investigate the effect of questionnaire design. You might bear in mind the issue of **response set** – in the paranormal scale, some items had reversed scoring. This is to prevent people becoming too accustomed to writing 1 or 5 all the time.

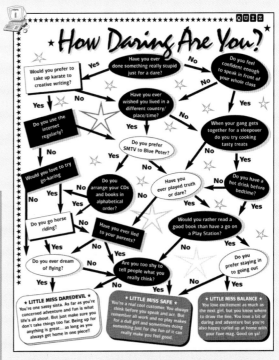

Does this questionnaire look as if it is testing sensation-seeking? If so, it has face validity.

KEY TERMS

Reliability
Internal validity

OTHER TERMS

Concurrent validity
External reliability
Face validity
Inter-interviewer reliability
Internal reliability
Replication
Response set
Split-half method
Test-retest method

DIY: A study using a correlational analysis

ESP: A 'sheep-goat effect'

People who believe in paranormal phenomena are the 'sheep'.

People who do not believe in paranormal phenomena are the 'goats'.

Various studies have looked at the relationship between paranormal beliefs and misjudgements of probability, e.g. that of Brugger *et al.* (1990). People who are sheep (believe in paranormal phenomena) are less good at probabilistic reasoning. Probabilistic reasoning refers to making judgements related to probability. For example, which is more likely:

- I throw 10 dice at the same time and get 10 sixes?

- I throw one dice 10 times in succession and get 10 successive sixes?

In fact, they are both equally likely – if you did not think so, it suggests you are not good at probabilistic reasoning. You probably also think you should never choose the numbers in the lottery that came up last time.

The link between probabilistic reasoning and paranormal belief is that some people like to have an explanation for the things that happen around them. For example, if a door bangs shut on a windless night, such people 'prefer' the explanation that there was a ghost, whereas others prefer to accept that there is no explanation. Those preferring the explanation of causes also do not find it easy to comprehend the idea of chance (probability).

Activity 15 — Investigating the sheep–goat effect

To investigate this, you need:

1. A measure of the degree to which someone believes in paranormal phenomena.

   You can use The Belief in the Paranormal Scale (on page 62) or produce your own questionnaire. A high score on the scale indicates that you believe in paranormal phenomena.

2. A measure of probabilistic reasoning.

   Ask participants to mimic the rolling of a dice by writing or saying a digit between 1 and 6. They should produce a string of 100 numbers.

   The way to score this is printed at the bottom of page 62. A high score indicates that they are not good at probabilistic reasoning.

To analyse your data

1. Draw a scattergraph to show the relationship between the co-variables (belief in the paranormal and probabilistic reasoning).

2. Calculate the correlation coefficient.

   What do the graph and correlation coefficient tell you about your findings? Is the correlation strong, moderate or weak?

3. Calculate the mean, median and mode for both sets of data (belief in the paranormal and probabilistic reasoning).

   Which measure of central tendency is the most useful? Why?

   Which measure of central tendency is the least useful? Why?

4. Sort your participants into three groups: sheep, goats and neutral. You need to decide how to define each group; e.g. you might decide that the sheep are all those who scored more than 45.

   Draw a bar chart to show the mean probabilistic reasoning score for each group.

   Compare the scattergraph and the bar chart. Which do you think is more informative?

A final word on correlation

The correlations we have looked at are all **linear** – in a perfect positive correlation (+1) all the values would lie in a *straight* line from the bottom left to the top right.

There is, however, a different kind of correlation – **a curvilinear correlation**. The relationship is not linear – it is curved – but there is still a predictable relationship. For example, stress and performance do not have a linear relationship. Performance on many tasks is depressed when stress is too high or too low; it is best when stress is moderate. The relationship between stress and performance was first identified by Yerkes and Dodson and thus called the Yerkes–Dodson Law. The graph on the right illustrates this relationship.

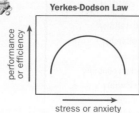

Yerkes-Dodson Law

performance or efficiency (y-axis)

stress or anxiety (x-axis)

Qs 32

1. Describe the aims of the sheep–goat study.

2. Would the hypothesis predict a positive or a negative correlation?

3. What conclusions can you draw from your findings?

OTHER TERMS

Curvilinear correlation
Linear correlation

Multiple choice questions

1. Data related to how people think and feel are called
   a. Qualitative data.
   b. Quantitative data.
   c. Questionnaire data.
   d. Both a and c.

2. Data that can be easily counted are called
   a. Qualitative data.
   b. Quantitative data.
   c. Questionnaire data.
   d. Both a and c.

3. Closed questions tend to produce
   a. Qualitative data.
   b. Quantitative data.
   c. Questionnaire data.
   d. Both a and c.

4. Open questions tend to produce
   a. Qualitative data.
   b. Quantitative data.
   c. Questionnaire data.
   d. Both a and c.

5. Respondents often answer questions in a way that makes them look good rather than being truthful. This is called
   a. A response set.
   b. A leading question.
   c. Social desirability bias.
   d. The Hawthorne effect.

6. One means of assessing people's attitudes is by using a scale from strongly agree to strongly disagree. This is called
   a. The semantic differential technique.
   b. A forced choice scale.
   c. A quantitative scale.
   d. The Likert Scale.

7. Which of the following is *not* an advantage of qualitative data?
   a. Represent thoughts and feelings that cannot be measured in an experiment.
   b. Easy to analyse the findings.
   c. Represents the true complexity of human behaviour.
   d. Means that unexpected information can be collected.

8. A clinical interview is a kind of
   a. Questionnaire.
   b. Structured interview.
   c. Unstructured interview.
   d. Correlation.

9. One advantage of an interview in comparison with a questionnaire is
   a. The interviewer can adapt questions as he or she goes along.
   b. People may feel more comfortable about revealing personal information.
   c. Interviews can be delivered by less skilled personnel.
   d. Social desirability bias is less of a problem.

10. Which of the following is false?
    a. A questionnaire can collect data from a large number of people in a short space of time.
    b. Questionnaires are less easy to analyse than interviews.
    c. Questionnaires do not require specialist administrators.
    d. Social desirability bias is a problem in a questionnaire.

11. A leading question is a question that
    a. Contains the answer in the question.
    b. Is the most important question on a questionnaire.
    c. Suggests what answer is desired.
    d. Tends to confuse respondents.

12. In a correlation you have
    a. An IV and a DV.
    b. Co-variables.
    c. Factors.
    d. Both a and b.

13. A negative correlation is when
    a. Two variables increase together.
    b. As one variable increases, the other decreases.
    c. There is a weak correlation between two variables.
    d. There is a strong correlation between two variables.

14. A correlation coefficient of $+0.65$ indicates.
    a. No correlation.
    b. A weak positive correlation.
    c. A moderate positive correlation.
    d. A strong positive correlation.

15. Which of the following could *not* be a correlation coefficient?
    a. 0
    b. $+0.79$
    c. $+1.28$
    d. -0.30

16. A scattergraph is
    a. A descriptive statistic.
    b. A graph that illustrates a correlation.
    c. A collection of dots where each dot represents a pair of scores.
    d. All of the above.

17. Which of the following is *not* an advantage of a study using a correlational analysis?
    a. Can be used when it is unethical or impractical to manipulate variables.
    b. Useful to help decide whether a more rigorous scientific investigation into the apparent relationship is justified.
    c. If no correlation can be found, you can rule out a causal relationship.
    d. Can demonstrate a causal relationship.

18. Internal reliability is a measure of the extent to which
    a. One measure of an object varies from another measure of the same object.
    b. How true or legitimate a measurement is.
    c. You obtain the result you were expecting.
    d. Something is consistent within itself.

19. One way to assess internal reliability is to
    a. Replicate the study.
    b. Use the test-retest method.
    c. Use the split-half method.
    d. Ask a friend.

20. Face validity is an assessment of whether a test
    a. Looks appealing to participants.
    b. Looks like it is measuring what it intends to measure.
    c. Produces a score similar to the score produced by another test measuring the same thing.
    d. All of the above.

Answers are on page 56

Exam-style question for chapter 3

1. A school decides to conduct a study on the healthy habits of the students in the school, using a questionnaire. They want to collect data about eating habits, exercise and smoking. It is important to know about (a) the students' habits and (b) their attitudes.

The school psychology department was asked to construct a suitable questionnaire. A part of this questionnaire is shown below.

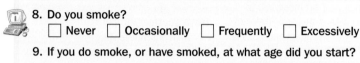

8. Do you smoke?

☐ Never ☐ Occasionally ☐ Frequently ☐ Excessively

9. If you do smoke, or have smoked, at what age did you start?

10. What do you think is the best reason not to smoke?

(a) (i) Define the terms 'qualitative data' and 'quantitative data'. **[2]**

(ii) Identify **one** question in the extract above that would provide qualitative data. **[1]**

(iii) With reference to the question you have identified in part (ii), explain why this question would produce qualitative data. **[2]**

(b) (i) Identify **one** sampling method that could have been used in this study. **[1]**

(ii) In the context of this study, explain **one** reason for using the sampling method identified in (i). **[2]**

(c) (i) The questions in the extract above can be criticised. Select **one** question and give one criticism of it. **[2]**

(ii) Re-write the question you selected so that it overcomes the criticism you identified in (i). **[2]**

(d) Describe **two** ways of making sure that this study would be carried out in an ethically acceptable way. **[4]**

(e) (i) Explain what is meant by validity in the context of research. **[2]**

(ii) Identify **one** problem with validity in this study. **[2]**

(iii) Explain how you would deal with the problem with validity identified in (ii) **[2]**

[Total 22 marks]

2. In your answers to this question you should include relevant information from the whole of your course, where appropriate.

(a) Outline **one** advantage and **one** disadvantage of using a questionnaire. **[4]**

(b) (i) An alternative way to collect data for individual participants is through an interview. What is the difference between structured and unstructured interviews? **[2]**

(ii) Describe **one** disadvantage of an unstructured interview compared to a structured interview. **[2]**

(iii) Describe **two** disadvantages of an unstructured interview compared to a structured interview. **[4]**

(c) Structured interviews can produce qualitative data. What level of measurement is the data likely to be and which measure of central tendency would you use with such data? **[2]**

[Total 14 marks]

[TOTAL FOR SECTION: 36 MARKS]

Examiner's tips

Question 1

(a) (i) Questions that simply ask you to define terms do arise, though more often you are asked to use your knowledge rather than just define it. In this question make sure that you have defined both of the terms - try not to use the term itself in the definition.

(a) (ii) To save yourself time, you can identify the question by its number, you don't have to copy the question from the extract out or explain why it would provide qualititave data; you do this in the next part of the question and it will not be credited in part (ii).

(a) (iii) There are 2 marks for this answer, which means you need to think hard about how you can provide sufficient detail. The question does not restrict you to give 'one' reason why the question would produce qualitative data so you can provide detail by giving a range of answers.

(b) (i) Any sampling method is acceptable but make sure you do give a reason in (ii) for the sampling method you named in (i).

(b) (ii) Watch out for the 'in the context': you must refer to some aspect of the study to get the full marks.

(c) If you select a question and do not provide an appropriate criticism, you get no marks for (i) and no marks for (ii).

(c) (ii) The question says 'rewrite' so don't just give vague details of what you would do; instead, present a new, alternative question – which must overcome the criticism given in (i).

(d) Being asked for 'two' of anything may stretch your knowledge. Think carefully, otherwise you are throwing away an important 4 marks.

Note that your answer must be contextualised and must focus on what you would do, not on what the issue is. Thus, just writing 'privacy' will get no marks because it is an issue. You need to explain what you would do.

(e) (i) You might want to use the definition of validity provided in this chapter rather than the one provided in chapter 2. In chapter 2, we were concerned with the validity of *experiments*, but that answer would also be acceptable.

(e) (ii) The 'problem' may relate to internal or external validity. Note that this question is worth 2 marks so you need to provide sufficient details.

(e) (iii) Clearly, the answer to (iii) must be linked to (ii). Any sensible answer will gain credit, although it must be explained.

Question 2

(a) When stating an advantage, be careful to provide sufficient detail and not just say 'a lot of data can be collected' – this could be said to be true for all methods. Remember, for all the questions with the word 'one' in them, that only your first answer may be marked by the examiner. Do not waste time providing more than one answer.

(b) (i) Note that this question is worth 2 marks. It hasn't asked for two points, so you could gain 2 marks either by making one point and elaborating it or by describing two differences.

(b) (ii) This question specifies one disadvantage, so you must elaborate your answer to get 2 marks. Bear in mind that the question says 'compared to ...'

(b) (iii) In this part of the question, each of the two points you make must be detailed (because each disadvantage is worth 2 marks). Remember that you might prompt yourself by thinking about the disadvantages as being opposites.

(c) Remember NOIR for levels of measurement, then use this to decide whether the appropriate measure of central tendency is the mean, median or mode.

Model answer for exam-style question

Question 1

(a) (i) Define the terms 'qualitative data' and quantitative data'. **[2]**

Qualitative data are descriptive rather than numbers. Quantitative data are measurable and numerical, such as scores on a test.

(a) (ii) Identify **one** question in the extract above that would provide qualitative data. **[1]**

Question 10.

(a) (iii) With reference to the question you have identified in part (ii), explain why this question would produce qualitative data. **[2]**

The answer would tell you what people think about smoking and would produce a range of answers that would not be easily quantifiable.

(b) (i) Identify **one** sampling method that could have been used in this study. **[1]**

An opportunity sample.

(ii) In the context of this study, explain **one** reason for using the sampling method you have identified in (i). **[2]**

Doing an opportunity sample means that you can obtain your participants easily because they are the first ones, rather than having to contact volunteers. This would mean it was quicker to complete the questionnaire.

(c) (i) The questions in the extract above can be criticised. Select **one** question and give **one** criticism of it. **[2]**

Question 8. The terms used aren't explained so different people may interpret them differently. One person might think 10 a day was excessive whereas someone else would rate this as moderate.

(ii) Rewrite the question you selected so that it overcomes the criticism you identified in (i). **[2]**

Instead of using the terms moderate, excessive, etc. I would use numbers, e.g. 0–5 a day, 6–10 a day, 11–20 a day, etc.

(d) Describe **two** ways of making sure that this study would be carried out in an ethically acceptable way. **[4]**

1. Confidentiality – I would ensure that people did not put their names on the questionnaires and would tell them about their rights of confidentiality as part of the informed consent.

2. Protection from psychological harm – I would make sure that there were no distressing questions, which could be checked during the pilot study.

(e) (i) Explain what is meant by validity in the context of research. **[2]**

Validity refers to the legitimacy of a study. It concerns both internal validity (the extent to which a study has measured what was intended to be measured) and external validity (the extent to which the findings can be generalised).

(ii) Identify **one** problem to validity in this study. **[2]**

The questionnaire may not collect the 'right' sort of data, e.g. people may not be truthful about their smoking habits and may lie to make themselves look better.

(iii) Explain how you would deal with the threat to validity identified in (ii). **[2]**

I would try to reduce dishonest answers by assuring them about confidentiality and that it was important to be honest so the healthy habits of school students could be properly assessed.

Examiner's comments

(a) (i) Qualitative data answer is just adequate. It would have been useful to have added the kinds of information that qualitative data tends to represent. Saying, for example, 'when participants describe their feelings rather than just ticking a box to say which emotion they are experiencing.' The definition of quantitative data is good.

(a) (ii) The other questions in the extract are all quantitative so would not be acceptable answers (and you would get zero for (ii)).

(a) (iii) An answer that omitted the last six words would only get 1 mark, and an answer that only mentioned '*what people think*' would not earn any marks.

(b) (i) Any sampling method could be chosen here.

(b) (ii) The first sentence is excellent. Notice how the explanation is made more detailed by making a comparison with another method. BUT there is no contextualisation in the first sentence (as required in the question) so the candidate has added another sentence.

(c) (i) The criticism is clearly explained. Just saying '*the words aren't clear*' would not have been detailed enough for 2 marks.

You might, alternatively, criticse the open-ended nature of Question 10 and provide some tick box answers.

(c) (ii) The choice of numbers (0–5, 6–10, 11–20) is a bit erratic but again sufficiently detailed for 2 marks. You do have to actually show what you would do.

(d) Ample detail for both answers, focused on what you would do about the ethical issue. Note that there is no mark for identifying the issue.

(e) (i) Detail has been gained by offering definitions of three aspects of validity.

(e) (ii) The first part of this sentence alone would possibly attract 1 mark, but it is fairly woolly. The 'e.g.' provides us with the important information. Either example would have been sufficient.

(e) (iii) An alternative solution might have been to lie about the aims of the study. Since the word 'one' is not in the answer, you could include a range of ways for the two marks and these would all be creditworthy.

Question 2

(a) Outline **one** advantage and **one** disadvantage of using a questionnaire

[4]

One advantage is that you can collect a lot of data from a lot of people quickly and relatively easily.

One disadvantage is that people may want to present themselves in a good light and therefore you don't get truthful (valid) answers.

(b) (i) An alternative way to collect data for individual participants is through an interview. What is the difference between structured and unstructured interviews? [2]

A structured interview has a set list of questions to follow so that every person is asked the same thing whereas in an un structured interview the interviewer responds to what is said with different questions.

(b) (ii) Describe **one** disadvantage of a structured interview compared to an unstructured interview. [2]

Because the questions are fixed, there may be things that would be useful to know but the interviewer cannot ask, so less varied information is gained than would be obtained from an unstructured interview..

(b) (iii) Describe **two** disadvantages of an unstructured interview compared to a structured interview. [4]

In an unstructured interview the interviewer may ask leading questions without realising they are, for example by the tone of their questions or their facial expression, so the participant's answers may be biased.

As the questions can change, the interviewer is more likely to encroach into personal information and the interviewee might not feel comfortable about answering them so might not be honest.

(c) Structured interviews can produce qualitative data. What level of measurement is it likely to be and which measure of central tendency would you use with such data? [2]

Oridinal data, so I would use a median.

Examiner's comments

(a) Saying that an advantage is that questionnaires are 'quick and easy' would receive no marks because it needs more explanation. You could argue that some experiments are also quick and easy.

The disadvantage given here may appear to be two answers (and then only the first would be credited) but the 'and' links two related points. There is no need to use the term 'social desirability bias' because there is enough for 2 marks as it stands – but it would make the answer clearer.

(b) (i) This answer makes the two key points, that structured interviews have fixed questions in contrast to unstructured interviews where the questions develop in the course of the interview. If the last three words had been missing, it would not have gained full marks.

(b) (ii) This answer makes the point that useful information may be missed and expands this by commenting on the limited range this technique imposes.

(b) (iii) The candidate has given two thorough answers. They are sufficiently detailed for the difference between the types of interview to be implicit.

(c) Nominal or (plastic) interval would also have been acceptable answers. The median is the best measure of central tendency to use with ordinal data. If the answer had been nominal or interval an answer of mode or mean (respectively) would have been correct. Note that it is necessary for this question to justify the decision to gain full marks.

Some exam hints to help with questions like these:

- Learn NOIR, and remember that N>O>I>R provides more information about data.

- Learn MMM (mode, median, mean). You need to remember what each one is, that is, what it represents about thee data set. You can probably remember what the mean is, for the other two, try remembering MOst=MOde and MEDian=MIDdle.

- There are several ethical issues that you can use when answering exam questions. It's helpful to know about a range of different ones as you may need them to apply to different studies or situations in examination questions. The key issues are:

  - deception
  - privacy
  - informed consent
  - protection
  - confidentiality
  - right to withdraw

See if you can make a word from the initial letters, or a rhyme that will remind you about each issue.

Crossword

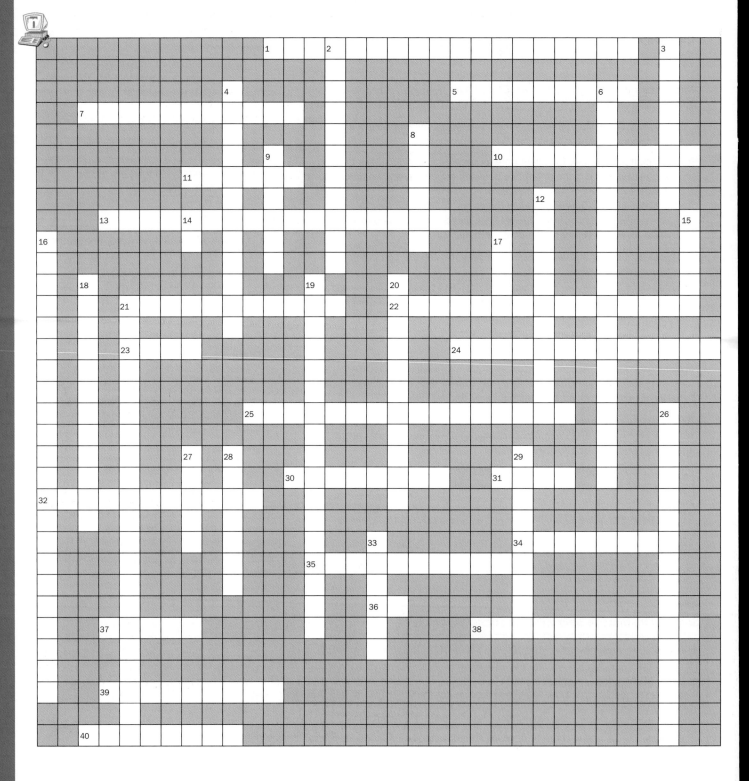

Clues

Across

1. Process of ensuring that variables are in a form that can be easily tested. (18)
5. An investigative method that generally involves a face-to-face interaction with another individual and results in the collection of data. (9)
7. The kind of data that express what people think or feel and cannot be counted. (11)
10. The mode is one measure of central tendency. Name two others. (4,6)
11. The middle value in a set of scores when they are placed in rank order. (6)
13. A statistical measure of the amount of variation in a set of scores around the mean. (8,9)
21. A research design in which neither the participant nor the experimenter is aware of the condition that an individual participant is receiving. (6,5)
22. The extent to which an observed effect can be attributed to the experimental manipulation rather than some other factor. (8,8)
23. The arithmetic average of a group of scores, calculated by dividing the sum of the scores by the number of scores. (4)
24. Data that represent how much, how long or how many, etc. there are of something; i.e. a behaviour is measured in numbers. (12)
25. An experimental technique designed to overcome order effects. (16)
30. The kind of reliability in which something is consistent within itself; e.g. all test items should be measuring the same thing. (8)
31. The most frequently occurring score in a set of data. (4)
32. Kind of sampling in which people are selected who are most easily available at the time of the study. (11)
34. A correlation between two variables such that, as the value of one co-variable increases, the other decreases. (8)
35. In a repeated measures design, a confounding variable arising from the sequence in which conditions are presented, e.g. a practice or fatigue effect. (5,6)
36. In an experiment, the variable that is manipulated by the experimenter (initials). (2)
37. An experiment in which the relationship between an independent and dependent variable is studied within the context in which the behaviour normally occurs, (usually) without the participants knowing they are part of a study. (5)
38. Predicts the kind of difference (e.g. more or less) or relationship (positive or negative) between two groups of participants or between different conditions: _____ hypothesis. (11)
39. A type of frequency distribution in which the number of scores in each category of continuous data are represented by vertical columns. (9)
40. Kind of correlation in which both variables increase together. (8)

Down

2. The extent to which two measures are consistent. (11)
3. A graph used to represent the frequency of data; the categories on the x axis have no fixed order, and there is no true zero. (3,5)
4. Term used to describe instructions or procedures that are the same for all participants to avoid investigator effects and enable replication of the study. (12)
6. A calculation of the extent to which a measure varies from another measure of the same thing. (8,11)
8. A way of conducting research in a systematic manner e.g. experiment or interview. Is this the design or the method? (6)
9. A technique for selecting participants such that every member of the population being tested has an equal chance of being selected. (6)
12. Shows a relationship between two variables. (11)
14. In an experiment, the variable that is measured by the experimenter (initials). (2)
15. A small-scale trial of a study run to test any aspects of the design, with a view to making improvements. (5)
16. A number between −1 and +1 that tells us how closely the co-variables in a correlational analysis are related. (11,11)
17. In an interview or questionnaire, questions that invite the respondents to provide their own answers rather than select one of those provided. (4)
18. A graphical representation of the relationship (i.e. the correlation) between two sets of scores. (12)
19. An experimental design in which participants are randomly allocated to two (or more) groups representing different conditions. (11,6)
20. A type of research design in which the participants are not aware of the research aims or of which condition of the experiment they are receiving. (6,5)
21. Features of an experiment that a participant unconsciously responds to when searching for clues about how to behave. (6,15)
26. A type of experimental design in which each participant takes part in every condition under test. (8,8)
27. A measure of dispersion that measures the difference between the highest and lowest score in a set of data. (5)
28. A type of investigation in which the experimenter cannot manipulate the independent variable directly, but in which it varies naturally. (7)
29. A sampling technique that relies solely on people who offer to participate, usually in response to an advertisement. (9)
33. The overall plan of action to maximise meaningful results and minimise ambiguity using research techniques such as control of variables and selection of participants. Is this the design or the method? (6)

Crossword answers are on page 63

Belief in the Paranormal Scale

This inventory represents an attempt to discover which of the various paranormal events and phenomena you believe to be most likely and which you believe to be least likely. There are no right or wrong answers. Moreover, this is not an attempt to belittle or make fun of your beliefs. Therefore, please indicate your true feelings as well as you can. If you are unsure or ambivalent, indicate this by marking 'undecided' and proceed to the next item. Indicate your answers in the following format:

1 = strongly disagree with this statement
2 = disagree with statement
3 = undecided or don't know
4 = agree with statement
5 = strongly agree with statement

1 2 3 4 5	1.	I believe psychic phenomena are real, and should become part of psychology and be studied scientifically.
1 2 3 4 5	2.	All UFO sightings are either other forms of physical phenomena (such as weather balloons) or simply hallucinations.
1 2 3 4 5	3.	I am convinced the Abominable Snowman of Tibet really exists.
1 2 3 4 5	4.	I firmly believe that ghosts and spirits do exist.
1 2 3 4 5	5.	Black magic really exists and should be dealt with in a serious manner.
1 2 3 4 5	6.	Witches and warlocks do exist.
1 2 3 4 5	7.	Only the uneducated or demented believe in the supernatural.
1 2 3 4 5	8.	Through psychic individuals it is possible to communicate with the dead.
1 2 3 4 5	9.	I believe the Loch Ness monster of Scotland exists.
1 2 3 4 5	10.	I believe that once a person dies his spirit may come back from time to time in the form of ghosts.
1 2 3 4 5	11.	Some individuals are able to levitate (lift objects) through mysterious mental forces.
1 2 3 4 5	12.	I believe that many special persons throughout the world have the ability to predict the future.
1 2 3 4 5	13.	The idea of being able to tell the future through the means of palm reading represents the beliefs of foolish and unreliable persons.
1 2 3 4 5	14.	I am firmly convinced that reincarnation has occurred throughout history.
1 2 3 4 5	15.	I firmly believe that, at least on some occasions, I can read another person's mind via ESP (extrasensory perception).
1 2 3 4 5	16.	ESP is an unusual gift that many persons have and should not be confused with elaborate tricks used by entertainers.
1 2 3 4 5	17.	Ghosts and witches do not exist outside the realm of the imagination.
1 2 3 4 5	18.	Supernatural phenomena should become part of scientific study, equal in importance to physical phenomena.
1 2 3 4 5	19.	All of the reports of "scientific proof" of psychic phenomena are strictly sensationalism with no factual basis.
1 2 3 4 5	20.	Through the use of mysterious formulas and incantations it is possible to cast spells on individuals.
1 2 3 4 5	21.	With proper training anyone could learn to read other people's minds.
1 2 3 4 5	22.	It is advisable to consult your horoscope daily.
1 2 3 4 5	23.	Plants can sense the feelings of people through a form of ESP.
1 2 3 4 5	24.	ESP has been scientifically proven to exist.
1 2 3 4 5	25.	There is a great deal we have yet to understand about the mind of man, so it is likely that many phenomena (such as ESP) will one day be proven to exist.

Scoring for the Belief in the Paranormal Scale (Jones et al., 1977)

Reverse responses for questions 2, 7, 13, 17, 19; i.e. for question 2, if a person responded with 5, then change this to 1; if 4, then change this to 2; 3 stays the same; 2 changes to 4; and 1 changes to 5.

Now add all the responses, giving a maximum score of 125.

In the trial of this scale (with 475 undergraduates) 10% scored less than 50 (low believers) and 10% scored more than 85 (high believers).

Scoring for the probabilistic task

Score this by placing a tick whenever a number is repeated consecutively. The participant's score is the total number of ticks.

Crossword answers

Across

1. OPERATIONALISATION – Process ensuring that variables are in a form that can be easily tested. (18)
5. INTERVIEW – An investigative method that generally involves a face-to-face interaction with another individual and results in the collection of data. (9)
7. QUALITATIVE – The kind of data that express what people think or feel and cannot be counted. (11)
10. MEAN, MEDIAN – The mode is one measure of central tendency. Name two others. (4,6)
11. MEDIAN – The middle value in a set of scores when they are placed in rank order. (6)
13. STANDARD DEVIATION – A statistical measure of the amount of variation in a set of scores around the mean. (8,9)
21. DOUBLE BLIND – A research design in which neither the participant nor the experimenter is aware of the condition that an individual participant is receiving. (6,5)
22. INTERNAL VALIDITY – The extent to which an observed effect can be attributed to the experimental manipulation rather than some other factor. (8,8)
23. MEAN – The arithmetic average of a group of scores, calculated by dividing the sum of the scores by the number of scores. (4)
24. QUANTITATIVE – Data that represent how much, how long or how many, etc. there are of something; i.e. a behaviour is measured in numbers. (12)
25. COUNTERBALANCING – An experimental technique designed to overcome order and practice effects. (16)
30. INTERNAL – The kind of reliability in which something is consistent within itself; e.g. all test items should be measuring the same thing. (8)
31. MODE – The most frequently occurring score in a set of data. (4)
32. OPPORTUNITY – Kind of sampling in which people are selected who are most easily available at the time of the study. (11)
34. NEGATIVE – A correlation between two variables such that, as the value of one co-variable increases, the other decreases. (8)
35. ORDER EFFECT – In a repeated measures design, a confounding variable arising from the sequence in which conditions are presented, e.g. a practice or fatigue effect. (5,6)
36. IV – In an experiment, the variable that is manipulated by the experimenter (initials). (2)
37. FIELD – An experiment in which the relationship between an independent and dependent variable is studied within the context in which the behaviour normally occurs, (usually) without the participants knowing they are part of a study. (5)
38. DIRECTIONAL – Predicts the kind of difference (e.g. more or less) or relationship (positive or negative) between two groups of participants or between different conditions: hypothesis. (11)
39. HISTOGRAM – A type of frequency distribution in which the number of scores in each category of continuous data are represented by vertical columns. (9)
40. POSITIVE – Kind of correlation in which both variables increase together. (8)

Down

2. RELIABILITY – The extent to which two measures are consistent. (11)
3. BAR CHART – A graph used to represent the frequency of data; the categories on the x axis have no fixed order, and there is no true zero. (3,5)
4. STANDARDISED – Term used to describe instructions or procedures that are the same for all participants to avoid investigator effects and enable replication of the study. (12)
6. EXTERNAL RELIABILITY – A calculation of the extent to which a measure varies from another measure of the same thing. (8,11)
8. METHOD – A way of conducting research in a systematic manner e.g. experiment or interview. Is this the design or the method? (6)
9. RANDOM – A technique for selecting participants such that every member of the population being tested has an equal chance of being selected. (6)
12. CORRELATION – Shows a relationship between two variables. (11)
14. DV – In an experiment, the variable that is measured by the experimenter (initials). (2)
15. PILOT – A small-scale trial of a study run to test any aspects of the design, with a view to making improvements. (5)
16. CORRELATION COEFFICIENT – A number between −1 and +1 that tells us how closely the co-variables in a correlational analysis are related. (11,11)
17. OPEN – In an interview or questionnaire, questions that invite the respondents to provide their own answers rather than select one of those provided. (4)
18. SCATTERGRAPH – A graphical representation of the relationship (i.e. the correlation) between two sets of scores. (12)
19. INDEPENDENT GROUPS – An experimental design in which participants are randomly allocated to two (or more) groups representing different conditions. (11,6)
20. SINGLE BLIND – A type of research design in which the participants are not aware of the research aims or of which condition of the experiment they are receiving. (6,5)
21. DEMAND CHARACTERISTICS – Features of an experiment that a participant unconsciously responds to when searching for clues about how to behave. (6,15)
26. REPEATED MEASURES – A type of experimental design in which each participant takes part in every condition under test. (8,8)
27. RANGE – A measure of dispersion that measures the difference between the highest and lowest score in a set of data. (5)
28. NATURAL – A type of investigation in which the experimenter cannot manipulate the independent variable directly, but in which it varies naturally. (7)
29. VOLUNTEER – A sampling technique that relies solely on people who offer to participate, usually in response to an advertisement. (9)
33. DESIGN – The overall plan of action to maximise meaningful results and minimise ambiguity using research techniques such as control of variables and selection of participants. Is this the design or the method? (6)

Contents

Observations
and a few other things

Observational methods

Observational studies are non-experimental. There is no independent variable (IV), although a hypothesis concerning an IV may be tested (i.e. you can investigate but not demonstrate causal relationships).

In an observational study, participants are observed engaging in whatever behaviour is being studied. The observations are recorded.

In a **naturalistic observation**, behaviour is studied in a natural situation where *everything* has been left as it *normally* is.

In a **controlled observation**, some variables are controlled by the researcher, reducing the 'naturalness' of the behaviour being studied. Participants are likely to know they are being studied, and the study may be conducted in a laboratory.

Observational studies use observation as a *method* of conducting research, but observational methods may also be used in an experiment – in which case observation is a **research technique** instead of a **research method**.

Observational methods, like other methods where variables are measured, should be unaffected by the opinions or feelings of the researcher. That is, observations should be **objective**. This is a particular problem in observational research because an observer may be biased and record what he or she expects to see. Objectivity can be improved by using **operationalisation** (see facing page).

When researchers are biased, for instance being influenced by their theoretical opinion, they are demonstrating **subjectivity**.

Activity 16   **Making observations**

Work with a partner and take it in turns to observe each other. One of you will be Person A, and the other will be Person B.

Person A should have a difficult task to do (e.g. answering one of the exam questions in this book!).

Person B should have a boring task to do (e.g. copying out the exam question).

Each person should spend 5 minutes on the task.

The person doing the observing should note down any aspect of their partner's behaviour.

See questions on this task below.

Qs   **33**

1. Answer the following questions about the observational study in Activity 16.
   a. Suggest a suitable hypothesis for the study.
   b. If you did the activity, summarise your observations.
   c. What uncontrolled factors might affect your findings?
   d. What can you conclude from your research?
   e. In this study, is 'observation' the method or the technique?
   f. Are the observations controlled or naturalistic?
   g. If you did conduct the observation, can you suggest **one or more** difficulties that you encountered?
2. With reference to the study by Lamb and Roopnarine (an example of a naturalistic observation), give **one** advantage and **one** disadvantage of studying children in this way.
3. With reference to the example of a controlled observation, give **one** advantage and **one** disadvantage of studying children in this way.

An example of a naturalistic observation

Do little boys criticise each other if they behave like girls? Do little boys 'reward' each other for sex-appropriate play? Is the same true for little girls?

One study observed boys and girls aged 3–5 years during their free play periods at nursery school. The researchers classified activities as male, female or neutral, and recorded how playmates responded. Praise and imitation constituted some of the positive responses; criticism and stopping play were some of the negative responses. They found that children generally reinforced peers for sex-appropriate play and were quick to criticise sex-inappropriate play (Lamb and Roopnarine, 1979).

An example of a controlled observation

The same research as described on the right could have been conducted by controlling some of the variables. For example, the researchers might have set up a special playroom in their laboratory with certain types of toys available (male, female and neutral). They could have observed the children through a **one-way mirror** so that the children would be unaware of being observed.

An example of an experiment with controlled observational techniques

In the 'Bobo doll study' described on page 25 (Bandura *et al.*, 1961), the children's aggressiveness was observed at the end of the experiment to see if those exposed to the aggressive model behaved more aggressively. At the end of the experiment, each child was taken to a room that contained some aggressive toys (e.g. a mallet and a dart gun), some non-aggressive toys (e.g. dolls and farm animals) and a 3-foot Bobo doll.

The experimenter stayed with the child while he or she played for 20 minutes, during which time the child was observed through a one-way mirror. The observers recorded what the child was doing every 5 seconds, using the following measures:

- *Imitation of physical aggression*: any specific acts that were imitated.
- *Imitative verbal aggression*: any phrases that were imitated, such as 'POW'.
- *Imitative non-aggressive verbal responses*: such as 'He keeps coming back for more.'
- *Non-imitative physical and verbal aggression*: aggressive acts directed at toys other than Bobo, e.g. saying things not said by the model, or were not demonstrated by the model playing with the gun.

Observation techniques

You might think that making observations is easy, but if you tried Activity 16, you should now realise it is difficult, for two main reasons:

1. It is difficult to work out what to record and what not to record.

2. It is difficult to record everything that is happening even if you do select what to record and what not to record.

Observational research, like all research, aims to be objective and rigorous. For this reason, it is necessary to use observational techniques and conduct systematic observations.

Observational systems

One of the hardest aspects of the observational method is deciding how different behaviours should be categorised. This is because our perception of behaviour is often seamless; when we watch somebody perform a particular action, we see a continuous stream of action rather than a series of separate behavioural components.

In order to conduct systematic observations, one needs to break this stream of behaviour up into different categories. A **coding system** (also called a **behaviour checklist**) is constructed when making preliminary observations. What is needed is **operationalisation** – breaking the behaviour being studied into a set of components. For example, when observing infant behaviour, have a list such as smiling, crying, sleeping, etc., or when observing facial expressions, have a list of different expressions as shown on page 70.

The coding system should:

- Be *objective* the observer should make an accurate and unbiased record of events that occur, and should record only explicit actions rather than making inferences about behaviour.

- Cover all *possible component behaviours* and avoid a 'waste basket' category.

- Each category should be *mutually exclusive*, meaning that you should not have to mark two categories at one time.

In **controlled observations**, it is the participant's environment that is controlled – not the techniques used to obtain observational data. **Systematic techniques** are used in **naturalistic and controlled observations**.

In **unstructured observations**, the researcher records all relevant behaviour but has no system. The behaviour to be studied is largely unpredictable.

One problem with this is that the behaviours recorded are often those which are most visible or eye-catching to the observer, but these may not necessarily be the most important or relevant behaviours.

In **systematic** or **structured observations**, the researcher uses various 'systems' to organise observations.

- **Research aims** Decide on an area to study.

- **Observational systems** How to record the behaviour you are interested in.

- **Sampling procedures** Who you are observing and when.

Sampling procedures

Continuous observation Record every instance of the behaviour you see in as much detail as possible. This is useful if the behaviours you are interested in do not occur very often.

In many situations continuous observation would not be possible because there would be too much data to record, therefore there must be a systematic method of sampling observations:

- **Event sampling** Counting the number of times a certain behaviour (event) occurs in a target individual or individuals.

- **Time sampling**. Recording behaviours in a given time frame. For example, noting what a target individual is doing every 30 seconds. You may select one or more categories from a checklist.

Activity 17   Making systematic observations

The coding system below is adapted from one used by Fick (1993) in a study looking at the effects of having a dog as a pet on the nature and frequency of social interactions in nursing home residents.

You can use this shortened version to make observations of other students in a common room or cafeteria. Shortened coding system:

- *Non-attentive behaviour*: Participant is not engaged in group activity.

- *Attentive listening*: Participant maintains eye contact with other group members.

- *Verbal interaction with another person*: Participant initiates or responds verbally to another person.

- *Non-verbal interaction with another person*: Participant touches, gestures, smiles, nods, etc. to another person.

1. Decide on your research aims; e.g. you could compare social interactions in the morning and afternoon, or differences between boys and girls, or between different environments (such as in class and in the cafeteria).

2. State your hypothesis.

3. Draw up a grid to record your observations.

4. Decide on a sampling procedure.

5. Conduct a pilot study.

Observational studies

Distinctions

Method and technique
Remember that all research involves making observations; however, in the case of some research, the overall *method* is observational, where the emphasis is on observing a relatively unconstrained segment of a person's freely chosen behaviour.

Controlled and naturalistic
In both cases, systematic methods are used to record observations. In a controlled observation, the environmental variables are controlled to some extent e.g. the setting may be moved from the person's normal environment, or some of the items in the environment may be deliberately chosen.

Participant and non-participant
In many cases, the observer is merely watching the behaviour of others and acts as a non-participant. In some studies, observers also participate, which may affect their objectivity. A classic example of a participant observation is described on the right.

Disclosed and undisclosed (overt and covert)
One-way mirrors are used to prevent participants being aware that they are being observed. This is called undisclosed (covert) observation. Knowing that your behaviour is being observed is likely to alter your behaviour. Observers often try to be as unobtrusive as possible.

Direct and indirect
In many studies, such as content analysis, observations are made of data that has already been collected, e.g. observing advertisements on TV to see what gender bias exists, or observing newspaper advertisements or children's books. This is indirect observation (see 'Content analysis' on page 71.)

An undisclosed observation: The eve of destruction

In the 1950s, the social psychologist Leon Festinger read a newspaper report about a religious cult that claimed to be receiving messages from outer space predicting that the end of the world would take place on a certain date in the form of a great flood. The cult members were going to be rescued by a flying saucer so they all gathered with their leader. Festinger was intrigued to know how the cult members would respond when they found that their beliefs were

Rescue ship for the religious cult who foretold the end of the world.

unfounded, especially as many of them had made their beliefs very public. In order to observe this at first hand, Festinger and some co-workers posed as converts to the cause and were present on the eve of destruction. When it was apparent that there would be no flood, the group leader said that their prayer had saved the city. Some cult members did not believe this and left the cult, whereas others took this as proof of the cult's beliefs (Festinger *et al.*, 1956).

Devices for managing and recording observations
The raw data gathered in an observational study can come in visual, audio or written form. To assist the collection of data you might use:

- Binoculars, if you are observing from any distance.
- One-way mirrors, for undisclosed observations.
- A video camera, if you want to replay behavioural sequences or observe people in an unobtrusive manner.
- An audio-cassette recorder, again for replaying sequences so they can be coded later.
- Paper for recording data using a coding system. This can be done 'live' or using video/audio-recording.

Analysis of observational data
Unstructured observations produce **qualitative** data.

Structured or systematic observations produce numerical data in categories (**quantitative**) that can be analysed using descriptive statistics. See page 15 and chapter 6 for details of quantitative analysis and page 73 for details of qualitative analysis.

Qs

34

1. Identify what kind of observational study was conducted by Festinger *et al.* (described top right).

2. In each of the following observations, state which sampling procedure would be most appropriate and explain how you would do it:
   a. Recording instances of aggressive behaviour in children playing in a school playground.
   b. Vocalisations (words, sounds) made by young children.
   c. Compliance with controlled pedestrian crossings by pedestrians.
   d. Litter-dropping in a public park.
   e. Behaviour of dog owners when walking their dogs.

3. *A group of students decided to study student behaviour in the school library.*
   a. Suggest **one or more** hypotheses that you might investigate.
   b. List **five** behaviours you might include in a behaviour checklist.
   c. Identify a suitable sampling procedure and explain how you would do it.
   d. How could you observe the students so that they were not aware that they were being observed?
   e. What ethical issues might be raised in this observational study?
   f. For each issue identified in your answer to (e), explain how you could deal with this issue and whether this would be acceptable.
   g. Explain in what way this would be a naturalistic observation.
   h. In this study, is observation a method or a technique?

4. *What distinguishes a successful teacher from an unsuccessful one? A group of students decide to observe various teachers while they are teaching.*
   a. Identify **two** ways in which you could operationalise 'successful teaching behaviour'.
   b. Describe **one** way in which you could minimise the intrusive nature of your observations.
   c. How would you record the data in this observational study?
   d. Suggest **one** advantage and **one** disadvantage of conducting an observational study in this context.
   e. Describe **two** ways of ensuring that this study would be carried out in an ethically acceptable manner.
   f. In this study, is observation a method or a technique?

Reliability

Observations should be consistent, which means that two observers should ideally produce the same record. The extent to which two (or more) observers agree is called inter-rater or **inter-observer reliability**. This is measured by correlating the observations of two or more observers (see 'Assessing reliability' below). A general rule is that if (Total agreements) ÷ (Total observations) > 0.80, the data have inter-observer reliability.

Dealing with low reliability

Observers should be trained in the use a coding system/behaviour checklist. They should practise using it and discuss their observations.

Training observers

The Behavioural Observation unit (BEO) at the University of Bern trains people in the use of observational techniques (BEO, 2004). They have a nursery school at the unit where the children can be observed through a one-way mirror. The data collected have been used for various studies such as comparing twins. The unit has devised a coding system (called KaSo 12):

No social participation
1. Occupied alone participation
2. Hanging around alone
3. Alone – onlooker
4. Alone – unclear

Social participation
5. Parallel behaviour 1
6. Parallel behaviour 2
7. Loosely associated but interactive
8. Role play – identifiable
9. Social participation unclear

Not identifiable
10. Child not in view, generally unclear

Validity

External validity

Observational studies are likely to have high **ecological validity** because they involve more natural behaviours (but remember the discussion in Chapter 2 – naturalness does not always mean greater ecological validity).

Population validity may be a problem if, for example, children are observed only in middle-class homes. The findings may not generalise to all children.

Internal validity

Observations will not be valid (or reliable) if the coding system/behaviour checklist is flawed. For example, some observations may belong in more than one category, or some behaviours may not be codeable.

The validity of observations is also affected by **observer bias** – what someone observes is influenced by their expectations. This reduces the objectivity of observations.

Dealing with low validity

Conducting observations in varied settings with varied participants (improves external validity).

Dealing with low reliability (improves internal validity).

Using more than one observer to reduce observer bias and averaging data across observers (balances out any biases).

Assessing reliability

The graph below show observations made of two children in the nursery class using KaSo 12. Each time, three observers were used (blue, red and green lines). The figures represent the relative duration of a specific behaviour category in per cent.

Child 1: Mean correlation of the 3 profiles: $r = 0.86$.

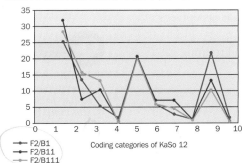

Coding categories of KaSo 12
F2/B1
F2/B11
F2/B111

Child 2: Showing a markedly different distribution of behaviour patterns but an even closer correlation: $r = 0.93$.

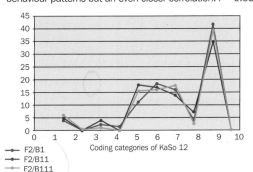

Coding categories of KaSo 12
F2/B1
F2/B11
F2/B111

Ethical issues

In a naturalistic observation, participants may be observed without their **informed consent**.

Some observations may be regarded as an invasion of **privacy**. Participant **confidentiality** should be respected.

The use of one-way mirrors involves **deception**/lack of informed consent.

Dealing with ethical issues

Informed consent: In some cases, it may be possible to obtain informed consent. For example, in the observations of nursery children by the BEO (see below left), parental permission was obtained for all children attending the nursery.

Invasion of privacy: **Ethical guidelines** generally advise that it is acceptable to observe people in public places (places where people expect to be seen by others).

Ethical committees can be used to approve observational designs.

 Qs **35**

1. On the left are two graphs showing the observations of two children by three observers. Do you think that the graphs indicate an acceptable level of inter-observer reliability?

2. *A psychologist decided to observe the non-verbal behaviours between two people having a conversation. (Non-verbal behaviours are those which do not involve language – such as smiling, touching, etc.)*

   a. Explain why it would be desirable to conduct a pilot study.

   b. If this is to be a naturalistic observation, *where* should the student researchers make their observations?

   c. Each conversation is observed by two students. Identify **one** way in which you could ensure reliability between the different observers and explain how you might put this into practice.

   d. Describe **two** features of the study that might reduce its validity.

   e. Explain how you could deal with these two features that might reduce validity.

   f. Draw a suitable table for recording observations, showing some of the possible categories.

   g. Describe **one** way of ensuring that this study would be carried out in an ethically acceptable manner.

   h. Evaluate your method of dealing with ethics.

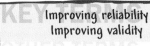

KEY TERMS
Improving reliability
Improving validity

OTHER TERMS
Inter-observer reliability
Non-participant observation
Observer bias
Undisclosed observations

Observational studies

Coding systems, categories and rating scales

Using a **coding system** (see right) means that a code is invented to represent each category of behaviour. A **behaviour checklist** is essentially the same thing, although a code may not be given to each behaviour.

A further method is to provide a list of behaviours or characteristics and ask observers to rate each one using a **rating scale** (see below).

Evaluating observational methods

Advantages

- What people say they do is often different from what they actually do so observations are more valid than questionnaires/interviews.

- The method offers a way to study behaviour when there are objections to manipulating variables, such as arranging for a child to spend time apart from his or her parent.

- Gives a more realistic picture of spontaneous behaviour. It is likely to have high ecological validity.

- A means of conducting preliminary investigations in a new area of research in order to produce hypotheses for future investigations.

Disadvantages

- There can be little or no control of extraneous variables.

- The observer may 'see' what he/she expects to see. This is called observer bias. This bias may mean that different observers 'see' different things, which leads to low **inter-observer reliability**.

- There are a number of ethical problems such as lack of **informed consent** and invasion of **privacy**.

- The method requires observer preparation and training.

Activity 18   DIY

Make your own coding system

A number of studies have looked at how males and females are represented in children's books. For example, Crabb and Bielawski (1994) examined American preschool books and found that female characters were more likely to be pictured using household objects, whereas males were more likely to be using production objects (e.g. items related to agriculture, construction, transportation – i.e. work outside the home).

Develop your own coding system to record the way in which males and females are represented in preschool children's books. Start by looking at some children's books and the activities that men and women, boys and girls are engaged in.

Once you have developed a coding system, you may investigate the hypothesis that children's books support gender stereotypes.

Facial Action Coding System (FACS) (Ekman and Friesen, 1978).

Paul Ekman and others have used this coding system to investigate how people display and recognise emotion using non-verbal cues and to study interpersonal deception.

For the full illustrations, see
www-2.cs.cmu.edu/afs/cs/project/face/www/facs.htm

Code	Description		Code	Description
1	Inner brow raiser		26	Jaw Drop
2	*Outer brow raiser		27	Mouth stretch
4	Brow lowerer		28	Lip suck
5	Upper lid raiser		41	Lid droop
6	Cheek raiser		42	Slit
7	Lid tightener		43	Eyes closed
9	Nose wrinkler		44	Squint
10	Upper lip raiser		45	Blink
11	Nasolabial deepener		46	Wink
12	Lip corner puller		51	Head turn left
13	Cheek puffer		52	Head turn right
14	Dimpler		53	Head up
15	Lip corner depressor		54	Head down
16	Lower lip depressor		55	Head tilt left
17	Chin raiser		56	Head tilt right
18	Lip puckerer		57	Head forward
20	Lip stretcher		58	Head back
22	Lip funneler		61	Eyes turn left
23	*Lip tightener		62	Eyes turn right
24	Lip pressor		63	Eyes up
25	Lips part		64	Eyes down

*Outer brow raiser

*Lip tightener

Naturalistic observation versus natural experiment

Both involve naturally occurring variables that have not been manipulated by the researcher. Both may involve an IV, but in a natural experiment the researcher is measuring a dependent variable (DV).

Qs   36

Imagine that you wished to investigate interpersonal deception to see if it was possible to use facial expressions to tell whether or not someone was lying.

1. Describe how you would design a study using observational techniques to investigate this. Identify and describe at least six design decisions and describe each one carefully.

2. Would you describe your study as a naturalistic observation, a controlled observation or a natural, field or lab experiment? Explain why.

3. How could same study be done using a different method?

4. What would be the relative advantages of doing this study as a naturalistic observation or as a lab experiment?

5. Identify **one** advantage of a natural experiment over a naturalistic observation.

6. Identify **one** advantage of a naturalistic observation over a natural experiment.

Content analysis

Indirect observations can be made of various media: books, films, TV shows, news programmes and interviews, CDs, etc. Content analysis may be used to explore issues such as aggression in children's stories, sexism in TV cartoons or racism in newspaper advertisements. Such observations are 'indirect' because they are observations of the communications produced by people. The data produced is quantitative when recording units, such as themes, tone or individual words are counted.

The process involved is similar to any observational study:

1. Decisions about a sampling method: what material to sample and how frequently (eg which TV channels and how many programmes).

2. Decisions about coding units: operational definitions of each type of item to be recorded. These may then be categorised.

3. As with observations, if there is a team of researchers it is important to ensure that they are applying criteria in the same way (see page 66)

Content analysis can also be used to follow changes over time (see longitudinal design page 76). For example:

- changing attitudes of teenagers to pre-marital sex or the use of condoms could be analysed through letters sent to the problem pages of magazines over many years

- levels of prejudice could be investigated by counting the number of racist or homophobic terms appearing in the lyrics of songs from different years or spoken by TV show hosts in archived programmes.

An example of content analysis: using lonely hearts ads

Evolutionary psychologists propose that men and women seek different things in a partner because of the basic differences between eggs and sperm. Women produce relatively few eggs, each at a physiological cost, so a female seeks a male partner who has 'resources' (such as being wealthy) to enhance her reproductive success. Men produce millions of sperm and should therefore seek youth and fertility in a partner to enhance the reproductive success of their genes. Features that are regarded as attractive in women are often things that are signs of health and youth (firm breasts, small waist, symmetrical face).

Various studies have analysed the contents of lonely hearts ads to see if what men and women advertise, and also what they seek, fits evolutionary predictions. For example, Waynforth and Dunbar (1995) analysed nearly 900 ads from 400 American newspapers. They looked at three behaviours: individuals seeking resources, seeking attractiveness and offering attractiveness. Age was also taken into account. Some of their findings are shown on page 75.

Evaluating content analysis

Advantages

- Has high ecological validity because based on direct observations of real media which are current and relevant, such as recent newspapers or children's books in print.

- When sources can be retained or accessed by others (e.g. back copies of magazines or videos of people giving speeches) findings can be replicated and so tested for reliability.

Disadvantages

- Researcher bias reduces the objectivity and validity of findings because use of coding units may be open to interpretation.

- If there is more than one observer and they are inconsistent in their application of operationalised coding units this would lower inter-rater reliability.

- Likely to be culture-dependent because interpretation of verbal or written content will be affected by language and society.

Activity 19 — DIY Content analysis

Many studies using content analysis consider the content of advertisements. For example, Lewis and Hill (1998) examined the ads for food that were shown between children's TV shows. They found that over half of the ads shown were for food products, most being for foods of 'dubious' nutritional value. The ads were designed to engage attention (e.g. used animation) and to produce an emotional response.

In order to replicate this study, you should:

1. Design an appropriate coding system/checklist. This might include the following sections, which need to be operationalised:
   - Product, e.g. cereals, sweets, savoury products.
   - Tone of advertisement, e.g. humour, fun, happiness, mood alteration.
   - Central character, e.g. man, woman, boy, girl (could rate these in terms of how 'stereotypical' they are).

2. Decide on when you will sample the ads, for how long and using what sampling method.

3. Divide the class to cover different channels, times and days.

4. Display your findings using one or more graphs.

Qs 37

1. Explain in what way a content analysis is a form of observation.

2. Suggest **one** advantage of doing this kind of research.

3. How might observer bias affect the findings of a content analysis?

4. In a study conducted on children's understanding of animism, child participants were asked to write a story about what would happen to a teddy bear that was wrapped up and sent through the post as a present but was lost on the way.

   a. Suggest **three** items that could be used as coding units in this study.

   b. Write operational definitions for **two** of these items.

   c. What **two** categories would you use to group the coding units to assist in analysis?

   d. How might you ensure that two researchers were applying the coding units reliably?

KEY TERMS

Advantages ☺ and disadvantages ☹ of
Observations
Content analysis
Coding units

Case Study

A case study is a research investigation that involves the detailed study of a single individual, institution or event. It uses information from a range of sources, such as interviews and observations, to obtain data. These findings are then selected and organised, for instance, to represent the individual's thoughts and emotions.

Case studies concern unique individuals or cases. The opportunity to study one case permits us to record rich details of human experience.

Evaluating case studies

Advantages

- The method offers rich, in-depth data, so information that may be overlooked using other methods is likely to be identified.

- Can be used to investigate atypical instances that may be rare, thus unusual information is accessible, for example in investigations of people with brain damage, which could not be generated experimentally.

- The complex interaction of many factors can be studied, in contrast to experiments where many variables are held constant.

- Triangulation (see facing page) increases the validity of findings.

Disadvantages

- It is difficult to generalise from individual cases as each different instances will not be identical. This uniqueness also means that cases cannot be replicated.

- Reliance on reports of past events cannot be validated as it is hard to uncover what did actually happen in the past.

- A researcher may lack objectivity as they get to know the case, or because of having a theoretical bias which may lead them to overlook aspects of the findings thus reducing validity.

- Variables cannot be controlled so this method cannot be used to deduce the causality of effects.

 Qs **38**

1. Suggest **one** advantage of doing case studies over experiments.

2. What advantages are there to case studies compared to structured interviews or questionnaires?

3. How might researcher bias affect the findings of case studies?

4. In which of the following situations would you recommend conducting a case study and why?

   a. A researcher wants to know if patients who are receiving help to cope with severe anxiety had any traumatic events in their early lives that could account for their symptoms.

   b. A hospital is interested to find out whether two of their head injury patients who have recently shown improvements have especially good relationships with their family or were particularly mentally active prior to their accidents.

Case studies of people receiving therapy

The case study allows researchers to gain in-depth information by interviewing individuals and their families. In the context of therapy this can provide detailed accounts of both the individual's current experiences and feelings and their previous experiences/feelings, such as childhood traumas and relationships. A researcher can look for links between the individual's past and present situation. This may lead to further interviews and can ultimately allow them to interpret the current experiences in the light of the individual's earlier life experiences. This technique, typical of **psychodynamic** therapy, can provide insights into unconscious motivation. However, it relies on the interpretation of the data obtained which may be subjective. For example, two therapists with different theoretical perspectives may analyse the meaning of a particular behaviour in different ways.

Case studies of brain damaged people

There are many case studies of patients with brain damage. These enable researchers to compare the behaviour and abilities of such individuals to typical cases and, in combination with investigations of the nature of their brain damage, the researchers can begin to suggest roles for particular parts of the brain. Evidence such as this cannot be used as evidence of a causal relationship between specific behavioural or cognitive functions and brain areas because the damage is not a deliberate manipulation – this would be unethical. However, such cases do provide additional evidence to support existing experimental studies. For example, case studies of HM (Scoville and Milner, 1957) and Clive Wearing (Blakemore, 1988) who were both amnesiac due to brain damage, support the existence of separate short and long term memories as proposed by the multi-store model.

Clive Wearing has brain damage to his hippocampus and cannot make new long term memories – what does that tell us about memory in the typical population?

Qualitative analysis

Research methods such as interviews, observations and case studies can be used to produce quantitative or qualitative data. Of course, results that have been obtained through *qualitative* methods can be 'reduced' to a quantitative form. For example, interviews with people about their dreams could produce qualitative data and then key themes could be identified and counted. This would generate *quantitative* data from a *qualitative* source.

Here, we are focusing on ways to anaylse qualitative data that preserve the richness and detail of the participant's responses and how to interpret this information.

Collaborative research and reflexive analysis

Summaries of qualitative data are an attempt by the researcher to represent the meaning intended by the participant. There are two alternative strategies for interpretation: collaborative research and reflexive analysis.

In **collaborative research** the participant and the researcher join forces. The participant reads and verifies the researcher's conclusions, improving **validity**. This process also improves **reliability** – if the participant has input into the reports of several investigators, as may happen when a team of clinicians are working with a single, rare case. They are more likely to generate consistently accurate representations of the situation if they collaborate.

Reflexive analysis allows the researcher to respond to the situation they are reporting – their 'reflex' or response to the situation. A counsellor may describe being saddened by a client's graphic description of their predicament or an observer may be horrified by a child's play. These subjective reports are of value because they represent the view of an involved individual – a participant in the exchange. This can be useful because it can provide a relatively external perspective because, if the client in counselling enters into certain interactions with the counsellor, this may provide corroboration for problems in other social interactions. For example, a client may engage in behaviour that threatens to upset people, which would explain why they are being avoided at work. Similarly a child may think he is being playful but the counsellor perceives this as threatening behaviour, offering an explanation for why the child has few friends.

Categorising and summarising

One problem with qualitative data is that it is hard to summarise. Quantitative data can be readily summarised with measures of central tendency and spread; it can then also be represented graphically. None of these options is possible with purely qualitative findings. Instead, qualitative data is summarised by identifying repeated themes. These should be based on the participants own meanings, that is they should be groupings as seen from the participant's perspective rather than ones imposed by the researcher. This **thematic analysis** enables the researcher to reduce the total material from the case study, for example hundreds of pages of transcribed interviews with a patient in therapy or hours of videoed play sessions with a child can be reduced to a few pages.

Qualitative analysis

collaborative research

reflexive analysis

triangulation

Activity 20 — DIY Qualitative analysis

Here are some quotes from the interview notes of a researcher working with an amnesic patient. Look for common themes or frequently occurring ideas and try to represent the patient's experience.

day 1: I feel like I'm in the middle of a big crowd where I don't know anyone. I keep looking round hoping that I'll notice someone I recognise. During the day I forget what I'm doing, I boil the kettle to make a cup of tea but by the time I put the water in, it's gone cold again.

day 14: This morning I turned the shower on but hadn't taken my towel into the bathroom. I went out to get it but must have got distracted and just dressed because when I went into the bathroom in the afternoon the shower was still running. In future I'm going to leave the light on to remind myself – I won't remember why I've done it but will have to go back in to turn the light off. I went out to the shops after that with a list – I always take a list now – but all I did for ages was look at the shop assistants in the hope that they would be familiar. It's so lonely.

day 28: I did really well today. I remembered you were coming to see me, well, I sort of did. I have a calendar where I write down everything that's going to happen. It's right by the kettle so I have to notice it even if I don't remember I put it there. I'm really glad you came here, I hate going to the hospital, everyone's unfamiliar, I just get lost among the people. I can use the map to find my way, that doesn't bother me, but it frightens me that everybody's faces look unfamiliar I feel like I'm on holiday in a foreign country all alone.

Improving validity: triangulation

Collaboration is one way to validate qualitative research and this can be extended to compare the findings obtained using data collected from several different sources – a technique called **triangulation**. For example, an instance of sleep disruption caused by shift work may be explored by interviewing a night worker, making detailed observations using equipment in a sleep laboratory and asking them to keep a sleep record. If these all generate similar findings with regard to their sleep disturbance, the validity of the findings is high.

Similarly triangulation may be used in an investigation of delay into a child's cognitive development by asking the parents to complete a questionnaire at regular intervals, collecting data by observing the child's behaviour and by interviewing their teacher.

Triangulation is a way to assess validity in qualitative research by comapring a number of different findings relating to a single case, each using different research methods.

Qs 39

1. Suggest **one** advantage of qualitative analysis over quantitative analysis.

2. How can findings from case studies be summarised?

3. How are the opinions of the participants represented in qualitative analysis?

4. What is triangulation and why is it useful?

Task 1

Look at the graphs on the right. For each one, identify the type of graph and draw **one or more** conclusions from each.

Task 2

A psychology class conduct a study on memory. Each student does a memory test first thing in the morning and then again in the afternoon. The table below shows how many items they got correct each time.

Student	1	2	3	4	5	6	7	8	9	10
Morning test	18	20	17	16	19	22	21	19	15	13
Afternoon test	20	18	15	12	18	20	16	16	17	14

(a) Calculate the mean, median, mode and range for each data set.

(b) What measure of central tendency would be most suitable to use to describe this data? Explain your answer.

(c) What measure of dispersion would be most suitable to use to describe this data? Explain your answer.

(d) Draw both a histogram and a scattergraph to represent the data from this study.

(e) From studying your graphs, what conclusions could you draw about this data?

Task 3

In this book, we have covered seven methods of research. Now let's see what you can remember!

When writing about strengths and weaknesses, try as far as possible to state a strength/weakness that is particular to the method, not one that could be applied to any method.

Research method	Two strengths	Two weaknesses	Two possible ethical issues
Lab experiment			
Field experiment			
Questionnaire			
Clinical Interview			
Investigation using a correlational analysis			
Observation			
Content analysis			
Case studies			

Task 4

You may recall that, right at the beginning of the book, there was a note on how learning about research methods was a bit like learning a foreign language – you have to learn a new set of words and what they mean. The best way to do this is to *use* your new language. The exercises throughout this book were intended to help you do this.

Write down now all the new words you have learned (those you can remember) and then check through your Research Methods Booklet to see what words you have forgotten. You might also check to see which terms were commonly forgotten. In fact, there's lots of scope for further analysis!

Work with a partner and, when you have finished, get another pair to check your list. See who in the class can correctly identify the most terms. You could even record the results in a bar chart!

Task 5

Test a friend on the key terms (or other terms). Read out a definition and see whether your friend can give the right term, You can do this using your Edexcel student workbook or the glossary at the end of this book. Or you can even make a game by constructing cards with the definitions on one side and the term on the reverse. (See 'Supplementary materials' on the Nelson Thornes website www.nelsonthornes.com/researchmethods for a Word file of the glossary.)

Task 6

Now that you have (just about) finished research methods, you could look back to the topic you found most challenging. To help you understand this better, create something memorable (for you and your class mates). It could be a PowerPoint presentation, a mobile, a poster for your classroom, a cartoon strip, a poem or even a rap.

1

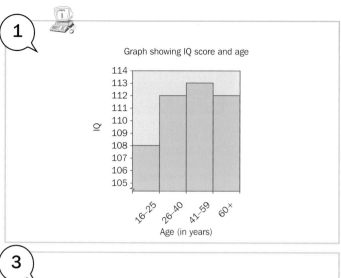

Graph showing IQ score and age

2

(a)

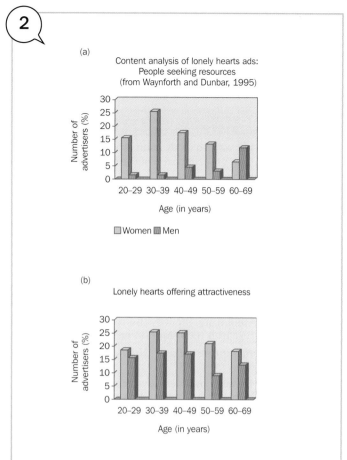

Content analysis of lonely hearts ads:
People seeking resources
(from Waynforth and Dunbar, 1995)

(b)

Lonely hearts offering attractiveness

3

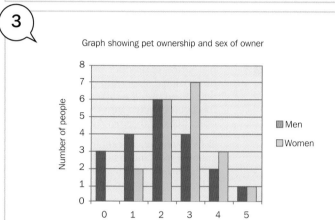

Graph showing pet ownership and sex of owner

4

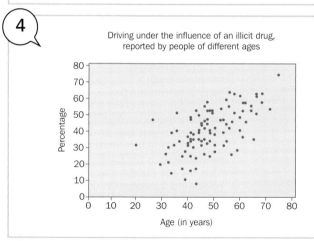

Driving under the influence of an illicit drug,
reported by people of different ages

5

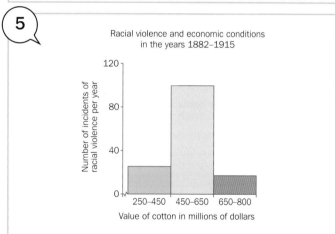

Racial violence and economic conditions
in the years 1882–1915

6

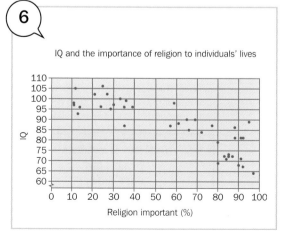

IQ and the importance of religion to individuals' lives

7

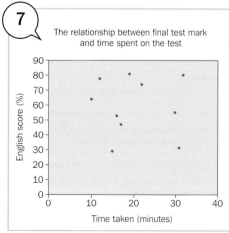

The relationship between final test mark
and time spent on the test

8

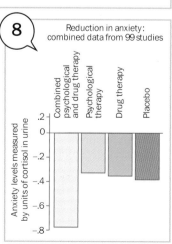

Reduction in anxiety:
combined data from 99 studies

A few other things

This book (and the A level specification) only covers some of the research methods designs used by psychologists. On this page, we will briefly mention some other methods and designs.

Lesioning

There are several ways to study brain structure and function, one of which is to damage (or 'lesion') specific parts of the brain and observe the effects of this damage on behaviour.

☺ One strength of lesioning is that damage can be caused to specific areas of the brain so that effects on behaviour can be observed.

☹ The most important weakness of lesioning is that it can only be deliberately performed on animals and there are ways in which the models are produced are not good explanations for human behaviour.

Qs   **41**

In each of the following, identify the research method and, where relevant, the research technique(s) or design.

1. Scores from a questionnaire 'How good is your memory' are related to GCSE results.
2. A male or female confederate stands by the roadside with broken-down car to see if people are more likely to help a male or female.
3. Children are shown two films: one that shows a child being helpful and another that shows a child not being helpful. They then are given free play time to see if they are more helpful.
4. Students are asked to explain what methods they find most successful for revision.
5. Interactions between first-time mothers and their newborn babies are compared with the interactions of mothers having a second baby.
6. A study on gambling is based around the experiences of one individual.
7. The onset of autism is investigated by following 90 children from birth to 5 years, looking for changes in behaviour at six-monthly intervals.
8. A study on homophobia is based on numbers of negative words used to refer to homosexuals in one week's editions of national tabloids
9. Rats have their hippocamus removed to investigate memory.
10. Brain activity when looking at maps is tested using geography and music students as participants.
11. Pictures drawn by children refered to their doctors for generalised anxiety are interpreted for indications of their fears.

Longitudinal and cross-sectional designs

When the same participants are studied repeatedly over a long period of time, a study is said to have a **longitudinal design**. Such studies aim to be able to observe long-term effects and compare the same individual at different ages.

An alternative way to do this (which takes less time) is to use a **cross-sectional design**. In this design, one group of participants of a young age are compared with another, older group of participants at the same moment in time.

☹ The problem with a cross-sectional study is that the two groups of participants may be quite different. The **participant variables** in a cross-sectional design are not controlled in the same way that they are not controlled in an **independent groups design** (in fact a cross-sectional design is an independent groups design, and a longitudinal design is a **repeated measures design**). This means that, in a cross-sectional design, differences between groups may be due to participant variables rather than the IV.

Recording brain activity: brain scanning and EEGs

There are a range of alternative ways to study the brain that can be performed on living people and animals. They use electrical, magnetic and radioactive techniques to provide information about both brain structure and function. These include the electroencephalogram (EEG), magnetic resonance imaging (MRI), computerised axial tomography (CAT) and positron emission tomography (PET). EEGs use electrodes on the scalp to measure the electrical activity of groups of neurones in the brain. MRI scans use a magnetic field to produce either structural images (of brain 'shape') or functional images (of brain activity). CAT scans use X-rays to produce detailed three-dimensional structural images. PET scans detect the use of a radioactive substance (that has been injected into the participant) during brain activity to generate functional images.

☺ In general, brain scanning is highly objective and, unlike lesioning, is non-invasive so can be used on humans. Scans can produce detailed images of brain function as well as structure.

☹ A participant in a scanner cannot perform many different activities, constraining their usefulness. CAT and PET scans also expose participants to radioactivity so their use must be limited.

Analysis of symbols

When psychologists want to investigate the unconscious they have to find entirely different ways to investigate people because, under normal circumstances, it is not possible to observe or to ask participants questions about their unconscious precisely because they are unaware of it. One technique used by **psychodynamic** psychologists is the interpretation of symbols. This is a way of exploring possible meanings behind the language (or drawings) used by an individual. This can be done as part of a wider study, such as a **case study** or an **experiment**.

☺ One strength of this technique is that it allows access to the unconscious which is otherwise difficult to study.

☹ A weakness is that the interpretation of any particular symbol is subjective – one researcher may analyse an individual's language (such as a description of a dream) entirely differently way from another. There is no way to independently verify the meaning of unconscious motives so the variables being investigated cannot be operationalised.

KEY TERMS

Analysis of symbols
Brain scan
Case study
EEG
Leisoning

OTHER TERMS

Cross-sectional design

Multiple choice questions

1. Observation is a
   a. Research method.
   b. Research technique.
   c. Form of experiment.
   d. Both a and b.

2. The key feature of a naturalistic observation is that
   a. No set categories are used to record behaviour.
   b. Behaviour is observed.
   c. There is an IV.
   d. Everything has been left as it normally is.

3. A coding system is a method used in observational research for
   a. Sampling behaviours.
   b. Making systematic observations.
   c. Analysing the findings.
   d. All of the above.

4. Which of the following is *not* a method of sampling observations?
   a. Continuous observation.
   b. Event sampling.
   c. Microscopic sampling.
   d. Time sampling.

5. Event sampling involves
   a. Noting what a target individual is doing every 30 seconds.
   b. Keeping a count of each time a target behaviour occurs.
   c. Making notes on all behaviours that occur.
   d. Noting what everyone is doing at a point in time.

6. A disclosed observation is where
   a. Observers do not participate in the study.
   b. Observers are also participants in the study.
   c. Participants know they are being observed.
   d. Participants do not know they are being observed.

7. When observations are made from data in a newspaper, this is called
   a. Direct observation.
   b. Indirect observation.
   c. Content analysis.
   d. Both b and c.

8. The reliability of observations may be affected by:
   a. Lack of agreement between several observers when observing the same thing.
   b. Lack of agreement between observations made by one observer on several occasions.
   c. Lack of agreement between several observers when observing different things.
   d. Both a and b.

9. The validity of observations may be affected by
   a. Observer bias.
   b. Low inter-observer reliability.
   c. Limited sample of participants.
   d. All of the above.

10. Low reliability can be dealt with by
    a. Using more than one observer.
    b. Conducting observations in varied settings with varied participants.
    c. Training observers to use the coding system.
    d. Both a and b.

11. Low validity can be dealt with by
    a. Using more than one observer.
    b. Conducting observations in varied settings with varied participants.
    c. Training observers to use the coding system.
    d. Both a and b.

12. Inter-observer reliability is the extent to which
    a. Two or more observers produce the same observations.
    b. Observers are not biased in the judgements they make.
    c. Observers do not drop out during an observational study.
    d. Both a and b.

13. Which of the following ethical issues is *not* likely to be a problem in a naturalistic observation?
    a. Informed consent.
    b. Privacy
    c. Confidentiality.
    d. Protection from psychological harm.

14. Which of the following is *not* a weakness of a naturalistic observation?
    a. Provides a less realistic picture of behaviour.
    b. Data are difficult to collect.
    c. Cannot investigate cause and effect.
    d. The method requires careful training.

15. Content analysis is:
    a. An experiment about how content people are.
    b. An indirect observation.
    c. An investigation of symbolism.
    d. A kind of field experiment.

16. A case study may concern
    a. A single individual.
    b. An institution.
    c. An event.
    d. All of the above.

17. Longitudinal design is like
    a. A repeated measures design.
    b. An independent groups design.
    c. A matched pairs design.
    d. Counterbalancing.

18. Which of the following is a non-experimental research method?
    a. Naturalistic observation.
    b. Interview.
    c. Investigation using correlational analysis.
    d. All of the above.

19. Which method makes it easier to obtain data from a large sample?
    a. Experiment.
    b. Questionnaire.
    c. Naturalistic observation.
    d. All of the above.

20. Which of the following has an IV and a DV?
    a. Experiment.
    b. Questionnaire.
    c. Naturalistic observation.
    d. Investigation using a correlational analysis.

Answers are on page 81

Exam-style question for chapter 4

1. SOURCE MATERIAL

A dental school was interested to find out what factors might reduce anxiety in dental patients. In one study, the focus was on anxiety level before the patients even got to see the dentist – looking at how the waiting room environment might affect anxiety. For example, some dentists have fish tanks in their waiting rooms, whereas others play soft music to help patients feel less anxious.

A naturalstic observation was designed involving a number of different dental practices. In each practice, observations were made of how anxious each patient was. These observations were recorded by the dental receptionist so that the participants were not aware that they were being observed. The observations were used to produce an anxiety score.

RESULTS
Some of the findings are shown in the graph below.

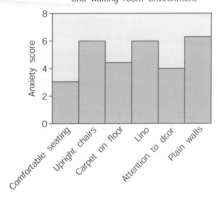

Graph showing relationship between anxiety and waiting room environment

(a) Describe the aim(s) of this study.   [2]

(b) (i) Explain why it was important that the participants were not aware that they were being observed.   [2]

    (ii) Outline **one** advantage and **one** disadvantage of observational studies other than the issue discussed in part (b) (i).   [4]

(c) What conclusion could you draw from the bar chart used to display the findings?   [2]

(d) (i) Suggest **two** ways in which anxiety could be measured.   [2]

    (ii) Describe how each of these measures of anxiety could be operationalised.   [2]

(e) (i) Identify **one** ethical issue raised by this study.   [1]

    (ii) Explain **how** this ethical issue is relevant in this study.   [2]

[total 17 marks]

In your answers to this question you should include relevant information from the whole of your course, where appropriate.

2. A researcher decides to conduct a content analysis investigating sexism in newspapers. they want to look at the use of positive and negative words in relation to males and females.

(a) Devise a detailed plan for conducting this investigation.   [6]

(b) (i) Outline how sexism could be investigated using any **one** other technique.   [3]

    (ii) Explain **two** possible ethical issues that could arise in the investigation you outlined in part (b) (i).   [4]

(c) (i) Describe **two** advantages of using content analysis to investigate sexism compared to any other named technique that could be used.   [4]

    (ii) Describe **one** disadvantage of using content analysis compared to this technique.   [2]

[total 19 marks]

[TOTAL FOR SECTION: 36 MARKS]

Examiner's tips

Question 1

(a) The aims can virtually be lifted from the stimulus material – but make sure you are writing aims and not a hypothesis.

(b) (i) Your answer needs to be contextualised – although it would be difficult to see how you could avoid doing this!

(b) (ii) This part of your answer does not need to be contexualised although you can use the source as an example to make your answer clear to ensure that you earn two marks for each point. Note that you cannot make the same point that is raised in (b) (i).

(c) The question requires only one conclusion for 2 marks so keep your answer fairly brief but do include *some* detail and do provide a conclusion and not just a finding (although it is OK to start with a finding and say '*This suggests that* …').

(d) (i) This is asking you to make a reasonable suggestion based on the information in the source.

(d) (ii) You need to describe how the variables you have identified could be made measurable.

(e) (i) Think about the BPS guidelines, in what ways must psychologists consider participants' welfare? You must indicate how your answer relates to the situation described.

(e) (ii) Note that *how* is in bold in the question. This is a hint to you from the examiner. You are not being asked to describe the issue itself but how it applies in this situation.

Question 2

(a) The plan must cover a range of methodological issues. Each step must move the procedure forwards.

(b) (i) Any reasonable technique can be described but it must be related to the investigation of sexism. A non-contextualised answer would score zero.

(b) (ii) The ethical issue must relate to the investigation you described in (b) (i) and there must be two of them. You can develop the procedure in order to make this issue evident and in order to earn marks.

(c) (i) Note that the advantages are worth two marks each – ensure that they are sufficiently detailed. You must identify another named technique and use this as a contrast. Note that it does not have to be the same technique as you described in (b) (i).

(c) (ii) This disadvantage is also worth two marks, so must be detailed. It must be in relation to the same method as content analysis was compared to in part (c) (i).

Model answer to exam-style question

Question 1

(a) Describe the aims of this study. **[2]**

The aims were to see if the décor of a dentist's waiting room was related to anxiety levels.

(b) (i) Explain why it was important that the participants were not aware that they were being observed. **[2]**

If participants know they are being watched, then they may behave in a different way.

(ii) Outline **one** advantage and **one** disadvantage of observational studies other than the issue discussed in (b)(i). **[4]**

One advantage is that you can collect information about how people behave in their everyday life rather than setting up some contrived situation to study behaviour.

One disadvantage is that the observations may be affected by observer bias – the expectations of an observer affect what he 'sees' so that the data lack validity.

(c) What conclusion could you draw from the bar chart used to display the findings? **[2]**

It appears that people feel less anxious in more comfortable surroundings (e.g. easy chairs and carpets).

(d) (i) Suggest **two** ways in which anxiety could be measured. **[2]**

Pacing.

Sweatiness because people sweat more when they are scared.

(ii) Describe how each of these measures of anxiety could be operationalised. **[2]**

Pacing could be operationalised by counting the distance travelled by each patient in a time interval such as one minute by recording the number of carpet tiles they crossed.

Sweatiness could be estimated by looking at shiny their faces were.

(e) (i) Identify **one** ethical issue raised by this study. **[1]**

Consent

(ii) Explain **how** this ethical issue is relevant in this study. **[2]**

The participants are in a vulnerable state and being watched, which they hadn't agreed to. If they were aware of someone watching them it might make them more nervous which isn't good for the participant.

Examiner's comments

(a) The answer satisfies the requirements of such questions – it is not a hypothesis and there is sufficient detail for two marks. Just saying *'To see if people were more anxious'* would only get 1 mark.

(b) (i) This answer is sufficiently clear for 2 marks. An answer worth 1 mark might simply say, *'It would change behaviour.'*

(b) (ii) Notice how details have been given both the advantage and disadvantage, rather than just saying *'one advantage is you can collect lots of information'* or *'one disadvantage is that observations may be affected by observer bias.'* Each of these examples would only be worth 1 mark because details have been omitted. Remember one way to provide detail is to make comparisons with methods other than observational studies.

(c) Note that the conclusion is about 'people' and not 'participants', and it is general statement rather than a note of particular findings – although some particular findings have been included for extra detail.

(d) (i) This only just gets 2 marks. It would be difficult to measure sweatiness by observation.

(d) (ii) The pacing answer is very thorough – it would offer enough for a 2 mark answer but the sweatiness suggestion does not earn marks because it is not realistic. Sweatiness could have been estimated by counting how many times the patient rubbed their hands on their clothing or mopped their brow.

(e) (i) Invasion of privacy or confidentiality were other possible alternative answers here.

(e) (ii) This answer gets 2 marks as it both identifies the participants' vulnerability and establishes why this is a problem.

Question 2

(a) Devise a detailed plan for conducting this investigation. **[6]**

I'd decide what words or phrases I was going to look for in the newspapers. I would try to find examples that explained 'positive' and 'negative' so that everyone understood, this would help to write operational definitions for the coding units. I would then decide which newspapers to use and how many. I'd try to use a range of broadsheets and tabloids and both weekday and weekend papers as they report in different ways. If I wasn't the only researcher I'd test inter-rater reliability. If there was a problem I'd try to improve the reliability by rewriting the operational definitions.

(b) (i) Outline how sexism could be investigated using any other technique. **[3]**

A questionnaire could be used to ask participants how they feel towards opposite sex colleagues, sporting personalities and other direct questions. These could be a mixture of closed ones, such as 'Is women's shot-put an appropriate sport?' and open ones such as 'How do you feel about women in more senior positions than yourself at work?'. I would then score the answers for sexism.

(ii) Explain **two** possible ethical issues that could arise in the investigation you outlined in part (b)(ii). **[2]**

I'd make sure that the records of individual's behaviour couldn't be linked to them, for example by identifying them by numbers not names or descriptions. Participants might be embarrassed about their sexist behaviour, or sexist behaviour towards them, and the questions might make them feel uncomfortable. This is against the guidelines of 'protection of participants from harm' so I would make sure that they knew they could withdraw at any time and were fully debriefed.

(c) (i) Describe **two** advantages of using content analysis to investigate sexism compared to any other named technique that could be used. **[4]**

It is better to use content analysis than interviews because content analyses can be replicated because the source of data (newspapers) can be reused. This increases reliability because you can test that the same results would happen every time. With open questions or unstructured interviews you might get different responses every time.

It is also good because the sources of data (newspapers) are real-world things, this means they are an accurate reflection of people's actual feelings. This increases reliability because you can test that the same results would happen every time. With open questions or unstructured interviews you might get different responses every time.

It is also good because the sources of data (newspapers) are real-world things, this means they are an accurate reflection of peoples actual feelings rather than an interview where they may be affected by leading questions or respond in socially desirable ways.

(ii) Describe **one** advantage of using content analysis compared to this technique. **[2]**

You cannot obtain rich, personal data. If the interviewer doesn't understand what a participant means, they can ask. This isn't possible in a content analysis, so questions may go unanswered.

Examiner's comments

(a) This answer earns full marks, although there would be many other ways to do so by expanding the answer. Examples of coding units or how to test inter-rater reliability could have been given.

(b) (i) Sensible answers could also include an interview or field study (for example an observation). Any answer must say how the research will be conducted, and it must be possible.

(b) (ii) Two issues are represented in this answer, and are explained inappropriate depth. Another possible issue would have been deception – it is unlikely that the participants would have been told beforehand that the study was about sexism, so they would have been deceived.

(c) (i) It is probably easiest to find suitable advantages and disadvantages for an unstructured interview although other methods, such as observations or questionnaires could have been compared.

(c) (ii) This answer is a bit 'chatty' but gets the point across that the data available in a content analysis is finite, whereas this is not true for interviews.

Contents

Coursework

CHAPTER 5

There are three guiding principles in producing your coursework:

1. Marks are awarded only for the report; *how you design, conduct and write up your study does matter too but there are no marks for the results you obtain – so don't worry if it 'doesn't work'!*

2. Choose an idea that you understand. *You need to be able to find and describe material for your introduction, write a suitable hypothesis and draw conclusions from the results. If the idea is too complex you are more likely to get muddled, though if it is very simple you may struggle to find enough to say in your results commentary and discussion.*

3. You should aim for full marks. *The coursework is worth 33% of your AS level mark and 16.5% of your final A level mark so this is an opportunity not to be missed. If you follow our guidelines here and listen to advice from your teachers then your hard work will lead to a better grade.*

Where do you begin?

Selecting a topic

Don't just dream up a hypothesis. Your starting point should be looking at previous research in a particular area. Such research (theories and/or studies) should enable you to select a possible hypothesis to test.

Your project should be related to the sub-sections you are studying (so you get a double benefit from the work). You are not required to choose a topic on the specification but your choice must be ethically acceptable and, unless it is chosen from the list provided by the examination board, you must submit a summary for it to be approved by them.

Your teacher may select the topic but you must design the investigation. You can replicate or adapt a previous study (e.g. change the stimulus material or some aspect of the design).

It is important that you chose a topic for which you can find some background information, either a study or theory that will help you to predict the possible outcome or to justify why it is worth investigating. Without this you cannot gain marks in the introduction section of the report.

You can either work alone or in a small group of up to four students. If you work with other students you must share between you all aspects of designing the project and collecting the data, **but you must write your reports individually**. Remember, copying from books or from the Internet is not allowed, although, if necessary, you can quote an extract from an original source, providing that this is clearly credited and referenced. The work you submit must be entirely your own.

Designing the study

- Select a method (e.g. field experiment, observation) and the design (e.g. repeated measures).
- Identify potential problems (bias and confounding variables).
- Identify ethical issues and consider how you will deal with them.
- Decide on a method of sampling.
- Consider what apparatus and/or materials will be necessary. Can you adapt these from material used in previous studies or will you have to design them yourself?
- Write down the standardised procedures and standardised instructions (briefing and debriefing).
- Consider conducting a small pilot study.
- Consider your descriptive statistics beforehand. Make sure that your choice allows you the opportunity to identify enough differences and patterns so that you can explain at least **four** key issues about the results (so you have enough material for sections 3b and 3d in the mark scheme).

Collecting data

You need sufficient participants to be able to make a meaningful judgement from your descriptive statistics – there's no point in averaging three scores! A guideline would be a minimum of 12 participants in a repeated measures design and 24 participants for an independent groups design.

It may be helpful to record any comments made by participants when they are debriefed because such qualitative data may be relevant to the discussion you write in the report.

Writing the report

In this chapter we will look at two reports: one a grade A report and the other a grade C. The grade A report is annotated with instructions about what should be included and how the report is marked. You do not need full marks for a grade A, but there are only 5 marks between a grade A and a grade B so every point counts. The grade C report is annotated with comments about where marks were lost. *There is a total word limit of 2000 words (excluding tables and appendices). If in an individual section you don't demonstrate sufficient selectivity or write concisely then there are 9 marks (out of 72) that you might lose. It is really quite a tight word limit, so don't waffle.*

An abbreviated version of the coursework mark scheme

Introduction

1a	Background research	1b	Rationale	1c	Aims	1d	Hypothesis(es)
0–2	Background research missing/ irrelevant	0	Link between student's study and background research is not clear or is missing	0	Irrelevant or missing	0	Hypothesis(es) irrelevant to study or missing
3–5	Brief description of somewhat relevant study/theory	1-3	Link is increasingly well explained	1	Stated but lack clarity/relevance	1	Relevant hypothesis(es)
6–7	Background study/theory is more relevant and accurate/ in depth	4	The rationale for the student's study is clear	2	Relevant aim(s) clearly stated	2	Hypothesis(es) relevant, clear, operationalised, concise and accurate
8–10	Background study/theory is relevant, accurate, and in depth but concise						

Method

2a	Method and design	2b	Variables	2c	Participants
0	Inappropriate or missing	0	No variables identified	0	Sampling method and participant details unclear, inappropriate or missing
1	Appropriate but not justified	1	Variable(s) identified and operationalised	1	Sampling method and participant details stated
2	Detailed, accurate and choice justified	2	Clear and full operationalisation of variable(s)	2	Sampling method and participant details clear and justified

2d	Apparatus	2e	Procedure	2f	Controls
0	Apparatus unsuitable or details missing	0	Unclear or missing, replication difficult/impossible	0	Identification of extraneous variables and control irrelevant/missing
1	Apparatus suitable, with scoring system and source if appropriate	1–2	Stated, replication possible	1	Identification of extraneous variables or ethical awareness
2	Apparatus suitable, description clear, choice justified	3–4	Clearly stated, easily replicated	2	Awareness of possible control of extraneous variables or ethical considerations

Results

3a	Summary table	3b	Summary table commentary	3c	Additional graphical description of results
0	Inappropriate or missing	0	Inappropriate or missing	0	Inappropriate choice or missing
1	Summary table or raw data attempted	1	Brief comments describing table	1	Suitable choice to describe data
2	Accurate, appropriate, labelled table with dispersion	2	Detailed, accurate and useful comments about trends in table	2	Appropriately measures of central tendency or labelled and clear

3d	Descriptive statistics commentary	3e	Relationship of results to hypothesis(es)
0	Inappropriate or missing	0	Inappropriate or missing
1	Brief comments on descriptive statistics	1–2	Increasingly accurate explanation given between results and hypothesis(es)
2	Detailed, accurate and useful comments about trends in graph	3	Detailed, clear, accurate explanation given relating results to hypothesis(es)

Discussion

4a	Validity	4b	Suggestions for improved validity	4c	Reliability	4d	Improving reliability
0	Missing	0	Inappropriate or missing	0	Missing	0	Inappropriate or missing
1	Brief reference to validity	1–2	Increasingly detailed account of how validity could have been improved	1	Reliability of study referred to	1–2	Increasingly suitable alternative techniques offered
2	Correct identification of operationalisation of variables or understanding of validity	2–4	Detailed account of how validity could have been improved including effects ideas might have on results	2	Reliability referred to with one link to study	2–4	Suitable suggestion of an alternative technique including possible effects on results
3	Validity linked to operationalisation of variables			3	Reliability discussed with reference to more than one methodological issue		
4	Informed, concise discussion assessing validity of operationalisation of variables			4	Reliability of study assessed with reference to a range of issues		

4e	Implications of study	4f	Generalisation of findings	4g	Application of Psychology to everyday life
0	No awareness of relationship between findings of study and background research	0	Missing	0	Missing
1–2	Attempts to relate findings situations to background research	1	Generalisation of findings made to target population	1	Brief links made with everyday situations
3–4	Detailed discussion of findings in relation to background research	2	Generalisation of findings made to target population and awareness of problems generalising beyond this	2	Detailed descriptions of how the study could be applied to real life

References, appendices, presentations of report

5a	References and appendices	5b	Presentation of report
0–1	References/appendices missing/incomplete	0	Incorrect format, poor communication skills, poor presentation
2–3	Increasingly accurate list of references, appendices of suitable materials included	1	Correct format, communication skills and presentation fairly clear, accurate and concise
		2	Correct format, good communication skills and high standard of presentation

Summary

Section heading	Section number	Marks
Introduction	1	18
Method	2	14
Results	3	11
Discussion	4	24
References, appendices and presentation	5	5
Total		72

Example 1: Levels of Processing

Grade A project: The Coursework Approval Request

COURSEWORK APPROVAL REQUEST

AS Unit 6763 Psychology Coursework Approval (CAR) Form

If your study is not one that has already been approved by Edexcel, then you must complete this form and send it to the Assessment Leader at Edexcel. Approval will be sought on your behalf from the Chief Examiner. Please allow at least FOUR weeks for obtaining permission.

Written approval will be given if your suggestion is acceptable; you should retain the written consent.

Proposed Coursework:

1. Title *The effect of levels of processing on recall of adverts*

2. Method (please tick) experiment ☑ observation ☐
   questionnaire ☐ interview ☐
   other (please explain) ....

3. Explain briefly who the participants will be, and the sampling method (including how the participants will be found).
They will be selected from family, friends and other students at my school. It will be across all ages. They will be selected by opportunity sample.

4. Explain how ethical issues will be dealt with (including consent, right to withdraw and debriefing).
Consent will be sought using a brief, explaining what the participants will have to do, i.e. remember content of adverts. Results will be treated confidentially.

5. Outline the procedure.
The participants will be shown approximately 12 adverts that should be processed structurally, phonemically or semantically. All adverts will be on A4 paper. The products will be novel brands. Each advert will be shown to the participant for 10 seconds. For recognition testing, the participants will be read out 24 statements such as "Gogey is bread, True/False?" and "Gogey is soap, True/False?" – two statements about each product. This will test the hypothesis "There will be a difference in the accuracy of recall of advertisements between structurally, phonemically and semantically processed advertisements".

Try to make the title informative without being too long – you only have one line!

The purpose of this form is to establish whether your proposed project is ethical; if it isn't ethically acceptable, you will not be allowed to submit it (or, if you do, it will not be marked so you will have a zero score for Unit 3). Bearing in mind that Unit 3 carries one third of the marks at AS, you don't want this to happen, so pay attention to this section. Consider also that if it is rejected, you will have to start again so will have lost valuable time — and wasted effort – this should be good motivation to design an ethically acceptable study!

When your coursework proposal is accepted, you will be given an approval log number (a long number that begins with your centre number). You need to enter this on the front sheet you will be given in readiness for submitting your coursework to the examination board.

Note that the exam board retains your original form. If you were to change your study from that which was approved, the project would be rejected so it is **vital that you stick to the study that you have proposed**.

You need to be:

- Confident that this is the study you want to conduct.
- Sure that the method is practical and does test what you intend it to.
- Certain that you have the time and resources to do it.
- Sure that sufficient background information exists for you to write your introduction.

State the target population and sampling method. Include any sources of participants you might use; if you don't use them it won't matter, but if you end up asking people from an ethically unacceptable source that you haven't recorded here, your project may be rejected.

It is important to show that you understand the need for briefing and debriefing participants, the need for confidentiality, why these are important to your study and whether there are any particular issues that your procedure will raise.

The outline of the procedure needs to be sufficiently detailed for an examiner to understand what participants will be expected to do. Details will be relevant if they help to make judgements about ethical issues. For example, in general word lists for memory experiments need not be included, but if you are testing recall of positive and negative words, it would be important to include the latter. If you are conducting a questionnaire about a sensitive issue attach a copy to your form.

Grade A project: Title page and introduction

Title page

AS Coursework
Carly Telford

Does the level of processing affect memory for adverts?

Front sheet (not shown)

You must fill in the coursework front sheet provided by the examination board. This will require the following information:

- your name
- candidate number
- centre number approval log number
- the title of your coursework
- your own signature
- the signature of your teacher and/or coursework supervisor.

Title page

You might like to set the scene for your coursework with a front cover, though this is not necessary and does not earn marks!

Page 1 of the report

1. Introduction

1a. Background research

Levels of Processing theory (LoP: Craik and Lockhart, 1972) says that the way information is encoded affects how it is recalled. They proposed three levels of processing – structural (visual), phonemic (auditory), and semantic (understanding). Structurally processed information is remembered the worst, phonemic somewhat better and semantically processed information is remembered best. LoP therefore implies that some advertisements will be recalled better than others.

Austin (1998) tested recall of verbal and pictorial advertisements in high or low involvement conditions. Pictorial messages gave better recall, in both conditions. Here, structurally processed information gives good recall, so contradicts LoP, suggesting that in my experiment I should find structural advertisements give better recall than phonemic ones.

Berg and Lippman (2001) tested how humour in radio advertising affected the recognition of brand names. Participants rated advertisements for amusement, then were given a surprise recognition test. Recall was better for humorous adverts. Humour depends on understanding, so semantic processing could account for this effect.

To investigate the influence of pictorial images on recall, Pieters et al. (2002) asked judges to rate advertisements for originality and familiarity. When tested on consumers, original advertisements were recalled better. Participants probably had to engage in semantic processing to understand the new (high originality) advertisements, but only had to see the unoriginal ones structurally.

Marks for the introduction are divided into 1a, 1b, 1c, and 1d

1a **Background research** *(10 marks)*

1b **Rationale** *(4 marks)*

1c **Aims** *(2 marks)*

1d **Hypothesis(es)** *(2 marks)*

1a Background research *(10 marks)*

The introduction should provide relevant, accurately reported and carefully selected psychological 'literature' (i.e. theories and/or studies). Theories, as well as studies, count as appropriate background research and the Levels of Processing theory is clearly relevant here. There should be no obvious omissions and it should be detailed yet concisely written. There is a trade-off between the number of studies and amount of detail – too many studies means too little detail.

The introduction should contain the studies that you originally looked at before formulating the hypothesis. Two studies or a study and a theory may be sufficient. No student should say, 'I don't know what to put in my introduction' – if that is true, where did your hypothesis appear from?

- → Don't copy an apparently relevant chunk out a textbook.
- → Make sure that you report sufficient details about each theory or study.
- → Select studies carefully, making sure they are relevant.
- → Keep your writing concise.

EXAMPLE 1: LEVELS OF PROCESSING

Grade A project: Introduction (continued) and method

Page 2 of the report

1b. Rationale
I have chosen a laboratory experiment because most similar studies have used this method and it allows good controls to be used. I am researching LoP but testing its effect on recall of adverts because previous research (e.g. Austin, 1998) suggests that the way adverts are processed affects recall.
I am partly replicating Berg and Lippman (2001) by conducting an experiment on novel brand advertisements but testing LoP rather than humour. Research such as Craik and Lockhart (1972) suggests that adverts requiring semantic processing to understand them will be recalled best although sometimes adverts that require only structural processing to be understood are recalled well (Austin, 1998).
As the results of the previous research conflicted my hypothesis is two-tailed, because I predict a difference in recall when advertisements are processed either structurally, phonemically or semantically but cannot say which will be better.

1c. Aim
I aim to investigate whether deeper processing of information about an advertisement affects recall accuracy for that advertisement.

1d. Hypotheses
Alternative – There is a difference in the number of advertisements recalled between structurally, phonemically and semantically presented advertisements.

Page 3 of the report

2. Method

2a. Method and Design
I chose a laboratory experiment because the level of processing can be manipulated by changing the style of the adverts while other factors are controlled so a causal effect on recall of the adverts can be measured. This is better than doing content analysis, where adverts could be assessed for their level of processing and people asked about how well they remembered them, because I could not control for factors such as exposure to the adverts that I can control in a lab experiment.
It is a repeated measures design to reduce participant variables such as familiarity with shopping (and therefore products) or TV (and therefore advertising).

2b. Variables
My IV is the type of presentation of the adverts. The levels will be determined by the requirement on the reader. They will be structural (visual images), phonemic (based on sounds) and semantic (requiring understanding).
My DV is the recall of fictitious brands mentioned in the adverts, measured with one question about each product that the participant must answer correctly from their recall of the advert (score out of 12 for each level).

2c. Participants
25 participants will be selected by opportunity sampling from the population of a girls' school (ages 11–18) from across the age ranges. I chose opportunity sampling because it allowed me to select participants that were available at the same time, so that they could be tested together as a group rather than individually which might have introduced error.

1b Rationale (4 marks)

This section should explain to the examiner what you have decided to do and how you reached this decision – what was the reasoning behind your choice, in relation to previous research. It should be clear why you have selected the method and topic of your project. This may also lead to a justification of a one- or two-tailed hypothesis.

1c Aims (2 marks)

The aims should be clear and relate directly to the background research and rationale.

→ Clunk-click:
The background research should buckle neatly into the aims.

1d Hypothesis(es) (2 marks)

To gain full marks the hypothesis should be clearly stated, concise and operationalised.

→ You only need to provide the alternative hypothesis, but you can include the null hypothesis if you wish. The 2 marks can be awarded for any one hypothesis.

Marks for the method are divided into 2a, 2b, 2c, 2d, 2e and 2f
2a **Method and design** (2 marks)
2b **Variables** (2 marks)
2c **Participants** (2 marks)
2d **Apparatus** (2 marks)
2e **Procedure** (4 marks)
2f **Controls/ethics** (2 marks)

2a Method and design (2 marks)

Be careful that you do identify your *research method*, not a technique that you are using. For instance you may be conducting a questionnaire in order to investigate differences between people's responses in two conditions – these are levels of the IV so your *method* is an experiment. For full marks you need to justify your choices of method and design – do this in relation to your own study rather than just stating the advantages of the technique in isolation. Here, both the design and method have been justified.

2b Variables (2 marks)

Both the IV and DV must be operationalised, as here.

2c Participants (2 marks)

The sample needs to be described. Also, the sampling technique must be stated and justified, as done here. The justification for opportunity sampling is sufficient, you cannot simply say 'I could get a large sample easily'.

Grade A project: Method (continued)

Page 4 of the report

2d. Apparatus

Overhead projector – To display the adverts. This is better than booklets because each participant sees each advert for an equal amount of time.

Stop clock – To measure the length of time the participants see the adverts.

Adverts (12) – Each will be the same size (A4), in colour, with novel brands. There will be 4 adverts for each level of the independent variable. Each different 'type' of advert (level of IV) needs a different level of processing to understand it – a structural, phonemic or semantic one. I designed more than I used and selected those that would produce only one type of processing, e.g. structural rather than structural and phonemic.

Question sheets x 25 - see appendix: "Questions about the adverts"

2e. Procedure

The room was set up with individual desks facing a screen. I first briefed the participants:

The brief:

"I am conducting an investigation into the effectiveness of adverts according to certain characteristics. In a moment I will project a series of 12 adverts on to that screen. Each advert will be shown for 10 seconds, with the next one immediately afterwards. It will take about 2 minutes. Afterwards you will be asked simple questions about the adverts. These questions are not a test of your ability and there are no right or wrong answers, so you can't 'do badly', you can only 'do well'. Please do not talk during the experiment. Your results will be confidential and you have the right to withdraw at any time."

Page 5 of the report

I ensured each participant could see the screen clearly before projecting each advert for 10 seconds. I then handed out the questions and asked participants to fill them in allowing them up to 10 minutes to answer the questions before taking in the papers and debriefing the participants:

The debrief:

'Thank you for participating. My study aimed to find out if the way you process adverts affects how well you remember them, so it was really a test of memory. I think that if the advert is based on pictures, you will not remember it very well. If it is to do with sounds, it will be remembered better, but if you have to understand the advert you will remember it the best. My adverts were a mixture of those things. If you had known what I was going to ask to begin with it may have affected my results, but if you want to withdraw your results you are allowed to do so. Are there any questions'

2f. Controls/ethics

I ensured that my product names were completely novel brands by testing them on non-participants before the experiment, altering if necessary so as to be unfamiliar. This will show that recall of products is due to type of processing rather than the product's name.

As I was using younger girls I obtained permission from the Headmistress and I reassured them that it was not a test and that there were no 'right answers'. This was to ensure that they were not harmed by the experiment.

2d Apparatus *(2 marks)*

The material and apparatus used should be described here and, if appropriate, actual examples should be placed in the appendix and described/referenced here. It is essential to justify why you chose the materials you eventually used. This has been done for both the OHP and the adverts.

All of the adverts were included in the Appendix; here are two examples:

2e Procedure *(4 marks)*

The main criterion for awarding marks in this section is whether you have provided sufficient detail for your study to be replicated (repeated) by someone else.

It is not just a matter of whether someone could conduct a similar study but whether they could do exactly the same study. The reason for this is because if one varies small details, such as the kind of participant, this may cause the findings to differ, so replication must be as far as possible identical in order to validate the original findings.

→ To achieve this, you will need to refer to standardised procedures (including how participants were allocated to conditions), controls and ethics.

→ Things to put in the appendix (as appropriate) are: standardised instructions (briefing and debriefing*), examples of materials, and maps.

Writing the procedure is like writing a recipe for a cake. You need to provide every detail so that someone else could do the same thing; this is replication.

*Note: It may be preferable to put the brief and debrief in an appendix to save on your word count. If you do this make sure they are referenced in the body of the report (e.g. 'see appendix 2').

2f Controls/ethics *(2 marks)*

For full marks in this section you can either describe control measures or describe how you dealt with possible ethical issues. You must both identify and explain the methodological or ethical issues *and* describe how they were overcome.

EXAMPLE 1: LEVELS OF PROCESSING

Grade A project: Results

Page 6 of the report

3. Results

3a. Summary table

Figure 3.1 Table of average number of questions about adverts correctly answered

	Median score*	Median %	Mean score*
Structurally presented adverts	9.0	75.0	7.6
Phonemically presented adverts	10.0	83.3	10.5
Semantically presented adverts	9.0	75.0	8.25
Total score	28.0	77.8	8.78

Median and mean scores are out of 12 for each type of processing, and out of 36 for the total score.

Figure 3.2 Table of dispersion (calculated using total scores out of 36)

	structural	phonemic	semantic	Total
Range	3–10	8–12	5–10	3–12

3b. Summary table commentary

Overall recall was good with correct information given about the advertisements 77.8% of the time. The ranges show that there was a large spread of scores, from 3/12 to fully correct (12/12). The spread was widest for the structural questions (3–10) and narrowest for phonemic presentation (8–12).

Page 7 of the report

3c. Additional graphical description of results

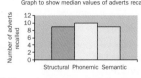
Graph to show median values of adverts recalled

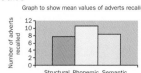
Graph to show mean values of adverts recalled

3d. Descriptive statistics commentary

From the graphs in 3c it is apparent that the type of presentation did affect recall of the advertisement. However, the differences are very small; there was only an 8.3% difference between medians for the best processing and the joint worst.

Phonemically presented adverts were remembered the best (83.3% accuracy of recall), with semantically and structurally presented advertisements the worst (both 75.0% accuracy), as shown in 3c. This is interesting because the phonemic adverts also produced the narrowest range. However the difference between actual scores was very small – phonemic 10.0 (out of 12) and semantic and structural 9.0.

3e. Relationship to hypotheses

The data show only a slight difference in recall between advertisements that have been structurally, phonemically or semantically presented. Phonemically presented advertisements were recalled the best, but neither semantically nor structurally presented advertisements were dramatically different. These findings support the null hypothesis rather than the alternative, i.e. that 'there is no difference in the accuracy of recall of advertisements between structurally, phonemically and semantically presented advertisements'. The findings seem to show that level of processing makes little difference to people's recall of advertisements.

Marks for the results are divided into 3a, 3b, 3c, 3d and 3e

3a **Summary table** *(2 marks)*

3b **Summary table commentary** *(2 marks)*

3c **Additional graphical description of results** *(2 marks)*

3d **Descriptive statistics commentary** *(2 marks)*

3e **Relationship of results to hypothesis(es)** *(2 marks)*

3a Summary table *(2 marks)*

Descriptive statistics allow us to 'eyeball' the data and draw some preliminary conclusions. You will need to use measures of central tendency and spread to give as much information about your results as you can. Make sure that your table row and column headings are complete and informative, that units are presented once in the first column or row and that each table has a title.

If you have interval data, you can quote the mean, median, mode and range – this will give you more to say about your results.

Your raw data table (if included) should be placed in an appendix and referred to in the results section.

Remember that you don't include tables in your word count.

3b Summary table commentary *(2 marks)*

This is exactly what the heading says, a commentary on the data – you need to describe (rather than explain) aspects of the data such as differences between means or ranges of results across conditions. You can quote actual figures from your table when you make comparisons, such as differences in the extent of the range or individual results from your raw data table (remember that these should not have names attached).

3c Additional graphical description of results *(2 marks)*

Whether you draw your graph(s) by hand or on a computer make sure that your scales are sensible, accurate and labelled and that each graph has a title. Resist the temptation to plot fancy graphs using a computer – your graph(s) must offer a clear description of your data. If in doubt, use the simplest graph you can, e.g. a bar chart of means.

3d Descriptive statistics commentary *(2 marks)*

Since your graph or graphs are representing the data presented in your table, you need to be careful that you don't simply repeat in 3d exactly what you have said in 3b. One way round this is to combine 3b and 3d, although you may find it easier to keep them separate. Your graphs may make comparison between means more obvious – ask yourself how much of a difference is there between conditions?

3e Relationship of results to hypothesis(es) *(2 marks)*

A trend in the data has been identified but, as it is small, the null hypothesis has appropriately been retained.

Page 8 of the report

4. Discussion

4a. Validity

Although students are familiar with looking at an overhead projector in a classroom, so the setting is valid, this is not how they would normally see adverts, so it is not a real-life task. Because people would expect to see printed adverts in magazines the ecological validity was reduced and participants may have paid less attention.

The time spent viewing the adverts may also be unrealistic because people can linger or flick pages in a magazine whereas my participants had a fixed length of time to view, this may have reduced their recall compared with real life.

I measured the recall of the adverts by asking true/false questions. The participants therefore had a 50% chance of getting the answer correct, and their answers may not have been what they could remember, but guesses.

I created 12 adverts, four each of structural, phonemic and semantic presentation. However, since I presented all my adverts visually, the participants may have only structurally processed adverts that were supposed to be phonemic or semantic, so affecting the validity of the levels of the IV.

4b. Suggestions for improved validity

To improve the validity, I could present the adverts in a magazine complete with articles, so that the participants would look at them for the length of time and with the amount of concentration that they would in real life. When reading in context, they may have paid more attention to the adverts so improved their results for the semantic ones.

Page 9 of the report

Instead of using true/false questions, I could ask direct questions, e.g. 'What is Gojey?' so the element of guesswork would be reduced. This would mean the results were what the participants could actually recall, demonstrating the effect of my IV rather than recognition.

To ensure each advert was processed as intended, I could present each level of the IV in a different way: structural adverts in a magazine; phonemic ones on the radio and semantic adverts in a task that required the advert to be understood, e.g. while looking at the adverts, 'how well do you think these products will sell?' This would be more likely to reveal a difference between the levels of the IV.

4c. Reliability

If I conducted my study again I do not think that I would get the same results, as the adverts were not clearly one type of processing and open to be interpreted differently by different people. For example, the advert for 'Howde's toothpaste' requires understanding that the two pictures are different, therefore it could be interpreted as either semantic on the basis of the ideas the picture conveyed (as intended) or structural (just on the basis of the image). My results are not reliable because the same person might interpret it differently on two separate occasions.

I had aimed to measure the recall of adverts by asking a series of questions but they might not all have been measuring participants' memory of my fictitious advert, some of the questions might have provided more cues. For example, if a participant's interpretation of a question related to a real product or television programme, then this could prompt their memory so the results for that question would not be internally consistent with others in the questionnaire, meaning the results are not reliable.

Grade A project: The discussion

Marks for the discussion are divided into 4a, 4b, 4c, 4d, 4e, 4f and 4g

4a **Validity** (4 marks)

4b **Suggestions for improved validity** (4 marks)

4c **Reliability** (4 marks)

4d **Improving reliability** (4 marks)

4e **Implications of the study** (4 marks)

4f **Generalisation of findings** (2 marks)

4g **Application of study to everyday life** (2 marks)

The main factors to remember in order gain marks in your discussion are to *discuss* the issues raised, and to be thorough. It is more about quality than quantity.

4a Validity (4 marks)

It may help you to think of the validity of your IV (did the technique you used to manipulate the experimental situation actually result in the different conditions you intended?) and the validity of your measure of the DV (were you measuring what you thought you were measuring?). The example opposite tackles both of these aspects, i.e. it considers whether the variables were successfully operationalised. In this section and 4c, you can either go for breadth or depth, i.e. cover four points (as here) or make fewer points in more detail.

4b Suggestions for improved validity (4 marks)

Each of the issues you raised in 4a should be discussed here. Your suggestions should be sufficiently detailed for the examiner to see what you would do and how it would overcome the problem identified, that is, you need to explain what effect you would expect each solution to have on the results. This last aspect could have been more explicit in the final section although there was already sufficient for full marks.

4c Reliability (4 marks)

You need to present *detailed* explanations of different methodological issues that could have affected reliability. Apparatus and methodology were discussed here; another option would have been to consider how well standardised the procedure was – participants were given printed questionnaires, so some could have dwelt on some questions longer than others.

In this section (unlike 4a) two points have been explored in detail. This is an alternative way to get 4 marks.

If you fail to identify suitable points here (or in 4a) you cannot gain corresponding marks in 4d (or 4b), so work at getting these right.

EXAMPLE 1: LEVELS OF PROCESSING

Page 10 of the report

4d. Improving reliability
To ensure the adverts were definitely one type of processing I could get independent sources to judge what type of processing they think each advert will use. They should not have been informed of which type of processing each advert is supposed to use. I would discard any that were not consistently judged.

I could conduct a split-half test of reliability on the questions and exclude any that were not reliable. I would make two 'half' versions of the questionnaire, with some questions for each level of presentation on each test. I would then get a new group of participants to complete the task and answer both sets of questions. If their scores on the two tests correlated, my questions have internal reliability. By excluding questions that did not provide consistent results, I could be sure that differences between recall for different adverts were due to the IV and not inconsistencies between the questions.

4e. Implications of the study
My results partially support Craik and Lockhart. LoP suggests that semantic processing gives the best recall, followed by phonemic and structural. My study offers some support for the idea that structural processing results in the worst recall. However, I found the best recall was from phonemic processing. All three were very close unlike LoP predicts. Pieters et al. (2002) and Berg and Lippman (2001) also found that semantic processing would produce the best recall, but I found it was not as good as phonemic.

I also failed to support Austin (1998), who found that structural processing should give better recall than phonemic. My study found that phonemic processing was better than structural.

Page 11 of the report

The implication of my findings is that semantic processing is not always the best to use in attempting to produce good memory for adverts. My findings reflect the disagreement that other studies have shown about which level of processing is best although the issues with validity and reliability discussed above cast doubt on my results.

4f. Generalisation of findings
My findings cannot be generalised to the population as a whole, because my sample was not a good cross-section – it was only female students, aged between 12 and 16 who all attended the same school. Gender might affect the kind of processing individuals prefer (for example it could be that men are better at semantic processing and women tend more towards phonemic processing) and gender/age might affect the understanding or recall of the stimuli. The findings therefore do not apply to those aged under 12 or over 16, men or non-students. As the participants were all volunteers, it cannot even be generalised to the school as a whole because non-volunteers might behave in a different way.

4g. Application of study to everyday life
Even though there was only a slight difference between conditions, my results could be applied to advertising. By using phonemic processing in adverts, e.g. through rhymes, consumers will remember products better, improving sales. Companies could use radio advertising (the best medium according to my study).

These findings can be applied to other situations such as education. Teachers should encourage students to use phonemic processing e.g. learning verses to help them revise, such as the song for the periodic table.

Grade A project: Discussion (continued)

4d Improving reliability *(4 marks)*
As with 4b this section must be detailed and explain the effects of the proposed changes on results. The example of testing for internal consistency is one possibility – though just explaining how you would do the test is not enough. You need to say what you would do as a result and how this would improve your study.

4e Implications of the study *(4 marks)*
This section should not only relate the findings of your study to the background research that you described in the introduction but indicate the *implications* of those results for people. In other words, how can your findings explain people's emotions, behaviour or cognition?

You can complete the sections in any order, but it makes sense to do them in the order suggested by the specification. Tackling part 4e after you have described the problems with validity and reliability may help you to explain or justify differences between your results and those you quoted in the introduction. Also, a lack of validity or reliability will affect your conclusions about the implications of the results for understanding how the independent variable affects people.

4f Generalisation of findings *(2 marks)*
The question to ask yourself is whether the results would apply to other situations. Can they be generalised beyond the immediate experimental set-up, do they apply to a wider population? You also need to consider the extent to which this generalisation is appropriate. More than one problem in relation to generalisation must be identified in order to gain full marks here. This is done in this example, with the aspects of the wider population that were not represented being identified.

4g Application of study to everyday life *(2 marks)*
This section must indicate how the findings can be used in the real world. This is more difficult if your study 'hasn't worked'. You could explain that either 'option' might be useful/beneficial or unhelpful/dangerous.

Note that even though the title for this section says 'application' (singular) you must mention more than one for full marks (see marking criteria).

Page 12 of the report

References

Austin, J.R. (1998) The power of pictorial images when ad processing involvement is low and subsequent brand evaluations are memory based. *Dissertation Abstracts International Section A:-Humanities and Social Sciences*, 59(1-A); 241

Berg, E.M. & Lippman, L.G. (2001) Does humour in advertising affect recognition of novel brand names? *The Journal of General Psychology* 128(2), 194-205

Craik, F.I.M. & Lockhart, E. (1972) Levels of processing: a framework for memory research. *Journal of Verbal Learning and Verbal Behaviour*, 11, 671-684

Pieters, R., Warlop, L. & Wedel, M. (2002) Breaking through the clutter: Benefits of advertisement originality and familiarity for brand attention and memory. *Management Science*, 48(6), 765-781

Appendix

This would contain:

- A copy of the questionnaires given to each group of participants.
- Copies of the other adverts not already included in the text
- Examples of adverts
- Examples of statements from the quesionnaire:

Answer true or false to each of the following statements:

1. Gogey is jam
2. Howde is toothpaste
3. Tellop is coffee
4. Rask is eggs
5. Chank is jewellery
6. Lingoy is shoe polish

We have not included all the contents of the appendix from the report in this book, but they would have to be present and complete to receive full marks.

Grade A project: References, appendices and presentation

Marks for references, appendices, presentation of report are divided into 5a and 5b

5a **References and appendices** (2 marks)

5b **Presentation of report** (2 marks)

5a References and appendices *(2 marks)*

All *references* were provided in a conventional way for both sources used and studies quoted in the text. If you use a secondary source (a textbook for example) this should be referenced appropriately, e.g. Craik & Lockhart (1972) in M. Jarvis, J. Russell & P. Gorman (2004) *Angles on Psychology*, Cheltenham: Nelson Thornes.

It is not sufficient just to give a bibliography (a list of resources you used); it must be the specific sources that you have referred to in your report.

Your *appendices* are likely to contain your standardised instructions, examples of any questionnaires or stimuli you used and possibly a raw data table.

They should not contain every single questionnaire from your participants or other bulky items.

5b Presentation of report *(2 marks)*

The report was concisely written, in an appropriate scientific style, using a broad range of specialist terms and logically organised into sections so demonstrated good use of communication skills and a high standard of presentation.

There were only minor errors in grammar, punctuation and spelling.

Finally, you must remember to package your project up as hole-punched sheets held together with treasury tags. Do not staple or paperclip your work or put it into plastic wallets or cardboard files.

This report is about 2000 words in length, the maximum word limit. Most importantly it is concise in all of the sections and therefore marks have not been lost through lack of conciseness (selectivity).

Example 2: Effects of priming on perception

Grade C project: The Coursework Approval Request

COURSEWORK APPROVAL REQUEST

AS Unit 6763 Psychology Coursework Approval (CAR) Form

If your study is not one that has already been approved by Edexcel, then you must complete this form and send it to the Assessment Leader at Edexcel. Approval will be sought on your behalf from the Chief Examiner. Please allow at least FOUR weeks for obtaining permission.

Written approval will be given if your suggestion is acceptable; you should retain the written consent.

Proposed Coursework:

1. Title *Does priming affect perception of ambiguous figures?*

2. Method (please tick)   experiment ☑   observation ☐
                              questionnaire ☐   interview ☐
                              other (please explain) ....

3. Explain briefly who the participants will be, and the sampling method (including how the participants will be found).
   The participants will be family and fellow students. The sampling method is an opportunity sample.

4. Explain how ethical issues will be dealt with (including consent, right to withdraw and debriefing).
   Participants will be given enough information about having to describe images to give their informed consent to participate. They will be allowed to withdraw at any time and will be debriefed about the experiment afterwards, with relation to what it was all about.

5. Outline the procedure.
   Participants will be shown the ambiguous 'duck-rabbit' image on an overhead projector and asked to identify it. One third will do this after being shown various duck pictures. Another third will be shown various rabbit pictures before the final image is shown and the last third will do this with no priming whatsoever.

What happens next?

After you send off your coursework submission you should get a response within 4 weeks. During this time you might write your introduction and method and collect together the apparatus and materials that you need to conduct the study (but you must not start to collect data). This will give you more time to complete your project **BUT** if your proposal is refused or if there are significant changes required, then you will have to start again.

In cases where the approval is subject to changes or advice is offered, remember to take heed of this in order to ensure that your completed project is acceptable.

Remember also that you must stick to the method that was approved; you cannot change what you are doing in ways that could affect participants. In some instances, minor changes might have to be made, such as in this case the use of an overhead projector to present stimuli was replaced with a computerised version. However, you must always seek the advice of your teacher.

AS Psychology CWK:

Does Priming Affect the Perception of an Ambiguous Image?

Laura Evans

A front cover of your own, such as this one, is not necessary but you must fill in a front sheet from the examination board (see page 87)

Grade C project: The method

Page 1 of the report

Introduction

1C Aim: I will investigate how priming affects the perception of an ambiguous stimulus.

1A Background Research:
Bugelski & Alampay (1961) showed half their participants a series of animal pictures and the other half none. All participants saw the ambiguous 'rat-man' image and reported what they saw. Usually, primed participants saw a rat, while non-primed participants saw a man. The image seen was brought about on the basis of context, linking to my aim because expectations affected the perception of an ambiguous stimulus.

Leeper (1935) presented participants with a figure (see below) of a young woman (A) followed by an ambiguous figure (C), or presented the old woman (B) followed by (C). The participant was asked what C was. When C came after A, it was viewed as a young woman. If shown after B, it was seen as an old woman, showing that priming affects the perception of an ambiguous stimulus – which is my aim.

A   B   C

Page 2 of the report

Bruner & Minturn (1955) demonstrated the effect of expectation on perception. When participants were shown '13' in a string of numbers participants said it was thirteen. When '13' was shown in a string of letters, participants said it was a 'B'. They were influenced by expectation, affecting what they recorded. This shows that context affects perception. In the present study, visual contexts will be provided by pictures of ducks and rabbits.

Palmer (1975) flashed various object images in front of a kitchen scene on a screen. The images were: a loaf shape, a U.S. mailbox and a drum kit. Participants were asked to identify them. The loaf was correctly identified 80% of the time, but participants identified the drums and mailbox 40% of the time, due to the expectations participants had about kitchens. Therefore, expectation and context affect perception. In my experiment, context will be provided by priming images leading to expectations about the ambiguous figure.

1B Rationale:
From previous research, it seems priming has an effect on the perception of ambiguous images, due to expectation gained during priming. I will test this idea by conducting a laboratory experiment, which will partly replicate Bugelski & Alampay, except that the ambiguous image will be 'duck-rabbit' (see appendix 1), not 'rat-man'. The IV levels will consist of pictures of ducks as priming, pictures of rabbits as priming and no priming at all. The hypothesis will be two-tailed because there will be a difference in the way the picture is viewed, depending on priming.

1D Hypotheses:
Alternative/experiment hypothesis: There is a difference in the perception of the ambiguous 'duck-rabbit' image depending on priming.

Null hypothesis: There is no difference in the animal seen in the ambiguous picture following priming with ducks, rabbits or no priming.

	Max mark	Mark given	Examiner's Comments
1c Aims	2	2–	This single sentence only just gets 2 marks (hence 2–). It is relevant and clearly stated but could have been more thorough, for example by indicating what was meant by 'priming' and 'perception' in the context of this experiment, i.e. the use of pictures and alternative possible perceptions in the figure used. Although the sections can be written in any order, if the aims had followed the background research and rationale, the evolution of the aims in this particular instance would have been more clearly expressed.
1a Background research	10	6	The background research that has been selected is relevant to the study being conducted and is accurately reported (criteria for 6–7 marks) but, on the other hand, each study has not been described in detail and several essentially present the same ideas. So, although the material is relevant, it is not 'in depth' so does not achieve the criteria for 8–10 marks. Nevertheless, the material could not be described as 'brief' and is certainly relevant and therefore gets 6 marks.
1b Rationale	4	2	Some of the content for the rationale was present in part 1a, but this 'shaping' was not used effectively in the rationale. The links were 'clear' but not well formulated here. The attempt to justify a two-tailed hypothesis is wrong. However, it is clear that the study is a partial replication and what the differences are between this study and the original, so the rationale is worth 2 marks.
1d Hypothesis(es)	2	1	Although both the alternative and null hypotheses are relevant and relate to the intended study, neither is adequately operationalised so they only earn 1 not 2 marks.

Total mark for Introduction is 11 out of 18 marks.

EXAMPLE 2: EFFECTS OF PRIMING ON PERCEPTION

Page 3 of the report

Method

2A Method and design

I used a lab experiment because it has a high level of control e.g. the amount of time the image is displayed. Therefore, I can be sure that priming is the only factor affecting perception of the duck-rabbit image. The setting can be easily replicated in case I need to repeat any IV levels. I used an independent groups design, with a different set of participants for each IV level. This is best for my investigation because if the same participants were used for each level, they would be expecting the ambiguous image and could opt for the animal they saw last time, regardless of priming received.

2B Variables

My independent variable was the priming that participants receive. There were three IV levels: priming consisting of a series of 10 pictures of ducks, pictures of 10 rabbits as priming and no priming. The dependent variable was which animal participants saw in the ambiguous image.

2C Participants

There were 15 participants for each IV level, making the total number of 45 participants. They were from the population of students at a school for girls aged 11 to 18. To be ethical I asked permission from the Headmistress as I was using younger girls. However, I excluded students from my psychology class, as they may have expectations about the experiment. I used an opportunity sample to select my participants so I could select participants on the basis of their availability, which is quicker than other methods.

2D Apparatus

I used: pens and forms for the participants to write how they view the ambiguous stimulus, 10 pictures of rabbits and 10 of ducks for priming, one copy of the ambiguous 'duck-rabbit' image (see appendix 1), a computer installed with Microsoft Power Point, projector and white screen, used for presenting clear images to all participants.

Appendix 1 (would be placed at the end of report)

Show the two priming pictures and the ambiguous duck-rabbit picture

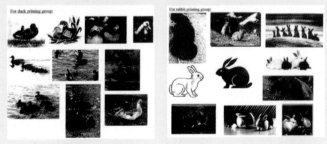

Grade C project: Method

	Max mark	Mark given	Examiner's Comments
2a Method and design	2	2	The attempt to justify the use of a lab experiment is good and there is some contextualised explanation, e.g. in relation to the amount of time the image is displayed to each participant. The design has also been justified, so this section earns 2 marks.
2b Variables	2	1	The IV is successfully operationalised but the DV is not. If you look at the images used, it is perfectly possible for someone to see both a duck and a rabbit. To overcome this, only the first image seen was recorded – this needed to be stated as part of the operationalisation.
2c Participants	2	1	Some participant details are given and the sampling method stated, earning 1 mark. However, the details of the sample are not complete, e.g. how many of each age were asked? Also, it is not clear how they were asked.
			The sampling technique is not fully justified; the explanation could have been expanded to say it is quicker because 'the researchers didn't have to go outside the school for participants', or by saying why it was a good choice ethically.
2d Apparatus	2	1	The materials were described (and included in an appendix) but were not fully justified. There was no explanation for the particular choices of pictures used (for example were they clear, coloured, sufficiently different from the ambiguous stimulus, etc.?) or where they came from (were they chosen because they were readily available as electronic files or were they scanned in?).

Page 4 of the report

Grade C project: Method (continued)

2E Procedure

The 15 participants selected for each IV level will be given a pen and standard form (see appendix 2). A white screen will be positioned where every participant has a clear view and the computer will be set up on Power Point. This brief will be read out to participants:

'This study is about perception, and you will not be harmed in any way. All results will be strictly confidential and no names are asked for. You will be asked to look at some pictures and answer a question. You have the right to withdraw from the experiment at any time. If you do not want to participate please say now.'

Participants will be given standardised instructions (see appendix 2). There are two versions because the instructions need to be different for those given priming and those not, as one group will write down the first thing they see, whilst the others will be primed first.

Participants may ask questions and then the lights will be switched off, allowing a clear view of the screen on which the priming images and the ambiguous image will be shown. Before the ambiguous image is shown, participants will be reminded that they must write down the first image that they see. The duck-rabbit image will appear for 10 seconds. For the group receiving no priming, the duck-rabbit image only will appear for 10 seconds. Lights will be switched on and forms and pens collected in. This debrief will then be read out:

'The aim of this experiment was to see if priming had any effect on the viewing of the ambiguous duck-rabbit image. We expect that any images you have seen before being shown the ambiguous duck-rabbit picture will have had an effect on whether you saw a duck or a rabbit. You are reminded that you may withdraw your results at any time. Thank you very much for your time. Are there any questions about the experiment? Further questions will be answered'

2F Controls

The number of images shown before the duck-rabbit picture must be the same for both priming groups, because if one group is shown more priming, it might increase the level of expectation. This could lead to a bias towards primed perception in one group but not the other.

I will follow ethical guidelines ensuring that participants are treated with respect. I will assure the confidentiality of participants by storing data securely and not asking for their names. This will prevent embarrassment or discomfort of participants. I will not deceive my participants and will use the brief to tell them enough about the aims of the study to give real consent. I will assure them that they will not be harmed in any way. Participants can, therefore, withdraw from the experiment if they are unsure or unhappy.

Discussion marks

	Max mark	Mark given	Examiner's comments
2e Procedure	4	2	The actual procedures described are incomplete. For example, where were the participants tested? How much time was each priming image shown for? How were the groups of 15 participants selected? Where did the other participants wait? There is no explanation of how the participants were allocated to levels of the IV. There is sufficient detail for reasonable replication – assuming that all the priming pictures and the ambiguous figure were included in the appendix. However, this replication would not be easy due to the omissions in detail; therefore this section only gains 2 marks. The brief and debrief, like the standardised instructions, should have been moved to an appendix and referred to here because this report is too lengthy and therefore the candidate will lose marks for lack of conciseness.
2f Controls	2	2	There is one form of control described and an awareness of several ethical issues.

Total mark for Method is 9 out of 14 marks.

Appendix 2 (would be placed at end of report)

Form used for all participants:

When shown the last image on the white screen (you will be told which image is the last by the experimenters), please write down the first thing you see and nothing else.

The thing I saw **first** was: _____

Standardised instructions:

For priming groups: 'We would be grateful if you do not talk to anybody until the experiment is over. You should have a form and pen in front of you. Soon, a number of images will appear on the white screen. Do not write anything whilst these images are being shown to you. The last image will be shown for 10 seconds and you must write down the first thing you see and nothing else. You will be reminded of this instruction just before the last image is shown.'

For groups without priming: 'We would be grateful if you do not talk to anybody until the experiment is over. You should have a form and pen in front of you. You will be shown an image on the white screen for 10 seconds. Please write down the first thing that you see and nothing else.'

COURSEWORK

EXAMPLE 2: EFFECTS OF PRIMING ON PERCEPTION

Page 5 of the report

Results

3A Summary Table

IV Level

	Duck Priming	Rabbit Priming	No Priming
Duck	11	11	12
Rabbit	3	2	1
Neither	1	2	2
Modal image seen	Duck	Duck	Duck

3B Summary table commentary

11 out of 15 participants that were given duck priming saw a duck first, the same number of participants saw a duck who were given rabbit priming. In the non-primed group only 1 participant saw a rabbit, compared to 12 who saw a duck. Therefore, most participants saw a duck first despite the priming given.

3C Additional graphical description of results

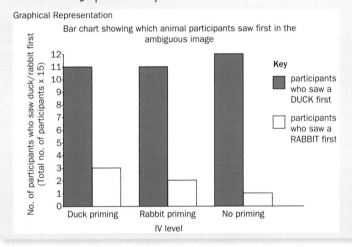

Graphical Representation

Page 6 of the report

3D Descriptive statistics commentary

Fewer participants saw neither a duck nor a rabbit when given duck priming than the other IV levels. Also, the IV level with the least participants seeing a rabbit first, was the group given no priming. More participants saw a rabbit, when given duck priming than both rabbit and no priming groups.

3E Relationship of results to hypothesis(es)

My alternative hypothesis that 'there is a difference in the perception of the ambiguous duck-rabbit image depending on priming' has not been supported. There is hardly any difference in the perception of the ambiguous image between different IV levels. Most participants saw a duck, despite the priming received. My null hypothesis, which says 'there is no difference any animal seen in the ambiguous picture following priming with duck, rabbits or no priming' is supported because whether the participant sees a rabbit or a duck is not affected by the priming received.

Grade C project: Results

	Max mark	Mark given	Examiner's Comments
3a Summary table	2	1	The table is well laid out and contains appropriate information, the correct measure of central tendency has been used for the level of measurement of the data. However, the table has no title; a heading such as 'Table to show the number of participants who first saw a duck, rabbit or neither image when shown the ambiguous figure' was needed. Also, the table is not correctly labelled – the rows need to indicate that they hold the number of participants who first saw 'duck', 'rabbit' or 'neither'. Without this the meaning of the figures in the table is unclear.
3b Summary table commentary	2	2	This commentary is good, even though the data are not especially interesting!
3c Additional graphical description results	2	2	This graph is suitable, clear and appropriately labelled. It earns full marks, showing that you don't of have to use computer graphics.
3d Descriptive statistics commentary	2	1	This section is too brief. Two points have been made, but they could have been more detailed and effective if they had used figures from the data to illustrate the differences being commented on.
3e Relationship results to hypothesis(es)	3	2	This explanation is clear and of accurate but not sufficiently detailed to gain the full 3 marks. It needed to go on to explain what the priming was supposed to do and why; therefore, the alternative hypothesis was not supported.

Total mark for Results is 8 out of 11 marks.

Page 7 of the report

Discussion

4E Implications
My findings disagree with Bugelski & Alampay (1961) and Leeper (1935), because priming had no effect on the perception of an ambiguous image in my experiment, but it did in the previous investigations. Bruner & Minturn's (1955) results conflicted with mine, as my visual contexts (duck and rabbit pictures) did not affect the perception of the ambiguous image, as they usually saw a duck regardless of priming. My results contradict Palmer (1975), as the expectation and context of my priming had no effect on the participants' perception.

4A Validity
My study was not valid because the image may have looked more like a duck than a rabbit, meaning the DV would not be measuring priming's effect on the perception of the ambiguous image, but simply displaying that participants could spot the most obvious animal in the image.

Participants may have seen the duck-rabbit image before, as it is a widely published picture. These participants may remember both animals visible in the image from their last viewing and could pick one from memory. Therefore, my DV would be measuring memory, not perception.

4B Suggestions for improved validity
I could choose a different version of the ambiguous image, making an equal portrayal of both animals, e.g. in colour. Or, I could select a different ambiguous image altogether by using a pilot study, ensuring both images can be viewed equally well. I would have to select an uncommon image to make sure that participants have not seen it before. To ensure this, I would have to design my own ambiguous image, e.g. a 'spider/sun.'

4C Reliability
My study was quite reliable, as I conducted it in the same environment for every IV group: over three lunchtimes, in the computer suite each time. However, the lighting was dim, as I used a projector and needed the lights switched off for clear viewing. The blinds did not keep out all the light so on a sunny day this could affect which image was clearest. Participants sat different distances away from the screen, affecting quality of viewing, and, therefore, what was seen first. I followed my brief, debrief and standardised instructions word-for-word with each group, so everyone was treated in the same way, increasing reliability.

Page 8 of the report

4D Improving reliability
Participants could use lamps to see what they were writing on the forms, so all lights could be switched off for a clearer view of the images. Participants could be seated at individual workstations making each person the same distance from the screen. I could use a random sample to select participants, making results representative to generalise to the population.

4F Generalisation
As I only used school students in my experiment, my findings cannot be generalised to the population as a whole, as they may not be typical of responses of males or older people.

4G Application of Psychology to everyday life
My findings can be used in everyday life, as depending on context you are more likely to see things, e.g. if you have been visually primed before entering a laboratory by a video/notice, it may cause you to spot dangers and hazards more easily. Therefore, my findings could be used as a safety procedure.

5A References
Bugelski & Alampay (1961) in J.Radford and E.Govier (1991) 'A text book of psychology', Routledge: London.
Bruner & Minturn (1955) in J.Radford and E.Govier (1991) 'A text book of psychology', Routledge: London.
Leeper (1935) in J.Radford and E.Govier (1991) 'A text book of psychology', Routledge: London.

Grade C project: The method

	Max mark	Mark given	Examiner's Comments
4a Validity	4	2	The ideas discussed here are appropriate but should have been expanded, for example by describing the effect each problem had on the results of this study.
4b Suggestions for improved validity	4	2	2 marks have been missed again. The ideas are well expressed but the effect of the suggestions on the results have not been described.
4c Reliability	4	2	There is an effective discussion of two points (relating to control of situational variables and standardised procedures). However, these needed to be more detailed or further issues considered.
4d Improving reliability	4	1	This discussion needed to consider limitations of the sample, in terms of gender, age, nationality, etc.
4e Implications of study	4	2	This discussion does relate the findings to the background research but should be more detailed. It does not consider the impact of the problems identified in sections 4a–4d on the conclusions drawn or how these could account for the differences in findings.
4f Generalisation of findings	2	1	This comment is too brief. It needs to consider particular ways in which the sample may have differed from the target population. The candidate could alternatively have suggested that the priming stimulus may have caused demand characteristics, 'instructing' the participants what to see.
4g Application of Psychology to everyday life	2	0	This section has no appropriate content. It has identified relevant everyday situations but has not linked these to the findings of the study.

Total mark for Discussion is 10 out of 22 marks.

	Max mark	Mark given	Examiner's Comments
5a References and appendices	3	2	The references are not complete (Palmer has been omitted), nor are they in alphabetical order.
5b Presentation of report	2	2	The report is written in an appropriate format using specialist terms. There were a few errors in grammar, punctuation and spelling, but not enough to affect the overall mark.

TOTAL MARKS 42/72

CHAPTER

Inferential statistics **6**

In this chapter we will look at how to choose and interpret inferential statistics. You do *not* need to use inferential statistics in your coursework (although some people do so); you do, however, need to understand how to choose statistical tests and how to interpret their results for the A2 Unit 5 examination.

Contents

Why use inferential statistics?

CHIP BIN CHIP BIN

Psychologists can draw conclusions from descriptive statistics (such as bar charts), in the way that you will have done in your AS coursework – you can see from a graph that one group did better than another group. But was this difference significant? Remember that significance is the extent to which something is particularly unusual.

Consider the following example*: At my local chippy I am convinced that they save money by giving some people rather thinner chips (means they can get more chips from each potato). I know there are two chip bins under the counter – they claim they are the same but I wonder if they are different. So I (sadly) tried an experiment. I asked for one bag of chips from bin 1 and one lot from bin 2, and I went home and measured the width of the chips in each bag.

The null hypothesis is 'The two bins contain chips of an equal average width'.
The alternative hypothesis is 'One bin has thinner chips on average than the other'.

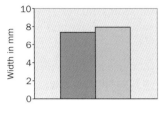

Graph showing the mean width for both bins

There was a very small difference between the average width of each bag (as you can see below) but nothing to write home about. We would expect small differences between samples (bags of chips) just because things do vary a little each time you do them – simply random variation or 'chance'. What we are looking for is a sufficiently large (significant) difference between samples to be sure that the bins are actually different. Otherwise we assume the bins (populations) are the same (accept the null hypothesis).

*Another gem from Hugh Coolican!

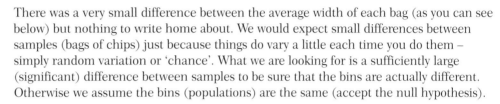

Width of chips in mm																				Mean
Bin 1 (fat chips)	4	4	5	5	6	7	7	7	7	8	8	8	8	8	9	9	9	9	9	10	7.35
Bin 2 (thin chips)	5	6	6	7	7	7	7	7	8	8	8	8	8	9	9	9	9	10	10	11	7.95

Significance levels and chance

What inferential statistics allow psychologists to do is draw conclusions based on the probability that a particular pattern of results could have arisen by chance. If it could have done, then it would be incorrect to conclude that the pattern in the data was caused by the independent variable or to conclude that there was a real correlation between two variables. If it could not have arisen by chance, then the pattern is described as a **significant** one.

Inferential tests of significance are based on some cunning maths that you don't need to know about. They permit you to work out, at a given probability, whether a pattern in the data from a study could have arisen by **chance** or whether the effect occurred because there was a real difference/correlation in the populations from which the samples were drawn.

But what do we mean by 'chance'? We simply decide on a **probability** that we will 'risk'. You can't be certain that an observed effect was not due to chance but you can state how certain you are. In general, psychologists use a probability of $p \leq 0.05$, this means that there is a 5% possibility that the results did occur by chance – in other words a 5% probability of the results occurring if there was no real difference/association between the populations from which the samples were drawn (the samples may differ but what we are really interested is knowing how likely it is that the populations must be different).

In some studies psychologists want to be more certain – such as when they are conducting a replication of a previous study or considering the effects of a new drug on health. Then, researchers use a more stringent probability, such as $p \leq 0.01$ or even $p \leq 0.001$. This chosen value of 'p' is called the **significance level**.

Qs 42

1. What letter is used to signify the significance level?

2. What is meant by the phrase 'significant at $p \leq 0.05$'?

3. Suggest why a researcher may choose to use $p \leq 0.01$ in preference to $p \leq 0.05$.

INFERENTIAL STATISTICS

Deciding which inferential test to use

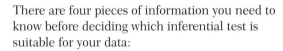

There are four pieces of information you need to know before deciding which inferential test is suitable for your data:

1. Are you looking to find out if your two samples are different or correlated?

2. Are your samples related (e.g. a repeated measures design was used) or are they independent (i.e. an independent groups design was used)?

3. What level of measurement was used? (This is explained below.)

4. Does my data fit parametric assumptions? (This is explained on the right.)

Levels of measurement

What are nominal, ordinal, interval and ratio data?

Nominal. The data are in separate categories, such as grouping people according to their favourite football team (e.g. Liverpool, Inverness Caledonian Thistle, etc.).

Ordinal. Data are ordered in some way, e.g. asking people to put a list of football teams in order of liking. Liverpool might be first, followed by Inverness, etc. The 'difference' between each item is not the same; i.e. the individual may like the first item a lot more than the second, but there might be only a small difference between the items ranked as second and third.

Interval. Data are measured using units of equal intervals, such as when counting correct answers or using any 'public' unit of measurement. Many psychological studies use *plastic interval scales* in which the intervals are arbitrarily determined so we cannot actually know for certain that there are equal intervals between the numbers. However, for the purposes of analysis, such data may be accepted as interval.

Ratio. There is a true zero point and equal interval between points on the scale, as in most measures of physical quantities such as cm or seconds.

NOIR is the way to remember all four levels of measurement

Parametric assumptions

Some inferential tests can only be used if the data fit parametric assumptions. These are:

1. The level of measurement is **interval** or **ratio**.

   See an explanation of levels of measurement on the left. **Plastic interval** scales are acceptable.

2. The data are drawn from a population that has a **normal distribution**.

   Note that it is not the *sample* that must be normally distributed but the **population**.

   A normal distribution is when most scores cluster around the mean with an equal number of scores above and below the mean, as illustrated below.

   We expect many physical and psychological characteristics to be normally distributed, such as IQ and shoe sizes.

3. The **variances** of the two samples are not significantly different.

   When looking at related samples, differences in variances should not distort the result (Coolican, 1996).

   When looking at independent samples, the best way to ensure similar variances is to collect samples that are similar in size.

However, **parametric tests are quite robust – they are reliable unless the parametric assumptions are met quite poorly.**

Normal distribution

We would expect shoe sizes of adult females to have a *normal distribution* – a lot of women have size 5 or 6 feet, and fewer have smaller or larger sizes. There is no reason for there to be more smaller than larger sizes so the data would be distributed equally either side of the mean.

Skewed distribution

In some populations scores are not distributed equally around the mean. Consider a test of depression where 0–50 represents normal behaviour, and 50+ represents chronic depression. We would expect most scores to be towards the low end rather than the high end of this score range. However a few high scores will affect the mean and produce a skewed distribution as illustrated below.

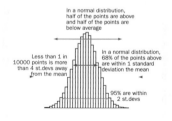

In a normal distribution, half of the points are above and half of the points are below average

Less than 1 in 10000 points is more than 4 st.devs away from the mean

In a normal distribution, 68% of the points above are within 1 standard deviation the mean

95% are within 2 st.devs

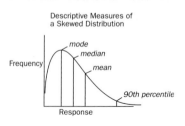

Descriptive Measures of a Skewed Distribution

Frequency

mode
median
mean

90th percentile

Response

Which test?

	Non-parametric		Parametric
Design/Data	Nominal data	Ordinal data	Interval data
Association/Correlation	Association: Chi-square test (see page 104)	Correlation: Spearman's (see page 108)	Correlation: Pearson's (see page 109)
Independent samples	Chi-square test	Mann–Whitney (see page 106)	Unrelated t-test (see page 110)
Repeated measures (and matched pairs)	Sign test (see page 105)	Wilcoxon (see page 107)	Related t-test (see page 111)

Justifying your choice

In an examination question in Unit 5, you may be asked to justify a choice of inferential test, either one that has been conducted on some data or one you would use in a given situation. Below are a variety of possible justifications for your choice of inferential test. In each case, full reference to the data has been made, as well mentioning other important criteria for deciding which test to use.

Chi-square test

As the data have been put into categories, they are classified as *nominal data*. The results are *independent* in each cell, and the expected frequencies in each cell are greater than 4. The appropriate inferential test to use is therefore a chi-square test (test of association, independent groups, nominal data, frequency/nominal data).

Sign test

A test of *difference* is required because the hypothesis predicts that there will be a difference between the two groups. As the data have been put into categories, they are classified as *nominal data*. This means we should use the sign test (test of difference, related groups, nominal data, non-parametric).

Spearman's rho

A test of correlation is needed as the hypothesis predicted a *correlation*. The data involved ratings made by participants that are *ordinal data*. This means we should use a non-parametric test so Spearman's rho is chosen (test of correlation, ordinal, i.e. non-parametric data).

Mann–Whitney U

A test of *difference* is required because the hypothesis predicts that there will be a difference between the two groups. The design is *independent groups* as participants were allocated to one of two treatment groups, and the data were scores on a test (*ordinal data*). Therefore the Mann–Whitney test is suitable (test of difference, independent groups, non-parametric).

Wilcoxon

A test of *difference* is required because the hypothesis predicts that there will be a difference between the two conditions. The design is *repeated measures* as all the participants were tested twice. The data were scores on an attitude scale, which are *ordinal data*. Therefore a Wilcoxon test was chosen (test of difference, related groups, non-parametric).

With the following designs and data, which test should you use?

a. An experiment with nominal data and an independent groups design.

b. An experiment with ratio data and a repeated measures design.

c. Ordinal data on both measures in a study to see if two measures are associated.

d. Interval data collected from an experiment with a matched pairs design.

e. An experiment with an independent groups design in which the DV is measured on a ratio scale.

f. A study using a correlational technique in which one measure is ordinal and the other is ratio.

g. A field experiment producing nominal data with an independent groups design.

h. A study testing an association using a nominal level of measurement.

i. A study using a correlational technique in which one measure is ratio and the other is ordinal.

Unrelated t-test

A test of *difference* is required because the hypothesis predicts that there will be a difference between the two conditions. The design is *independent groups* as each participant was tested on only one condition, and the data were reaction times, which are *ratio data* (a true zero). It is reasonable to assume that the data were drawn from a population that was *normally distributed* and we assume that the *variances* are similar because the samples were similar in size. Thus it is acceptable to use a *parametric* inferential test and the independent t-test was chosen (test of difference, independent groups, data fit parametric assumptions).

Related t-test

A test of *difference* is required because the hypothesis predicts that there will be a difference between the two conditions. The design is *repeated measures* as each participants' recall was tested in the morning and afternoon. The data are *interval data* (a true zero). Memory scores are likely to be *normally distributed,* and related samples differences in *variances* should not distort the result (Coolican, 1996). Thus it is acceptable to use a *parametric* inferential test and the related t-test was chosen (test of difference, repeated measures, data fit parametric assumptions).

Pearson

A test of correlation is needed as the hypothesis predicted a *correlation*. The data fit *parametric assumptions*: it is *interval level* (reaction times and score on a memory test are measured on scales with a true zero and equal intervals), come from populations that are likely to be *normally distributed* and, since the pairs of scores come from the same individual the *variances* are likely to be similar. Thus we would use the Pearson product-moment test of correlation (test of correlation, data fit parametric assumptions).

Note: Parametric tests are preferred, where justified, because they 'detect' smaller differences/relationships.

The chi-square test

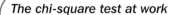

The chi-square test at work

Alternative hypothesis: Belief in the paranormal (believing or not believing) is associated with a correct assessment of coincidence (non-directional, two-tailed). This hypothesis is related to the sheep and goats study on page 54

Null hypothesis: There is no association between belief in the paranormal and correct assessment of coincidence.

The data are displayed in a contingency table (below)

In this case the table is 2×2 (count the number of rows first, then columns)

Assessment of chance	Belief in the paranormal		
	High	**Low**	**Totals**
Right	5	12	17
Wrong	10	9	19
Totals	15	21	36

Find critical value of χ^2

The data in the table are used to calculate a single observed value (called χ^2).

In this case the observed value of $\chi^2 = 1.984$.
(*Such calculations are done using a formula given in books such as those cited on page 000.*)

In order to look up a critical value for chi squared, you need to know the number of degrees of freedom (**df**): calculate (rows – 1) $\times$ (columns – 1) = 1.

For this data, **df** = 1.

Look up the value in a table of critical values (on the right).

For a two-tailed test the critical value of χ^2 ($p \leq 0.05$) = 3.84 ($p < 0.05$) (two-tailed test)

Conclusion

As the observed value (1.984) is less than the critical value (3.84), we cannot reject the null hypothesis and must conclude that there is no association between belief in the paranormal and correct assessment of coincidence.

When to use the chi-square test

The hypothesis predicts a *difference* between two conditions or an *association* between variables.

The sets of data must be independent (no individual should have a score in more than one 'cell').

The data are in frequencies (*nominal* level of measurement – see page 102 for an explanation)

Note: This test is unreliable when the expected frequencies fall below 5 in any cell, i.e. you need at least 20 participants for a 2×2 contingency table.

Critical values of chi squared (χ^2) at 5% level ($p \leq 0.05$)

df	One-tailed test	Two-tailed test
1	2.71	3.84
2	4.60	5.99
3	6.25	7.82
4	7.78	9.49
5	9.24	11.07

Observed value of χ^2 must be EQUAL TO or GREATER THAN the critical value in this table for significance to be shown.

Source: *abridged from R.A. Fisher and F. Yates (1974) Statistical tables for biological, agricultural and medical research (6th edition).* Longman.

Bigger or smaller?

The observed value should be greater than the critical value for:

Spearman, Pearson, Chi-Squared, Related t-test, Unrelated t-test (each test name, like the word 'greater' has a letter 'r')

The observed value should be **less** than the critical value for:

Wilcoxon, Mann Whitney, Sign (there is no letter 'r' to be found!)

In an exam question, if you are asked to decide whether the test is significant, you will be provided with an extract of a table of critical values. You will also be provided with information about whether the observed value needs to be greater or less than the critical value for significance to be shown.

Understanding observed and critcal values

Each inferential test produces a single number, the test statistic or **observed value** (so called because it is based on the observations made). To decide if this observed value is significant this figure is compared to another number, found in a table of critical values; this is called the **calculated** or **critical value**. There are different tables of critical values for each different inferential test (see, for example, table of critical values above). To find the appropriate critical value in a table you need to know several pieces of information about the data:

- the number of participants in the study (N). In studies using an independent groups design there are two values for N – which may be different – they are called N_1 and N_2. In other situations, *df* (degrees of freedom) is used instead of N, and is calculated easily)

- whether the hypothesis was one-or two-tailed

- the significance level eg $p \leq 0.05$

When looking up critical values you need to be sure that you are using the correct table and that you are following the right column and row.

Finally, some tests are significant when the observed value is equal to or exceeds the critical value, for others it is the reverse (the size of the difference between the two is irrelevant).

Qs 44

1. What is the general name for the value that is worked out using an inferential test?

2. What is the general name given to the number, found in a significance table, that is used to judge the observed value produced by an inferential test?

3. What three pieces of information are needed to find this value?

The sign test

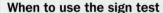

When to use the sign test

The hypothesis predicts a *difference* between two sets of data or when you have a choice of two possible answers for each participant (e.g. yes/no, plus/minus).

The two sets of data are pairs of scores from one person (or a matched pair) = *related*.

The data are nominal or reduced to *nominal data*, e.g. + and –.

The sign test at work

Alternative hypothesis: When there is no traffic visible, more participants cross at a pedestrian crossing showing a red 'man' than wait for the green man (directional, one-tailed).

Null hypothesis: There is no difference between the number of participants who cross on a red man and those who wait for a green man.

The data are presented in a table

Participant	1	2	3	4	5	6	7	8	9	10	11	12
Cross on red man	+	–	–	–	–	+	+	–	+	–	–	–

The table may have numbers or plus and minus signs in it. These are used to calculate the observed value of **S**.

In this case S=4.   (*Such calculations are done using a formula given in books such as those cited on page 111.*)

Find critical value of S

Look up the critical value in a table of critical values (on the right).

For a one-tailed test and N = 12; the critical value of **S** = 2 ($p \leq 0.05$) (one-tailed test)

Conclusion

As the observed value (4) is greater than the critical value (2), we must therefore retain the null hypothesis and conclude that there is no difference between the number of participants who cross on a red man and those who wait for a green man.

Critical values of S at 5% level ($p \leq 0.05$)

N =	One-tailed test	Two-tailed test
5	0	
6	0	0
7	0	0
8	1	0
9	1	1
10	1	1
11	2	1
12	2	2
13	3	2
14	3	2
15	3	3
16	4	3
17	4	4
18	5	4
19	5	4
20	5	5
25	7	7
30	10	9
35	12	11

Observed value of S must be EQUAL TO or LESS THAN the critical value in this table for significance to be shown.

Source: F. Clegg (1982) *Simple statistics.* Cambridge University Press. With permission of the publishers.

Qs 45

1. A student conducts a study based on previous research. This research suggests that there will be an association between parenting style (authoritarian, authoritative or permissive) and adjustment in adolescence (high, medium or low). She performs a chi-square test on her data. Her contingency table is 3×3 and she obtains an observed value of 8.13. Her hypothesis was two-tailed.

   a. Select an appropriate significance level.

   b. What is meant by '*df*'?

   c. Work out *df*.

   d. Determine the appropriate critical value.

   e. Should she retain or reject her null hypothesis?

   f. What would she do if she had a one-tailed hypothesis?

2. In another study the observed value of chi-square was 3.16. The contingency table was 2×2. Would the results be significant at $p \leq 0.05$ if the hypothesis was two-tailed?

3. A sign test generates an observed value of 3.

   a. Would this be significant with 10 participants and a one-tailed hypothesis at $p \leq 0.05$?

   b. Would it be significant if there were 20 participants?

Probability of snow - 20%

Probability of warm barn - 2%

The Mann-Whitney U test

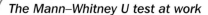

The Mann–Whitney U test at work

Alternative hypothesis: Male participants interviewed on a high bridge give higher ratings of the attractiveness of a female interviewer than those interviewed on a low bridge (directional, one-tailed).

Null hypothesis: There is difference in the ratings of attractiveness between those interviewed on a high or low bridge.

The data are presented in a table (on right)

The data in the table are used to calculate the observed value of **U**.

In this case the observed value of **U** = 5.   (*Such calculations are done using a formula given in books such as those cited on page 111.*)

Find critical value of U

N_1 = number of participants in one group.

N_2 = number of participants in other group.

Look up the critical value in a table of critical values (below).

For a one-tailed test, N_1 = 10 and N_2 = 14, and the critical value of **U** = 41 ($p \leq 0.05$) (one-tailed test)

Note: When you have a one-tailed hypothesis, remember to check whether the difference is in the direction that you predicted. If it is not, you cannot not reject the null hypothesis.

Conclusion

As the observed value (5) is less than the critical value (41), we can reject the null hypothesis and therefore conclude that participants interviewed on a high bridge give higher ratings of attractiveness to a female interviewer than those interviewed on a low bridge.

When to use the Mann–Whitney test

The hypothesis predicts a *difference* between two sets of data.

The two sets of data are from separate groups of participants = *independent groups*.

The data are *ordinal* or *interval* (see page 102 for an explanation).

Attractiveness ratings given by high bridge group	Points	Attractiveness ratings given by low bridge group	Points
7	1.5	4	10.0
10	0	6	8.5
8	1.0	2	10.0
6	3.5	5	9.5
5	7.0	3	10.0
8	1.0	5	9.5
9	0.5	6	8.5
7	1.5	4	10.0
10	0	5	9.5
9	0.5	7	7.0
		9	3.0
		3	10.0
		5	9.5
		6	8.5
N_1 = 10	16.5	N_2 = 14	123.5

Critical values of U at 5% level ($p \leq 0.05$) for a one-tailed test

	N_1	2	3	4	5	6	7	8	9	10	11	12	13	14	15
N_2	2				0	0	0	1	1	1	1	2	2	2	3
	3		0	0	1	2	2	3	3	4	5	5	6	7	7
	4		0	1	2	3	4	5	6	7	8	9	10	11	12
	5	0	1	2	4	5	6	8	9	11	12	13	15	16	18
	6	0	2	3	5	7	8	10	12	14	16	17	19	21	23
	7	0	2	4	6	8	11	13	15	17	19	21	24	26	28
	8	1	3	5	8	10	13	15	18	20	23	26	28	31	33
	9	1	3	6	9	12	15	18	21	24	27	30	33	36	39
	10	1	4	7	11	14	17	20	24	27	31	34	37	41	44
	11	1	5	8	12	16	19	23	27	31	34	38	42	46	50
	12	2	5	9	13	17	21	26	30	34	38	42	47	51	55
	13	2	6	10	15	19	24	28	33	37	42	47	51	56	61
	14	2	7	11	16	21	26	31	36	41	46	51	56	61	66
	15	3	7	12	18	23	28	33	39	44	50	55	61	66	72

Critical values of U at 5% level ($p \leq 0.05$) for a two-tailed test

	N_1	2	3	4	5	6	7	8	9	10	11	12	13	14	15
N_2	2							0	0	0	0	1	1	1	1
	3			0	1	1	2	2	3	3	4	4	5	5
	4		0	1	2	3	4	4	5	6	7	8	9	10
	5		0	1	2	3	5	6	7	8	9	11	12	13	14
	6		1	2	3	5	6	8	10	11	13	14	16	17	19
	7		1	3	5	6	8	10	12	14	16	18	20	22	24
	8	0	2	4	6	8	10	13	15	17	19	22	24	26	29
	9	0	2	4	7	10	12	15	17	20	23	26	28	31	34
	10	0	3	5	8	11	14	17	20	23	26	29	33	36	39
	11	0	3	6	9	13	16	19	23	26	30	33	37	40	44
	12	1	4	7	11	14	18	22	26	29	33	37	41	45	49
	13	1	4	8	12	16	20	24	28	33	37	41	45	50	54
	14	1	5	9	13	17	22	26	31	36	40	45	50	55	59
	15	1	5	10	14	19	24	29	34	39	44	49	54	59	64

For any N_1 and N_2, the observed value of U must be EQUAL TO or LESS THAN the critical value in this table for significance to be shown.

Source: R. Runyon and A. Haber (1976) *Fundamentals of behavioural statistics* (3rd edition). Reading, Mass: McGraw-Hill.

The Wilcoxon test

Frank Wilcoxon
(1892–1965)

When to use the Wilcoxon test

The hypothesis predicts a *difference* between two sets of data.

The two sets of data are pairs of scores from one person (or a matched pair) = *related*.

The data are *ordinal* or *interval* (see page 102 for an explanation).

The Wilcoxon signed pairs matched ranks test at work

Alternative hypothesis: There is a difference in a person's score on a short-term memory test when it is taken in the morning or in the afternoon (non-directional, two-tailed).

Null hypothesis: There is no difference in a person's score on a short-term memory test when it is taken in the morning or in the afternoon.

The data are presented in a table

Participant	Score on test taken in morning	Score on test taken in afternoon
1	15	12
2	14	15
3	6	8
4	15	15
5	16	12
6	10	14
7	8	10
8	16	15
8	17	19
10	16	17
11	10	15
12	14	8

In this case the observed value of **T** = 26.5.   (*Such calculations are done using a formula given in books such as those cited on page 111.*)

Find critical value of **T**

Look up the critical value in a table of critical values (on the right).

For a two-tailed test, N = 11; the critical value of **T** = 10 ($p \leq 0.05$) (two-tailed test)

Conclusion

As the observed value (26.5) is greater than the critical value (10), we must retain the null hypothesis and conclude that here is no difference in a person's score on a short-term memory test when it is taken in the morning or in the afternoon.

Critical values of T at 5% level ($p \leq 0.05$)

N	One-tailed test	Two-tailed test
5	$T \leq 0$	
6	2	0
7	3	2
8	5	3
9	8	5
10	11	8
11	13	10
12	17	13
13	21	17
14	25	21
15	30	25
16	35	29
17	41	34
18	47	40
19	53	46
20	60	52
21	67	58
22	75	65
23	83	73
24	91	81
25	100	89
26	110	98
27	119	107
28	130	116
29	141	125
30	151	137
31	163	147
32	175	159
33	187	170

Observed value of T must be EQUAL TO or LESS THAN the critical value in this table for significance to be shown.

Source: R. Meddis (1975) *Statistical handbook for non-statisticians*. London: McGraw Hill.

 Qs   46

1. A researcher suggested that boys might score lower on a personality test than girls, and this was what she found. There were 10 boys and 13 girls in the sample. To see whether there was a significant difference she used an inferential test and calculated an observed value of 2.
   a. What inferential test would she have used?
   b. Would she use a one-tailed or two-tailed test?
   c. Would the results be significant at $p \leq 0.05$?
2. In another study, a researcher compares how boys do on two different personality tests. She expects the scores to be different but is not sure which test will produce a higher score. There were 10 boys in the sample. The observed value was 9.
   a. What inferential test would the researcher have used?
   b. Would she use a one-tailed or two-tailed test?
   c. Would the results be significant at $p \leq 0.05$?
   d. Should she retain or reject her null hypothesis?
3. A Wilcoxon test generates an observed value of 30. Would this be significant with 15 participants and a one tailed hypothesis at $p \leq 0.05$?

The Spearman's rank correlation

Charles Edward Spearman (1863-1945)

When to use Spearman's rank correlation test

The hypothesis predicts a *correlation* between two variables.

The two sets of data are pairs of scores from one person or thing = *related*.

The data are *ordinal* or *interval* (see page 102 for an explanation).

The Spearman's rank correlation test at work

Alternative hypothesis: Participants' recall on a memory test is positively correlated to their GCSE exam performance, a participant with a high score on the memory test would have a high GCSE score and a participant with a low score on the memory test would have a low GCSE score (directional, one-tailed).

Null hypothesis: There is no correlation between recall on a memory test and GCSE exam performance.

The data are presented in a table

Each participant's scores on the two variables that have been measured appear in the two columns.

Participant	Memory score	GCSE score
1	18	8
2	14	16
3	17	10
4	13	9
5	10	15
6	8	14
7	15	12
8	16	8
9	9	17
N = 10	14	5

These results are used to calculate the observed value for the Spearman Rank correlation test, which is called **rho** (or r_s).

In this case, the observed value of **rho** = −0.58. (*Such calculations are done using a formula given in books such as those cited on page 111.*)

Note that this is a negative correlation – when comparing this figure to the critical value, only the value, not the sign, is important. The sign does, however, tell you whether the correlation is positive or negative. If the prediction was one-tailed and the sign (and therefore the correlation) is not as predicted, then the null hypothesis must be retained.

Find critical value of *rho*

Look up the critical value in a table of critical values (on the right).

For a one-tailed test, N = 10, and the critical value of **rho** = 0.564 ($p \leq 0.05$) (one-tailed test).

Conclusion

As the observed value (0.58) is greater than the critical value (0.564 AND the value of the statistic is negative (not the predicted direction), we must retain the null hypothesis and conclude that there is no correlation between recall on a memory test and GCSE exam performance.

Critical values of rho at 5% level ($p \leq 0.05$)

N =	One-tailed test	Two-tailed test
4	1.000	
5	0.900	1.000
6	0.829	0.886
7	0.714	0.786
8	0.643	0.738
9	0.600	0.700
10	0.564	0.648
11	0.536	0.618
12	0.503	0.587
13	0.484	0.560
14	0.464	0.538
15	0.443	0.521
16	0.429	0.503
17	0.414	0.485
18	0.401	0.472
19	0.391	0.460
20	0.380	0.447
21	0.370	0.435
22	0.361	0.425
23	0.353	0.415
24	0.344	0.406
25	0.337	0.398
26	0.331	0.390
27	0.324	0.382
28	0.317	0.375
29	0.312	0.368
30	0.306	0.362

Observed value of **rho** must be EQUAL TO or GREATER THAN the critical value in this table for significance to be shown.

Source: J.H. Zhar (1972) Significance testing of the Spearman rank correlation coefficient. *Journal of the American Statistical Association*, 67, 578–80. With kind permission of the publisher.

The Pearson's product-moment correlation test

When to use Pearson's product-moment correlation

The hypothesis predicts a *correlation* between two variables

The two sets of data are pairs of scores from one person or thing = *related*.

The data fit *parametric assumptions* (see page 102 for an explanation).

The Pearson's product-moment correlation at work

Alternative hypothesis: A person's age is positively correlated with the number of items they can remember on a memory test, an older person would have a high score on the memory test and a younger person would have a lower score on the memory test (directional, one-tailed).

Null hypothesis: There is no correlation between age and recall on a memory test.

The data are presented in a table

Participant	Age (in years)	Score on memory test
1	12	46
2	27	64
3	20	53
4	18	40
5	33	72
6	36	68
7	16	52
8	13	48
9	15	55
10	39	70
N = 10		

The data in the table are used to calculate the observed value of **r**.

In this case the observed value of **r** = 0.497. *(Such calculations are done using a formula given in books such as those list on page 111.)*

Find critical value of r

Look up critical value in table of critical values (on the right).

For a one-tailed test, N = 10, the critical value of **r** = 0.497 ($p \leq 0.05$) (one-tailed test).

Conclusion

As the observed value (0.888) is greater than the critical value (0.497) we can reject the null hypothesis and accept the alternative hypothesis that a person's age is positively correlated with the number of items they can remember on a memory test.

Critical values of r at 5% level ($p \leq 0.05$)

N =	One-tailed test	Two-tailed test
2	0.9000	0.9500
3	0.805	0.878
4	0.729	0.811
5	0.669	0.754
6	0.621	0.707
7	0.582	0.666
8	0.549	0.632
9	0.521	0.602
10	0.497	0.576
11	0.476	0.553
12	0.475	0.532
13	0.441	0.514
14	0.426	0.497
15	0.412	0.482
16	0.400	0.468
17	0.389	0.456
18	0.378	0.444
19	0.369	0.433
20	0.360	0.423
25	0.323	0.381
30	0.296	0.349
35	0.275	0.325
40	0.257	0.304
45	0.243	0.288
50	0.231	0.273
50	0.211	0.250
70	0.195	0.232
80	0.183	0.217
90	0.173	0.205
100	0.164	0.195

Observed value of *r* must be EQUAL TO or GREATER THAN the critical value in this table for significance to be shown.

Source: J.F.C. Powell (1976) *Cambridge Mathematical and Statistical Tables* Cambridge University Press. With kind permission of the author and publishers.

Qs 47

1. A research study investigates the correlation between a person's scores on two personality tests, expecting to find a positive correlation. There were 20 participants involved in the study. The observed value that was calculated was 0.433.

   a. Are these data parametric or non-parametric?

   b. What test would have been used to calculate the observed value?

   c. Is this hypothesis directional or non-directional?

   d. Should you use a one-tailed or two-tailed test?

   e. Select an appropriate significance level.

   f. Determine the appropriate critical value.

   g. Should the null hypothesis be retained?

2. Another study investigates the correlation between a person's reaction time and score on a memory test, expecting to find a negative correlation because reaction times are lower the faster you get. 15 participants were tested and the observed value that was calculated was 0.521. Answer the questions a–g above.

The unrelated *t*-test

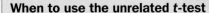

INFERENTIAL STATISTICS

When to use the unrelated *t*-test
The hypothesis predicts a *difference* between two sets of data.

The two sets of data are from separate groups of participants = *independent samples*.

The data fit *parametric assumptions* (see page 102).

The unrelated t-test at work
Alternative hypothesis: Female confederates receive help more quickly than male confederates (directional, one-tailed).

Null hypothesis: There is no difference in the time taken to give help to female and male confederates.

The data are presented in a table

Time (in seconds) for males to be helped	Time (in seconds) for females to be helped
56	64
34	96
49	83
74	65
61	40
30	22
52	97
83	121
110	96
43	73
	93
	62
$N_A = 10$	$N_B = 12$

The data in the table are used to calculate the observed value of *t*.

In this case the observed value of $t = -0.0548$.

> (*Such calculations are done using a formula given in books such as those cited on page 111.*)

Find critical value of t
Calculating N: $N = N_A + N_B - 2 = 10 + 12 - 2 = 20$

For a one-tailed test, N = 20, the critical value of $t = 1.725$ ($p \leq 0.05$) (one-tailed test).

Conclusion
As the observed value (–0.0548) is less than the critical value (1.725) AND the value of the statistic is negative (not the predicted direction), we must retain the null hypothesis and conclude that there is no difference in the time taken to give help to female and male confederates.

When using the unrelated or related *t*-test, remember to check whether the sign of t is in the predicted direction. If it is not, and the prediction is one-tailed (directional), you must accept the null hypothesis.

Why should you use a parametric test when non-parametric tests are easier to calculate?

Parametric tests are more *powerful*, which means that if a non-parametric test does not find a significant difference/correlation between samples a parametric test may do so because it is more *sensitive*.

Critical values of t at 5% level ($p \leq 0.05$)

N =	One-tailed test	Two-tailed test
1	6.314	12.706
2	2.920	4.303
3	2.353	3.182
4	2.132	2.776
5	2.015	2.571
6	1.943	2.447
7	1.895	2.365
8	1.860	2.306
9	1.833	2.262
10	1.812	2.228
11	1.796	2.201
12	1.782	2.179
13	1.771	2.160
14	1.761	2.145
15	1.753	2.131
16	1.746	2.120
17	1.740	2.110
18	1.734	2.101
19	1.729	2.093
20	1.725	2.086
21	1.721	2.080
22	1.717	2.074
23	1.714	2.069
24	1.711	2.064
25	1.708	2.060
26	1.706	2.056
27	1.703	2.052
28	1.701	2.048
29	1.699	2.045
30	1.697	2.042
40	1.684	2.021
60	1.671	2.000
120	1.658	1.980

Observed value of rho must be EQUAL TO or GREATER THAN the critical value in this table for significance to be shown.

Source: J.H. Zhar (1972) Significance testing of the Spearman rank correlation coefficient. Journal of the American Statistical Association, 67, 578–80. With kind permission of the publisher.

The related *t*-test

When to use the related *t*-test

The hypothesis predicts a *difference* between two sets of data.

The two sets of data are pairs of scores from one person (or a matched pair) = *related*.

The data fit *parametric assumptions* (see page 102).

The related t-test at work

Alternative hypothesis: People remember more words that are deeply processed (semantic condition) than words that are shallowly processed (rhyme condition) (directional, one-tailed).

Null hypothesis: There is no difference in the number of words remembered in the deeply processed or shallowly processed conditions.

The data are presented in a table

Participant	number of words recalled	
	semantic condition	rhyme condition
1	21	18
2	18	19
3	25	22
4	12	16
5	16	13
6	8	9
7	18	16
8	24	20
9	21	14
10	16	17
N = 10		

The data in the table are used to calculate the observed value of **t**.

In this case the observed value of **t** = 1.812.   (*Such calculations are done using a formula given in books such as those cited below.*)

Note: Check whether the sign of *t* is in the predicted direction. In this case, if the sign was negative, we could not reject the null hypothesis.

Find critical value of *t*

Look up critical value in table of critical values (on the left).

For a one-tailed test, N = 10, the critical value of **t** = 1.812 ($p \leq 0.05$) (one-tailed test).

Conclusion

As the observed value (1.877) is greater than the critical value (1.812) we can reject the null hypothesis and conclude that people remember more words that are deeply processed than words that are shallowly processed.

If you want help with inferential tests that we have not covered here or further suggestions about coursework, consult:

- M. Cardwell & H. Coolican (2003) *A–Z Psychology: Coursework* (2nd edition). *Handbook.* London: Hodder.
- J. Russell & C Roberts (2001) *Angles on Psychological Research.* Cheltenham: Nelson Thornes.

Qs   48

1. In a study on memory, participants are given two word lists to learn. One list is organised into categories and the other is unorganised. The researcher expects to find a difference in the recall of the two lists.

   a. Is the hypothesis directional or non-directional?

   b. What would be a suitable inferential test to use with this data? Explain your answer.

   c. If there were 12 participants and the significance level was set at $p \leq 0.05$, what is the lowest observed value that would be significant?

2. The same study is repeated but this time two groups of participants are used – one group is given the organised list and the other group is given the disorganised list. In the first study it was found that participants remembered more from the organised list.

   a. Is the hypothesis directional or non-directional?

   b. Give **two** reasons why you would use a parametric test for this data.

   c. There were 10 participants in each group. Calculate N for this number of participants.

   d. If the significance level was set at $p \leq 0.05$, would the results be significant if the observed value of the statistic was 1.931?

3. Some students investigate whether students have faster reaction times in the morning or in the afternoon. They predict that reactions times will be faster in the morning. The observed value of **t** for 20 students is calculated to be –1.92.

   a. Is the hypothesis directional or non-directional?

   b. What would be a suitable inferential test to use with this data? Explain your answer.

   c. If the significance level was set at $p \leq 0.05$, would the observed value be significant?

   d. Would you reject or retain the null hypothesis?

Exam-style question for chapter 6

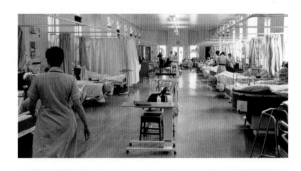

1. SOURCE MATERIAL

A local hospital decides to have mixed wards rather than separate wards for men and women. Before introducing this new scheme to all wards, the hospital management decide to compare the effects of mixed versus separate wards on patient well-being. They offer participants the choice of whether they are in mixed or single-sexed wards.

The hospital employs a psychologist to conduct a study into the effects of mixed versus single-sex wards on the health and happiness of the patients. Health outcomes could be determined by looking at whether patients recover more quickly in one type of ward than another, and also at whether they have better signs of health (e.g. lower blood pressure).

(a) Write a suitable non-directional hypothesis for this study. **[2]**

(b) (i) Identify the independent variable and the dependent variable in this study. **[2]**

(ii) Suggest **one** way in which you could operationalise the dependent variable. **[1]**

(c) (i) Identify the experimental design used in this study. **[1]**

(ii) Describe **one** disadvantage of this design in the context of this study. **[2]**

(iii) Explain **one** way of dealing with this disadvantage. **[2]**

(d) (i) Identify **one** variable that could have been controlled in this experiment. **[1]**

(ii) Describe how this variable could have been controlled. **[2]**

(e) The psychologist uses a Mann Whitney U test to check whether there is a significant difference between the recovery rates of 12 patients on mixed and 12 patients on single-sex wards.

(i) Explain why the psychologist chose this test. **[3]**

(ii) The test produced an observed (calculated) value of U=29. Using the table below, explain whether the results support the hypothesis that you proposed in part (a) (i). **[3]**

Critical values of U at 5% level (p ≤ 0.05) for a two-tailed test

		N^1					
		10	11	12	13	14	15
N^2	10	23	26	29	33	36	39
	11	26	30	33	37	40	44
	12	29	33	37	41	45	49
	13	33	37	41	45	50	54
	14	36	40	45	50	55	59
	15	39	44	49	54	59	64

For any N_1 and N_2 , the observed value of U must be EQUAL TO or LESS THAN the critical value in this table for significance to be shown.

Question 1 continued

(f) Which would be the best test to use to compare blood pressure rates for patients on mixed and single-sex wards? Justify your answer. **[2]**

[Total 21 marks]

2. **In your answers to this question you should include relevant information from the whole of your course, where appropriate.**

An alternative way to find out about people's preferences for hospital accommodation would be to conduct a survey.

(a) Explain **one** advantage and **one** disadvantage of conducting the investigation in this way. **[4]**

(b) Imagine that you have been asked to plan how this survey might be conducted.

(i) What method would you use to collect data? **[1]**

(ii) Which sampling method would be most appropriate in this instance? Justify your decision. **[2]**

(iii) Write a plan for conducting this study, taking into account both procedural and ethical issues. **[5]**

(iv) Explain **one** ethical issue that you have considered in your plan. **[2]**

[Total 15 marks]

[TOTAL FOR SECTION: 36 MARKS]

Examiner's tips

Question 1

(a) If you produce a directional hypothesis, you will score zero marks for both parts of this question.

(b) (ii) This is testing your understanding of 'operationalisation'. How would you make the DV into something you could test or measure
in some way? There are hints in the source material.

(c) (iii) Don't just identify a way to deal with the problem: *explain* how you would do this.

(d) Answer carefully – information that would be correct for one part of the answer but is placed in the wrong 'part' won't score marks. For example if you describe 'how' in part (i) then you won't receive marks and your answer won't be 'exported' to (ii).

Make sure you provide sufficient detail for any 2-mark sections. Don't give a 'knee-jerk' answer like *'noise'*. Think of a more likely variable – noise would not really be an extraneous variable here – unless you can explain why.

(e) (i) There are 3 marks, so think about the kind of relationship being predicted by the hypothesis, the design of the study and the
level of measurement.

(e) (ii) Again, there are 3 marks. You need to indicate clearly the pieces of information you have used to come to your conclusion. Say how you have found a value in the table, how you compared it to the value given in the question, and state your conclusion.

(f) Consider why your reasoning here will be different from the way you justified using a Mann–Whitney test in your answer to (e) (ii).

Question 2

(a) Note that there are 4 marks – provide sufficient detail.

(b) (i) The terms 'method' and 'research method' are used interchangeably in exam questions – they mean the same thing. You need to know the possible answers, e.g. experiment, observation, questionnaire, interview, case study, content analysis (these are the methods listed in the specification). Take care not to confuse a method with a technique (e.g. a questionnaire can be used as a method for measuring the DV in an experiment; in such a case the method would be an experiment and not a questionnaire).

(b) (ii) One mark for identifying a sensible method of selecting participants (any reasonable choice) and 1 mark for justifying this choice.

(b) (iii) Take note of the hint – you won't be able to get full marks for this section unless you tackle both practical (procedural) and ethical points. Make sure you write sufficient – this is a 5-mark question.

(b) (iv) Identify the issue (there are often marks for making this clear) and say both *why* it is an issue and *how* you would deal with it.

Model answer for exam-style question

Question 1

(a) Write a suitable non-directional hypothesis for this study. **[2]**

Patients on mixed wards will have different health outcomes in terms of speed of recovery. from those on single-sex wards.

(b) (i) Identify the independent variable and the dependent variable in this study. **[2]**

The IV is type of ward and the DV is the effect on health and happiness.

(ii) Suggest **two** ways in which you could operationalise the dependent variable. **[2 + 2]**

One way is to measure recovery rates as the time taken in days for the person to be discharged from the hospital. Another way is to measure blood pressure (in mm Hg) at the same time each day after rest.

(c) (i) Identify the experimental design used in this study. **[1]**

Independent groups.

(ii) Describe **one** disadvantage of this design in the context of this study. **[2]**

One disadvantage is that there is no control for participant variables – it could be that the patients in one group were healthier at the outset, which is why they got better faster.

(iii) Explain **one** way of dealing with this disadvantage. **[2]**

Use a matched participants design and exclude all participants who were not matched.

(d) (i) Identify **one** variable that could have been controlled in this experiment. **[1]**

One possible extraneous variable would be that people who opt for the mixed-sex wards have a more outgoing personality, which would affect the DV.

(ii) Describe how this variable could have been controlled. **[2]**

You could deal with this by matching participants, so that each member of one group had a similar personality to a member of the other group.

(e) The psychologist uses a Mann–Whitney U test to check whether there is a significant difference between the recovery rates of 12 patients on mixed and 12 patients on single-sex wards.
(i) Explain why the psychologist chose this test. **[3]**

The design was independent groups, they were looking for differences between male and female wards and the results were ordinal data.

(ii) The test produced an observed (calculated) value of U=29. Using the table below, explain whether the results support the hypothesis that you proposed in part (a) (i). **[3]**

The observed value of 29 is less than the critical value of 37 for a two-tailed test at $p \leq 0.05$ so there is a significant difference between the recovery of patients on mixed and single sex wards. The alternative hypothesis can therefore be accepted.

(f) Which would be the best test to use to compare blood pressure rates for patients on mixed and single-sexed wards? Justify your answer. **[2]**

The independent t-test because it's still an experiment with independent groups but blood pressurre is a natural scale so is a ratio measure.

Examiner's comments

(a) You would only get 1 mark for writing '*Patients on mixed wards will have different health outcomes*'. The DV (health outcomes) could be expressed in lots of ways, for example '*raised blood pressure*' or '*quicker recovery*'.

(b) (i) There is no need for any more detail.

(b) (ii) There are two examples of operationalisation given even though only one is required. Both are taken from the stimulus material though you could provide your own, such as time spent out of bed or a score from a questionnaire to assess happiness.

(c) (i) RIM.

(c) (ii) An answer that is not contextualised would only get 1 mark, e.g. '*There is no control for participant variables – participants in one group may differ from those in the other group which might explain why they do better.*'

(d) (i) There is sufficient detail in this answer, although there is much more one could write. Saying '*It could show you aspects of the design that didn't work*' would not gain marks as there is no reference to this study.

(d) (ii) The answer to d(ii) relates to d(i), which it has to in order to earn marks. Any sensible control measure will gain marks.

(e) (i) The first point is correct, the second gains a mark as, although the candidate has mis-reported the two conditions, they know that the Mann–Whitney test is used to test for differences (if the words '*between male and female wards*' had not been there, they would still have gained the mark). The third point is correct, although interval or ratio data would also have been accepted as the source does not provide enough information to decide which has been generated.

(e) (ii) This answer is correct and well expressed. It contains the three essential pieces of information: the correctly identified critical value, an appropriate comparison of the two values and the right selection of hypothesis has been made.

(f) '*Independant t-test*' is another name for unrelated *t*-test and is an acceptable answer. The second mark is for correctly observing that the DV of blood pressure is a ratio level of measurement (so a parametric test can be used).

Model answer for exam-style question

Question 2

(a) Explain **one** advantage and **one** disadvantage of conducting the investigation in this way. **[4]**

One advantage is that, by asking people questions, you can gain information about things you can't find out just by physiological measures (like blood pressure) such as their emotions. One disadvantage is that the participants might be more aware that they were being tested as it's normal to have blood pressure taken in a hospital but you don't normally get asked to fill in a questionnaire about how you feel about being there.

(b) Imagine that you have been asked to plan how this survey might be conducted.

(i) What method would you use to collect data? **[1]**

Questionnaire.

(ii) Which sampling method would be most appropriate in this instance? Justify your decision. **[2]**

Volunteer sampling, because people might not want to participate when they are unwell.

(iii) Write a plan for conducting this study, taking into account both procedural and ethical issues. **[5]**

Potential participants would be asked if they wanted to join in with some questions about whether they liked the hospital layout. This means they would know what they were going to have to do – answer questions about their preferences about the wards, but they wouldn't know the aims. This allows participants to give informed consent without giving away too much and causing the participants to react to demand characteristics. They would then be asked by interview whether they liked being on the ward, and if they did or didn't why/why not. The answers to this open question could then be scored for positive and negative comments about the ward system. After answering the questions, the patients would be debriefed by telling them that the study was really about attitudes to mixed-sex wards and that they could ask any questions and withdraw their results if they liked. They would also be told that their results would be kept confidential.

(iv) Explain **one** ethical issue that you have considered in your plan. **[3]**

Confidentiality – this is important as the answers to the questions could be quite personal and they should therefore not be revealed to anyone else. The participants could feel that they were being made fun of or that the information would prejudice their healthcare if they thought other people could find out what they had said. It was therefore important that they were reassured so that they did not suffer distress from participating in the experiment.

Examiner's comments

(a) The question is phrased to refer to the investigation described, rather than just any investigation, so your answer must relate to *this* situation.

(b) (i) 'Interview' would be an equally valid answer here.

(b) (ii) A good answer. Others were possible, such as *'opportunity sampling – using those patients walking to the day room, because they would be away from other patients who could overhear'*.

(b) (iii) This answer gives ample detail. It tackles more ethical issues than procedural ones, but is sufficient in both respects.

(b) (iv) This answer explains what the issue is and relates it successfully to the situation, offering sufficient detail. Note that the candidate could have gone on to explain how the issue would be dealt with, for example, by recording data without names and keeping the responses in a safe, secure place.

As the candidate also described consent in (b) (iii), they could alternatively have used this issue for part (b) (iv).

Review exercises

The intention of this chapter is to provide ideas and materials to enable you to practise your knowledge throughout the course. You will have spent a some time covering the basics of research methods in the first four chapters of the book. It is equally important to continue to rehearse and gain greater understanding as you progress through your AS and A2 courses.

Contents

Task 1 Quizzes

Write your own quiz

Look at the specification in Appendix I. Divide your class into groups and give each group a part of the specification. Their task is to write some quiz questions on their part of the specification. These can be MCQs, fill-in-the-blank or exam-style questions.

If each student writes 10–15 questions (and answers), you can then pool the questions and take the quizzes.

Swap quizzes between groups and see which group gets the highest percentage score on their quiz.

You may decide that some questions are not legitimate, but that's all part of studying for the research methods exam.

A bank of quizzes

Keep your own score

There are an assortment of quizzes on the following pages, loosely related to specific topics. Students might take one quiz every 2 weeks, and keep a running score of how they do.

One way to mark the quizzes is to ask other students to mark the answers.

You can use the following mark schemes:

2 marks	Accurate and elaborated
1 mark	Accurate but not elaborated
0 marks	Wrong

3 marks	Accurate and elaborated
2 marks	Not worth 3 marks but also not 1 mark! Not enough detail
1 mark	Accurate but not elaborated
0 marks	Wrong

Quiz no:	1	2	3	4	5	6	7	8	9	10	TOTAL
My score											
Total possible	50	50	50	50	50	50	50	50	50	50	500

QUIZ 1

Variables and other things

1. What do the letters IV and DV stand for? [2]

2. In the following list, which is the IV and which the DV?

    (a) In an experiment to test the relationship between imagery and memory, the two variables are performance on a memory test and instruction about how to process the stimulus words (rehearsal or imagery). [2]

    (b) In an experiment to see if physical attractiveness makes a person more likeable, the two variables are the attractiveness of a person's photograph and whether they are rated as more or less likeable. [2]

    (c) In an experiment to find out if people think blondes are less intelligent, the two variables are an estimate of IQ and a photo of a person in a blonde or a brunette wig. [2]

3. Explain the difference between an IV and a DV. [3]

4. What is an extraneous variable? [3]

5. What is a confounding variable? [2]

6. What is the difference between a confounding variable and an extraneous variable? [3]

7. Explain in what way a confounding variable acts like an independent variable. [2]

8. What is an experiment? [3]

9. Explain how a laboratory experiment differs from a natural experiment. [3]

10. *A psychologist aims to investigate context-dependent recall by arranging for students to be given a lesson on Freud in their normal classroom and then assessing their recall of this material in their teaching room or in the examination hall.*

    (a) Identify the IV and DV in this study. [2]

    (b) How could you operationalise the DV? [2]

    (c) Think of at least **one** extraneous variable that should be controlled. [3]

    (d) How might you control this extraneous variable? [2]

11. *In a research study, psychologists showed participants a set of photographs and then asked them a week later to identify the photographs they had seen out of a larger set of photographs. The original set consisted of photographs of people and of scenery. They expected to find that participants were more likely to remember the photographs of people.*

    (a) Identify the IV and DV in this study. [2]

    (b) Think of at least **one** extraneous variable that should be controlled. [3]

    (c) How might you control this extraneous variable? [2]

12. Why are standardised instructions needed in a study? [3]

13. Is there a IV and a DV in a correlation and if not, what is there instead? [2]

14. *A research study looked at the relationship between mother's age and length of time breastfeeding.*

    What are the co-variables in this study? [2]

QUIZ 2

Aims and hypotheses

1. What are the 'aims' of a study? [2]

2. Define the term 'hypothesis'. [2]

3. What is the difference between an experimental hypothesis and a null hypothesis? [2]

4. Why would a psychologist choose to use a directional hypothesis? [2]

5. When would a non-directional hypothesis be appropriate? [2]

6. Explain the difference between a directional and a non-directional hypothesis. [3]

7. In the examples below, state whether the hypothesis is directional or non-directional.

    (a) Men have a better recall of words than women. [1]

    (b) In STM memory, words are recalled acoustically rather than semantically. [1]

    (c) STM and LTM differ in the way in which memory is encoded. [1]

    (d) The presence of cues affects recall. [1]

8. Write a suitable alternative hypothesis for the following research ideas or questions:

    (a) A psychologist wishes to find out whether Therapy A is better than Therapy B for treating patients with depression. [2]

    (b) Do older people sleep more or less than young people? [2]

    (c) Do children perform better on intelligence tests if they have done some practice tests? [2]

9. Select **one** research study you are familiar with.

    (a) State the aims of the study. [2]

    (b) State a suitable hypothesis for this study. [2]

    (c) Is this hypothesis directional or non-directional? [1]

    (d) Write a different hypothesis (directional or non-directional). [2]

10. *A team of psychologists decides to conduct research into the effects of eating sweets on children's heath. Previous research suggests that children who eat more sweets have more illness than children who eat fewer sweets so they decide to use a directional hypothesis for their study.*

    (a) What is meant by the phrase a 'directional hypothesis' in the context of this study? [2]

    (b) Write a suitable directional hypothesis suitable for a correlational analysis. [2]

    (c) Why did they choose a directional hypothesis rather than a non-directional one? [2]

    (d) Write a suitable non-directional hypothesis for this study. [2]

11. For each of the following behaviours, suggest **two** ways in which they could be operationalised:

    (a) Hunger [2]

    (b) Embarrassment [2]

    (c) Being stressed [2]

    (d) Anger [2]

    (e) Memory [2]

    (f) Affection [2]

QUIZ 3

Sampling

1. What is a target population? [2]

2. Why is it desirable to obtain a representative sample for a research study? [2]

3. What is a random sample? [2]

4. How would you obtain a random sample? (State at least **two** steps that would be involved.) [2]

5. What is an opportunity sample? [2]

6. How would you obtain an opportunity sample? (State at least **two** steps that would be involved.) [2]

7. What is a volunteer sample? [2]

8. How would you obtain a volunteer sample? (State at least **two** steps that would be involved.) [2]

9. Give **one** advantage and **one** disadvantage of each of the three sampling methods named above. [6]

10. Why do very few studies use random sampling as a method, whereas the other two methods are more common? [3]

11. Why might a volunteer sample be preferable to an opportunity sample? [2]

12. What is the difference between a random sample and a systematic sample? [3]

13. What is a quota sample? [2]

14. Why might an opportunity sample be preferable to a volunteer sample? [2]

15. Identify the sampling method used in each of the following examples.

    (a) A group of psychology students interview shoppers in a local shopping centre about attitudes towards dieting. [1]

    (b) Psychology students advertise for people willing to fill out their questionnaire. [1]

    (c) The researchers post questionnaires to pupils in a school by selecting the first five names in each class register. [1]

    (d) Participants for a memory test are obtained by placing the names of everyone in the school in a box and selecting 30 names. [1]

16. *In an observational study, the research question is 'To what extent do primary school children behave helpfully?'*

    (a) Suggest **two** suitable behavioural categories that could be used to record how helpful children are. [2]

    (b) The researchers have to decide on a sampling technique for collecting their data. There are three observers. Suggest **one** suitable method of observing children in a playground and explain how you would do it. [4]

    (c) Suggest **one** advantage and **one** disadvantage of using this method. [4]

    (d) What is the advantage of using more than one observer? [2]

QUIZ 4

Validity, reliability and generalisability

1. Explain what is meant by validity, reliability and generalisability. [6]

2. Identify and distinguish between **two** kinds of validity. [3]

3. Identify and distinguish between **two** kinds of reliability. [3]

4. *A psychologist conducts interviews with mothers about their attitudes towards day care.*

    (a) Describe **two** features of the study that might affect the validity of the data being collected. [4]

    (b) Explain how you could improve the validity of the study. [2]

5. *A psychologist conducts a study to see if students do more homework in the winter or spring term. To do this, he asks students to keep a diary of how much time they spend on homework each week.*

    (a) Describe **two** features of the study that might affect the validity of the data being collected. [4]

    (b) Explain how you could improve the validity of the study. [2]

6. *A psychologist wishes to discover what factors are associated with bullying on the school playground. To do this, he observes primary school children during their playtimes for 1 month.*

    (a) Describe **two** features of the study that might affect the validity of the data being collected. [4]

    (b) Explain how you could improve the validity of the study. [2]

7. *A psychologist intends to use a repeated measures design to test participants' memories in the morning and afternoon. He uses two tests of memory.*

    (a) Suggest how he can ensure that both tests are measuring the same thing (internal reliability). [2]

    (b) Suggest **two** advantages of this experimental design in this study. [2]

8. *A psychologist interviews teenage girls about their dieting.*

    (a) Outline **one** way in which she could check the reliability of the data she collects in her interviews with the girls. [2]

    (b) Suggest **one** factor that could affect the validity of the interviews with the girls. [2]

    (c) Explain how you could deal with this problem. [2]

9. *Some psychology students plan to conduct an observational study on the effects of different dress styles – to see if men look more at girls dressed casually or smartly.*

    (a) Identify **two** ways in which you could operationalise 'being dressed casually'. [2]

    (b) Identify **one** way in which you could ensure reliability between the different observers. [2]

    (c) Explain how you would put this into practice. [2]

    (d) Explain **one** feature of the study that might affect the validity of the data being collected. [2]

    (e) Write a fully operationalised alternative hypothesis for this study. [2]

QUIZ 5

Experimental control

1. Explain the difference between an experimental group and a control group. [3]

2. Explain the difference between an experimental group and an experimental condition. [3]

3. What are standardised instructions? [2]

4. In what way are standardised instructions important for experimental control? [2]

5. What are situational variables? [2]

6. Why are controls important in an experiment? [3]

7. Suggest **two** ways in which an experimenter might allocate participants to experimental groups. [4]

8. Why is counterbalancing used? [2]

9. Describe **one** way of counterbalancing conditions. [3]

10. Name **three** kinds of experimental design. [3]

11. What are demand characteristics and why do they matter? [2]

12. Which experimental design(s) avoid order effects? [1]

13. Which experimental design(s) control participant variables? [1]

14. Which experimental design(s) avoid participants guessing the purpose of the study? [1]

15. Name **two** order effects. [2]

16. *A psychological study investigates how caffeine affects memory. The researcher gives participants a memory test before and another one after drinking a cup of coffee. Each test consists of a list of 20 five-letter words. All the words in the lists are equally common.*

    (a) What kind of design was this? [1]

    (b) Which was the experimental condition, and which was the control condition? [2]

    (c) The experimenter used words that were all of similar length and frequency. Give **one** reason why. [2]

    (d) Identify **one** order effect that might affect the result. Explain how. [2]

    (e) Suggest an alternative experimental design that would avoid this. [1]

17. *In an experiment, participants are given two word lists to compare whether it is easier to learn familiar or unfamiliar words.*

    (a) The experimenter wants to ensure that the word lists (one of common words and one of uncommon ones) are equivalent. Suggest **two** methods of doing this. [2]

    (b) If a repeated measures design were used, how could the experimenter counterbalance the lists? [3]

    (c) How might the selection of materials in the study affect the outcome (you can use examples to illustrate your answer)? [3]

QUIZ 6

Data analysis

1. Explain the difference between a bar chart and a histogram. [3]

2. Susan Morgan asks 20 people to take part in a memory and imagery experiment. Ten participants are tested in Condition A (they are told to just rehearse the words to be recalled) and 10 in Condition B (they are asked to form an image of each word). The number of words remembered in each condition were:

   Group A (rehearsal)   4 5 5 7 6 4 6 6 6 3 8

   Group B (imagery)   6 5 9 6 5 8 7 6 9 7.

   Susan drew two graphs to show her findings.

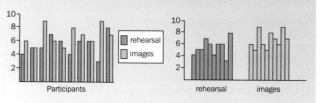

   (a) Which graph is meaningless? Why? [3]

   (b) What information is missing from both charts? [3]

   (c) Are these bar charts or histograms? [1]

   (d) What can you conclude from the graphs? [3]

   (e) Using the raw data, calculate the mean, mode and median for each experimental condition. [3]

   (f) Draw a bar chart of the means alone. Do you think this is a better way to represent the data? Why or why not? [6]

3. Label the scattergraphs below as positive, negative or zero. [3]

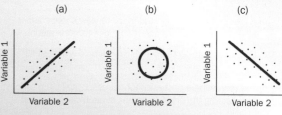

   (a)   (b)   (c)

4. What is a correlation coefficient? [2]

5. What is the difference between a correlation and a correlation coefficient? [3]

6. What does a correlation coefficient tell you about a set of data? [2]

7. Give an example of a positive correlation coefficient and a negative correlation coefficient. [4]

8. Explain what the following correlation coefficients mean:

   (a) +1.00   (d) −0.60

   (b) −1.00   (e) +0.40

   (c) 0.00   [2 each]

9. How are correlations used in twin studies? [1]

10. Give **one** advantage and **one** disadvantage of a study using a correlational analysis. [4]

QUIZ 7

Inferential statistics and drawing conclusions from data

1. Is the standard deviation a measure of central tendency or spread? [1]

2. What does the standard deviation measure? [2]

3. How does standard deviation differ from variance? [1]

4. When is variance used to help to make a choice of statistical test? [2]

5. (a) When an inferential stats test is conducted, it produces one figure. What is it called? [1]

   (b) What is the name of the 'table' figure that this is compared with in order to judge significance? [1]

6. What is meant by 'significance level'? [1]

7. (a) What are the criteria for using a parametric test? [3]

   (b) Which tests should be used only with parametric data? [3]

8. Which inferential tests can be used for repeated measures designs? [3]

9. Which inferential tests can be used for independent groups designs? [3]

10. Which inferential tests can be used for correlational designs? [2]

11. Which inferential tests can be used for matched pairs designs? [2]

12. *A student designed an experiment that used a repeated measures design to investigate obedience to male and female teachers. The student decided to do this by observing how pupils behaved with different teachers. She asked various friends to record teacher behaviours in their classrooms.*

    (a) State a possible directional hypothesis for this study. [2]

    (b) What are situational variables? [2]

    (c) Suggest two possible situational variables that might be a problem for this study and describe the possible effects they could have. [4]

    (d) What is meant by objectivity? [2]

    (e) Suggest two ways in which objectivity could be affected in this situation. [2]

13. *Rob Jones designs a set of questions to collect data about smoker's and non-smoker's attitudes to smoking.*

    (a) Write **one** open and **one** closed question he might use. [2]

    (b) Suggest **one** advantage and **one** disadvantage of presenting the questions in writing rather than conducting face-to-face interviews. [4]

    (c) Why would standardised instructions be necessary? [2]

    (d) What inferential test might Rob use? Justify the choice. [3]

    (e) How might demand characteristics be a problem in this study? [2]

QUIZ 8

Methods of conducting research

1. Explain the difference between:

   (a) A case study and a content analysis. [3]

   (b) A field experiment and a laboratory experiment. [3]

   (c) An observation and an experiment. [3]

   (d) An investigation using a correlational analysis and an experiment. [3]

   (e) An interview and a questionnaire. [3]

2. Give **one** advantage and **one** disadvantage of content analysis. [2]

3. Explain why a field experiment may or may not have greater ecological validity than a laboratory experiment. [3]

4. Explain **two** advantages and **one** disadvantage of a case study. [3]

5. In what way can cross-cultural studies be classified as natural experiments? [3]

6. Give **one** advantage and **one** disadvantage of using interviews as a way of collecting data. [4]

7. The person conducting the interviews may have a set of questions that he or she will ask. What kind of interview is this (a structured or unstructured interview)? [1]

8. If you were going to collect data about day care experiences using a questionnaire, write **one** question that would collect quantitative data and **one** question that would elicit qualitative data. [4]

9. If you wanted to find out about attitudes towards dieting, why would it be preferable to conduct an questionnaire rather than an interview? [3]

10. Why might it be better to conduct an interview rather than a questionnaire? [3]

11. In the following list, state what research method could be used:

    (a) A researcher records the behaviour of male and female birds during courtship. [1]

    (b) An investigation to demonstrate that rats in a maze without food will learn the layout as quickly as rats that receive food. [1]

    (c) A study of newborn infants to see if they looked longer at a black or a chequered square. [1]

    (d) A researcher uses a charity-collecting tin to see whether people will give more money if the researcher has a child with him. [1]

    (e) An investigation to look at the relationship between IQ and age. [1]

    (f) A study using the exam results from two schools to see whether streaming (used in School A) was better than no streaming (used in School B). [1]

    (g) A researcher approaches pedestrians and asks them questions about local shopping facilities. [1]

    (h) An investigation into the frequency of positive and negative stereotypes of working mothers in newspapers. [1]

    (i) A researcher wants to look at the cognitive impairments of a woman who has suffered a severe head injury. [1]

QUIZ 9

Ethical issues and other things

1. What is 'debriefing'? [3]

2. What ethical issue(s) can be resolved by debriefing? [3]

3. Consider the 12 studies you learned about at AS. Can you think of one which raises no ethical issues? Explain why. [3]

4. For each of the following, identify **one** ethical issue that might have arisen in this study and suggest how the researcher might have dealt with it.

    (a) A correlation of pupil IQ scores and GCSE results. [3]

    (b) Interviewing teenage girls about their dieting habits. [3]

    (c) An observational study of the way in which children cross the road going to and from school. [3]

    (d) A psychologist decides to conduct a field experiment to see whether people are more likely to obey someone wearing a uniform or dressed in a casual suit. [3]

    (e) A school decides to conduct a natural experiment to see if the students doing a new maths programme do better in their GCSE maths exam than a group of students using the traditional learning methods. [3]

    (f) An experiment to test the effect of self-esteem on performance. Participants are given a self-esteem questionnaire and then given a false score (told they have either high or low self-esteem). [3]

    (g) A teacher asks her students to take part in a research project, telling them it is about eating habits whereas it is really about eating disorders. [3]

5. Which body produces ethical guidelines to help psychologists in Britain? [1]

6. What protection exists to ensure that animals involved in psychological research are treated ethically? [2]

7. *A psychologist is interested in the development of attachment between ewes and their lambs. This could be based on visual, auditory or olfactory cues. In order to find out, she has a group of ewes and their lambs, some of which are deprived of visual, auditory or olfactory cues by lesioning nerves from the sensory organs to the brain, some pairs are treated as controls. In order to measure the effect, she records how often the lambs feed from the ewes.*

    (a) Identify **three** different ways in which this study could raise issues about the ethical treatment of animals and explain why they are problematic. [6]

    (b) For **two** of the issues you have identified, say what the researcher could have done to resolve the issue [4]

8. *A conservation group fear that a new motorway is affecting the ability of fledglings from the local population of rare birds to learn how to search for food. They think that the birds might either be distressed by the noise or their brains may be affected by the pollution. They ask a university psychology department to help them to design an observational study of the birds to see if their behaviour differs from earlier records.*

    (a) Identify and explain **two** additional ethical issues raised by this study that you have not considered in answer to question 7. [4]

    (b) What should the researchers do about **one** of these issues? [3]

QUIZ 10

General review

1. What is research? [2]

2. Why do psychologists conduct research? [2]

3. Which variable is manipulated by the experimenter – the independent or the dependent variable? [1]

4. Do longitudinal or cross-sectional studies control participant variables? [1]

5. In an experiment, what should be the only thing that affects the behaviour of the participant? [1]

6. Explain the difference between qualitative and quantitative data. [2]

7. Give **one** advantage and **one** disadvantage of using qualitative data. [4]

8. Give **one** advantage and **one** disadvantage of using quantitative data. [4]

9. You are conducting research on eating disorders. Give **one** advantage of collecting quantitative data *in the context of this study* and **one** disadvantage of collecting qualitative data *in the context of this study*. [4]

10. In the context of this study, why might it be preferable to collect quantitative data? [2]

11. Is content analysis, an example of qualitative or quantitative analysis? [1]

12. How can 'leading questions' be a problem in interviews or questionnaires? [2]

13. Give an example of a leading question and explain why it is 'leading'. [2]

14. What is 'subjectivity'? [2]

15. *A psychological study looked at the effect of different teaching styles on children's ability to learn. To do this, children were given a lesson, using either traditional or more pupil-centred teaching methods, on how the moon was formed. The children were tested the day before the lesson and again a week later using the same test to see how much they knew about the moon. Participants were drawn from three different year groups and randomly assigned to experimental conditions.*

    (a) What is the experimental design of this study? [1]

    (b) Give **two** advantages of using this experimental design. [4]

    (c) Why was it desirable to give the tests a week apart? [2]

    (d) Why did the experimenter choose classes from three different year groups? [3]

    (e) What were the two experimental conditions in this study? [2]

    (f) What does 'randomly allocated to experimental conditions' mean? [1]

    (g) Think of **one** way in which the experimental conditions might have differed from what the experimenter intended. [1]

16. In the analysis of quantitative data, the findings are categorised and summarised.

    (a) Why is it necessary to categorise and summarise qualitative data? [2]

    (b) Describe how qualitative data are categorised. [2]

17. Suggest two ways in which validity in studies collecting qualitative data may be improved. [2]

2 Research methods key terms

An exam question may occasionally require you to 'simply' define or explain a term such as 'validity' or 'laboratory experiment' (rather than using your knowledge of such terms to answer contextualised questions). Questions that require a definition or explanation are likely to be worth 2 or 3 marks.

It pays to be ready with an answer to such questions, and learning such definitions should increase your understanding.

For each key term, you should record three points that you need to remember. Three points should provide you with sufficient information to write 3 marks' worth.

Produce a table like the blue one below and record three points for each of the key terms in the purple box below that. There is a third column for additional information that might be useful to remember.

Key term	Three points describing each term	Additional information, such as
	Note that some of these of very simple concepts and you may not be able to write 3 marks' worth. If necessary, you can use examples as a method of elaborating definitions.	• Advantages and/or disadvantages • How might a researcher deal with this problem? • How would you do it?
Validity	• • •	

Key terms you need to know
All of these terms are included in the specification.

Aim	Ethical issues	Measures of central tendency	Random sample
Calculated value	Experiment	Nominal data	Range
Case study	Experimental/alternative hypothesis	Normal distribution	Ratio data
Clinical interview	Field experiment	Null hypothesis	Reliability
Confidentiality	Generalisability	Objectivity	Repeated measures design
Consent	Hypothesis	Observation	Right to withdraw
Content Analysis	Independent groups design	One-tailed hypothesis	Sampling technique
Control	Independent variable	Operationalisation	Significance
Correlational design	Inferential statistics	Opportunity sample	Situational variable
Counterbalancing	Interval data	Ordinal data	Standard deviation
Critical value	Interview	Participant (experimental) design	Subjectivity
Debriefing	Laboratory experiment	Participant variable	Systematic sample
Dependent variable	Level of measurement	Qualitative data	Two-tailed hypothesis
Directional hypothesis	Level of significance	Quantitative data	Validity
Ethical guidelines	Matched pairs design	Questionnaire	Variance
		Quota sample	Volunteer sample

3 Using studies to revise research methods

For your AS you will have learned (at least) two 'studies in detail' for each of the six approaches named in the specification. Some of these studies are named in the specification, including the research of Piaget, Freud and Milgram. In addition there are many others that many students choose to learn, such as Peterson and Peterson, Craik and Tulving, and Hofling. For each of your 12 studies, you need to know the aims, procedures, findings, conclusions and some strengths and weaknesses. But you can also use these as a way of revising research methods. (This exercise will also help you revise your studies for either your AS exams or for the synoptic paper (Unit 6) at A2.)

Select any research studies you have studied in detail during your AS and A2 course and for each of them:

- Identify the research method that was used (note that a study may involve observations or questionnaires as a way of collecting data but the *method* may be an experiment because there is an IV/DV; or, if there isn't an IV/DV, the method is an observation, questionnaire or interview).

- If it is an experiment, state the IV and DV.

- You should also state the aim of the research – what were they trying to find out?

- Finally, you should note at least two points of evaluation, you can consider methodological or ethical issues.

So you can fill in a table that looks like the one below. The first one has been filled in for you. (A copy of the full table for you to fill in can be found on the website www.nelsonthornes.com/researchmethods.)

One thing you will discover is just how few studies fall into a neat category!

Short-term memory Peterson and Peterson (1959) 'Trigrams'	**Method:** Laboratory experiment (IV: retention intervals, DV: recall)
	Aim: Recall is reduced as retention intervals get longer. (Directional)
	Evaluation: This is a repeated measures design. Rehearsal was controlled during the retention interval by participants counting backwards.
Another study	**Method:**
	Aim:
	Evaluation:

Looking at ecological validity (or validity in general, reliability or generalisibility)

You can choose your own studies to use in this table.

For each of the studies below, present arguments about whether it has high or low ecological validity.

Study	Arguments about why it may have *high* ecological validity	Arguments about why it may have *low* ecological validity
Milgram (1963) Obedience to authority		
Piaget (1954) object permance		
Freud (1909) Little Hans		

And finally, some research methods questions about 'key' studies that you may have encountered at AS or A2 – but remember, these may *not* be ones you have learned.

Milgram – a study into obedience to authority

1. Explain why this could be seen to be a laboratory experiment.
2. Describe **one** advantage of using a laboratory experiment in the context of this study.
3. Describe **one** disadvantage of using a laboratory experiment in the context of this study.
4. Describe **two** possible threats to the validity of this study.
5. Suggest how you could deal with these problems.
6. What sampling method was used?
7. Describe **one** advantage and **one** disadvantage of this sampling method in the context of this study.
8. Explain **three** ethical issues that arose in this study.
9. Explain **two** ethically sound aspects of Milgram's procedure.
10. Explain **one** reason why Milgram's results would generalise to a wider population and one reason why they would not.

Piaget – a study of object permanence

1. Explain in what way this study is an experiment.
2. Explain **one** research technique used in this study
3. Identify and operationalise the IV and DV in this study.
4. Write an operationalised experimental hypothesis for this study.
5. Is your hypothesis one- or two-tailed?
6. Explain why you chose a one- or two-tailed hypothesis.
7. Some of the participants Piaget studied were his own children, whom he followed throughout their early years. This is a longitudinal study. Are longitudinal studies repeated measures or independent groups designs?
8. Why do psychologists conduct longitudinal studies?
9. An alternative design to use when comparing age groups is to use a cross-sectional method. Are cross-sectional studies repeated measures or independent groups designs?

Freud – a study of the Oedipus Complex

1. What research method was used by Freud to investigate Hans?
2. Describe **two** advantages of using this method in this context.
3. Describe **two** disadvantages of using this method in this context.
4. Identify and explain **one** ethical issue that could have arisen in this situation.
5. In what way was this study likely to suffer from subjectivity?
6. How could the study have been made more objective?
7. If the study were to be repeated, parents could be interviewed about their children's early experiences. How could you assess the reliability of the interviews?
8. Describe the advantages of conducting interviews rather than using questionnaires.
9. What is the difference between open and closed questions?
10. Which type of question would be used to generate qualitative data?

Dement and Kleitman – a study of dreaming

1. In what respect was this an experiment?
2. What were the IVs being tested?
3. What DVs were measured and how were they operationalised?
4. What is a participant variable?
5. How were participant variables reduced in this study?
6. Why was it important to control the participant variables you have identified?
7. Identify **one** other control imposed in this study and explain its purpose.
8. Explain whether the sample was representative of the population. Explain how your answer affects the generalisibility of the results.

Skinner – a study of superstition in pigeons

1. In what respect was this an observational study?
2. Describe the **two** conflicting values that led to an ethical issue in this study.
3. How was learning operationalised in this study?
4. The Skinner box is used to reduce situational variables. What are situational variables?
5. Superstition has also been studied in humans. Design an experiment to test a newly acquired superstitious behaviour such as learning to press a computer key in the belief that it stops an annoying buzzing noise.
6 What ethical dilemma could arise in the study that you have designed?

Loftus and Palmer – a study into the role of leading questions in EWT

1. Identify the IV and DV in this study.
2. Is this a repeated measures design or an independent groups design?
3. Give **one** advantage and **one** disadvantage of this design in this study.
4. How could participants have been allocated to conditions?
5. Describe any demand characteristics that may have occurred in this study.
6. What other threats to validity might have been present?
7. Identify **one** ethical issue that may have arisen in this study.
8. Describe how this ethical issue could be dealt with.

Watson and Rayner – a study of classically conditioned fear

1. In was respect was this an observational study?
2. How was fear operationalised in this study?
3. Describe the **two** conflicting values that led to an ethical issue in this study.
4. Do you think this means that the study should not have been conducted?
5. How might this ethical issue have been resolved?
6. If you were going to conduct a study such as this, what would you tell parents beforehand in order to obtain their informed consent?
7. Do you think that asking for their informed consent absolves the researchers of any responsibility for taking further steps towards good ethical practice?

Make up your own

You can write question cards for the other studies from your course, to help revise research methods. Just writing the questions is good revision.

Marking exercises: specimen paper

1. SOURCE MATERIAL

Thirty students were gathered into a classroom, and were presented with a list of 27 letters. They looked at them for a specified amount of time, and were then asked to recall them on a sheet of paper, in any order. There were two conditions. The list of 27 letters was divided up into 9 groups of 3 letters, with spaces between. In one condition the groups of 3 letters contained initials which had 'meaning' (for example, fbi, phd, twa). In the other condition, although the same letters were used overall, the groups of 3 had no meaning (for example, bfd, hpa, wdt). Each student had either one list or the other, and a blank sheet of paper on which to write the letters they recalled.

Results

The table on the right shows the results of the study, recording the number of letters recalled in the two conditions. Condition One was where the stimulus letters were in meaningful groups, and Condition Two where the groups had no meaning.

It was found that the students given a list with 'meaningful' groups of letters recalled more than the students given letters with no 'meaning'. A statistical test was carried out and was significant at $p \leq 0.01$.

(a) Write down a suitable experimental hypothesis for the above study. **[2]**

(b) Give the independent and the dependent variable in the study. **[2]**

(c) From the table of results it is possible to work out what design was used. Decide from the information in the table what design was used, and give a reason for your decision. **[2]**

(d) Give **one** advantage and **one** disadvantage of the use of this design in psychological studies. **[4]**

(e) Analyse the data from the descriptive statistics given in the table of results. **[2]**

(f) Describe **one** example of a control used in this study. **[4]**

(g) What statistical test is likely to have been chosen? Give reasons for your choice. **[3]**

(h) In order to see if the result of a statistical test is significant, it is necessary to know whether the alternative or experimental hypothesis involves a one- or two-tailed prediction. What does 'one- or two-tailed' mean? **[2]**

(i) What does the expression 'a statistical test …was significant at $p \leq 0.01$' mean? **[1]**

(Total 22 marks)

In your answers to this question you should include relevant information from the whole of your course, where appropriate.

2. **Imagine you are going to carry out a study investigate a person's memory. The experimental method described in Question 1 is not suitable.**

   You are interested, for example, in a person's everyday memories, including what they remember about the past and how they remember what they have to do in the future.

(a) Outline a suitable method to use for your study. **[2]**

(b) Explain why the method you have chosen is suitable. **[4]**

(c) Describe how to plan and conduct your study. (You must take account of ethical issues.) **[5]**

(d) Explain **one** ethical issue that you have considered in your study. **[3]**

(Total 14 marks)

TOTAL FOR SECTION : 36 MARKS

Condition One: with 'meaningful' groups		Condition Two: with non-meaningful groups	
Student Number	Number of letters recalled out of 27	Student Number	Number of letters recalled out of 27
1	15	16	10
2	18	17	7
3	20	18	14
4	15	19	8
5	16	20	10
6	11	21	7
7	25	22	9
8	21	23	11
9	24	24	15
10	18	25	9
11	19	26	4
12	19	27	8
13	23	28	12
14	21	29	10
15	15	30	10
Mean	18.67	Mean	9.6
Median	18	Median	10
Mode	15	Mode	10
Range	14	Range	11

Examiner's tips

Question 1

(b) Must be detailed.

(e) Asks for analysis, so the answer must compare data from the two conditions, not just quote figures.

(f) Must elaborate answer to get both marks, e.g. by explaining how control is achieved or why it is important.

(g) Must make three relevant points to get full marks.

(h) Need to explain *both* for 2 marks.

Question 2

(a) 'Outline' is asking for more than just identification of the method.

(b) Need to make four separate points for full marks, or two points which are elaborated.

(c) Plan must be detailed and include at least one consideration of ethics.

(d) Issue must have been identified in part (c).

Specimen Paper: Answer from Candidate A

Question 1

(a) There will be a difference between recall of people who read meaningful and nonsense syllables.

(b) IV: The meaningfulness of letter sequences, either meaningful or nonsense.

DV: the participants' recall.

(c) Independent groups.

(d) Participants are less likely to work out the purpose of the study because they only see it once and don't experience both levels of the IV, which would affect their behaviour and so this is better than repeated measures but a problem is that there may be participant variables making the results different in the two levels of the IV.

(e) The mean, median and mode all show that people who read meaningful letter combinations had better recall for the lists. However, their results were more variable because the range was bigger.

(f) All letter combinations were three letters long.

(g) Independent t-test

(h) One-tailed means you can predict the direction of an effect, e.g. whether scores will be better or worse on one condition than the other.

Two-tailed means you can't tell, the effect could push the results to make the participant's performance either better or worse in each condition.

(i) That there is a less than 10% probability that the results obtained are due to chance.

Question 2

(a) Diary method

(b) Participants could write down the things they have to remember during the day, then in the evening record those things they remembered or forgot about.

(c) Each participant will be given a diary in which they are asked to record twice daily what they have to remember that day (in the morning), what they did remember (in the evening) and three things from their past, which would be used for content analysis. It is important that they are informed beforehand that the study is looking at memory and that they will be asked to record information about their remembering and forgetting, that they do not have to record everything and if there are items they would like to leave out they are free to do so. Also that if they want to drop out at any time they can. At the end it would be important to debrief the participants as some may have recalled things that upset them or been bothered about how much they forgot. The information in the diaries would be analysed. Operational definitions for 'items forgotten' and 'items remembered' would be decided, and the remembered and forgotten items could be grouped into categories to look for trends in the types of everyday memories that are recalled or lost.

(d) Psychological harm.

It was important to debrief participants as some may have recalled things that upset them or been bothered about how much they forgot and it is important that participants at the end of the study are in the same state that they were in the beginning, i.e. that they haven't been negatively affected by participating.

Examiner commentary on Candidate A's answer

Question 1

(a) This hypothesis is correctly an experimental hypothesis and is two-tailed because no previous evidence was presented. It has also operationalised the IV. However, the DV has not been operationalised; 'recall' is not sufficient.

(b) The IV has been operationalised but the DV has not: it needed to include a statement such as 'measured as the number of letters recalled out of 27'.

(c) There is no explanation offered, for example 'Because the participant numbers are different for the people in the second condition'.

(d) Note that the candidate doesn't use the term 'demand characteristics' but doesn't need to because they have given a full explanation. However, they needed to say more about participant variables.

(e) This answer is fine so far but does not say enough for 4 marks. The mean and median were higher than the mode suggesting that although there was a cluster of participants scoring 15, there were many different higher scores than this. The candidate needed to go on to draw a conclusion.

(f) Could alternatively have talked about the same letters being used overall or there being the same number of letter groups in each list.

(g) Should also mention why – because the level of measurement was interval and the design was independent groups.

(h) This answer indicates that the candidate understands although it could have been more effectively expressed.

(i) This answer is correct except that it should be 1% not 10% – watch out for zeros.

Question 2

(a) This question had 2 marks available so required more information about the method than this.

(b) This method only tells us about the immediate past, but, more importantly, the answer doesn't justify the choice of the method – it doesn't explain why the method is suitable.

(c) This is more than enough for 5 marks.

(d) Another good answer. If appropriate you can repeat information from the previous answer or, alternatively, identify and explain an issue that you had not mentioned in (c).

Marks given on page 138

Specimen Paper: Answer from Candidate B

Question 1

(a) Participants presented with lists of meaningful three-letter groups subsequently recall more of the letter groups than those presented with a nonsense three-letter list.

(b) The IV is the number of three-letter sequences correctly recalled out of 9.

The DV is whether the letter groups within the list were in random threes or organised into meaningful threes.

(c) The student numbers go from 1 to 15 in condition 1 and 16 to 30 in the other but also in the text it says that 'each student had either one list or the other' so it is an independent variables design.

(d) One problem with this design is that participant variables can affect the results because the people in each condition might be different in ways that matter; for example in this experiment the participants in one level of the IV might happen to have better memories. However, it is a good design because the participants can't suffer from order effects because they only do one condition which is better than repeated measures because they can't get fatigued or learn the three-letter sequences, which would distort the results.

(e) The median and mean are quite similar in both conditions (18.86 and 18 for one condition compared with 9.6 and 10 for the other). One mode is quite different and much lower (15) than the mean and median for the 'meaningful' group but this is not really in the 'middle' of the data. The range of scores is bigger for the meaningful group, the best scores were much better than the 'no meaning' group and the 'no meaning' group's scores went much lower than the lowest in the other group. This suggests that meaning helped with recall.

(f) The same letters were used in each set of 27. This means that any effects were not due to other factors such as one set having lots of distinctive letters such as x and z that might be easier to remember.

(g) It is a design that compares two different groups of people and the level of measurement is interval so the right test is an independent t-test.

(h) If a hypothesis is one-tailed you know which way it's going, but if it's two-tailed you don't.

(i) This means that there is a 1% possibility that the distribution of results found in the experiment could have arisen by chance.

Question 2

(a) Longitudinal study, where the participants record the things that are important to them to remember and identify incidents of forgetting.

(b) This enables the researcher to find out about the participants' strategies for remembering and whether they work because they can check whether the things they made an effort to remember were, in fact, recalled better. For example, participants could identify the things they need to remember to do and then the researchers use these records to check whether they have done them. By using a longitudinal study they would encounter lots of examples of real remembering and forgetting which would be better than an cross-sectional study where only one period of time could be considered.

(c) Participants would be asked to identify three things they had to remember each day and record the next day whether they had or not. At the end of each week the researcher would compare the kinds of things they had remembered or forgotten. The participants would have to be told that they didn't have to record personal things they remembered or forgot because this would invade their privacy. They would also need to know that what they did write down would be kept confidential which means the researchers couldn't show other people the exact records.

(d) Invasion of privacy. This is important as the participants might be embarrassed about things they had to remember or had forgotten to do and recording it might make them feel worse. It matters because participants must not suffer psychological harm from being in a study.

Examiner commentary on Candidate B's answer

Question 1

(a) This hypothesis is one-tailed which is acceptable as the question does not specify and it successfully operationalises both the IV and DV.

(b) The IV and DV are reversed, so no marks can be awarded even though each has been operationalised very well.

(c) The candidate has correctly identified the evidence from the table (although the sentence from the text is not what was required by the question). However, they have then used the wrong term (it should be independent groups not independent variables) – watch out for making predictable mistakes.

(d) Note that the error in (c) doesn't matter because it is clear that the candidate is talking about independent groups so the candidate can still get credit for part (d).

The issue of participant variables is dealt with well and earns 2 of the 4 marks. The advantage, relating to order effects is also appropriate.

(e) The candidate has made effective comparisons between the data sets and reached an appropriate conclusion.

(f) This is a good, elaborated answer.

(g) The choice and justification is correct. Note that the candidate has described independent groups rather than giving the name of the design, but this is sufficient to gain the marks.

(h) Although this candidate probably does know what two-tailed means, this isn't clear from their answer – you must not presume that the examiner will guess what you mean.

(i) This is almost a good answer – but it must say 'less than'.

Question 2

(a) This contains just sufficient detail for 2 marks. The candidate could also have said they would record what steps they took to remember and any recall they had of past events.

(b) This answer indicates that the candidate does know why this is a good choice of method, and their comparison is good.

(c) This is a good, concise, answer.

(d) This answer identifies the issue, explains why it matters to the participants and why it matters in terms of the ethical guidelines.

Marks given on page 138

Marking exercise: January 2003

1. SOURCE MATERIAL

A group of students decided to conduct some research into the effect that smiling at teachers has on the number of jokes teachers told in class. In their college there were two psychology groups, each taught by a different teacher. The students counted the number of jokes each teacher told in a typical lesson, which was approximately the same for both teachers. Students in one of the groups started to smile more often than they would normally. Students in the other group behaved as usual. For the next six weeks they counted the number of jokes each teacher told in class.

Their results are illustrated in the graph, below.

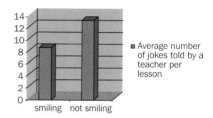

■ Average number of jokes told by a teacher per lesson

(a) (i) What type of experiment were the students conducting? **[1]**
(ii) Outline **one** advantage and **one** disadvantage of this method. **[4]**
(b) (i) What is the independent variable in this study? **[1]**
(ii) What is the dependent variable in this study? **[1]**
(iii) Identify **one** problem associated with measuring the dependent variable in this study. **[1]**
(c) What is the level of measurement for the data in this study? **[1]**
(d) Suggest a null hypothesis for this study **[2]**
(e) Suggest an experimental hypothesis for this study. **[2]**
(f) Why was it important to begin by counting how many jokes a teacher told in a typical lesson? **[2]**
(g) (i) What is meant by **operationalisation** when it applies to experimental variables? **[2]**
(ii) Why would the independent variable have been difficult to operationalise in this study? **[2]**

[Total 19 marks]

In your answer to this question you should include relevant information from the whole of your course, where appropriate.

2. **It has been suggested that looking at pictures before going to sleep affects images in dreams. Researchers decided to investigate whether looking at different colour combinations would affect the colours experienced in dreams. Participants were shown one of four possible colour combinations: 'red and white', 'green and white', 'blue and white', or 'black and white'. They looked at these colours before going to sleep. The next morning they recorded the predominant colour in their dreams.**

(a) (i) Which participant design was used in this study? **[1]**
(ii) Outline **one** advantage and **one** disadvantage of the design you named in (i). **[4]**
(b) (i) Define the term **participant variable**. **[2]**
(ii) Describe a participant variable which might have arisen in this study. **[3]**
(c) (i) Identify **two** BPS ethical guidelines which might have relevance to this study. **[2]**
(ii) For **one** of the ethical guidelines in (i), explain how it is relevant to the study. **[2]**
(iii) Suggest **one** way in which you could ensure that this study would be conducted in an ethical manner. **[3]**

[Total 17 marks]

TOTAL FOR SECTION : 36 MARKS

Examiner's tips

Question 1

(a) (i) Only the first answer will count.

(a) (ii) 2 marks for advantages and 2 for disadvantages. The second mark is for elaborating the idea stated.

If (a) (i) was wrong but the answer here matches it and is correct, it can earn marks.

(b) (i) Must state both levels of the IV.

(b) (ii) Must operationalise the DV.

(b) (iii) Any reasonable criticism but must be related to this study.

(c) Only the first answer will count.

(d) Must be a null hypothesis not an experimental hypothesis. For 2 marks the IV and DV must be clear.

(e) Must be an experimental hypothesis not a null hypothesis. For 2 marks the IV and DV must be clear. May be one- or two-tailed.

(f) The question doesn't state 'one' so the second mark can be for a second idea or for elaborating the first idea.

(g) (i) The second mark is for elaborating the basic definition. A correct example would gain 1 mark as it demonstrates an understanding of the concept.

(g) (ii) 2 marks for an elaborated answer.

Question 2

(a) (i) Single word answers are acceptable.

(a) (ii) If (a) (i) was wrong but the answer here matches it and is correct, it can earn marks.

(b) (i) Two marks for an elaborated answer.

(b) (ii) Second and third marks for elaboration and detail. If more than one variable is discussed, credit the best.

(c) (i) 1 mark per guideline.

(c) (ii) 1 marks for an elaborated answer. To gain marks the answer must make at least one reference to the study. If (c) (i) is blank or incorrect, marks can be gained in (c) (ii) if a guideline is clear.

(c) (iii) Second and third marks for elaboration. To gain marks the answer must make at least one reference to the study.

January 2003: Answer from Candidate A

Question 1

(a) (i) An experiment, a field experiment.

(ii) One advantage of field experiments is that the participants, in this case the teachers, are in their normal environment (the classroom) so will behave naturally. A disadvantage of this method is that the teachers might have responses to something else and you can't control all the variables so you wouldn't know.

(b) (i) If the students smiled or not.

(ii) How much the teachers told jokes over 6 weeks.

(iii) Different people might think different things were funny.

(c) Ordinal

(d) There is no difference between the IV of smiling and the DV of jokes.

(e) There is a difference between the number of jokes told by a teacher when the students smile more than usual and when they smile like they normally would.

(f) In case some teachers told more jokes to begin with.

(g) (i) Operationalisation is when experimental variables can be measured or changed precisely, e.g. counting the number of jokes as a way to measure the DV exactly.

(ii) It would be really difficult to control the amount of smiling because if you were supposed to be not smiling and got a fit of the giggles you might smile too much.

Question 2

(a) (i) Independent groups design.

(ii) An advantage is that the students are in their usual environment of the classroom so would act in a normal way. A disadvantage is that participant variables might cause differences as different people perform in the different IV conditions.

(b) (i) The different characteristics of people in the sample such as how vividly they normally dream.

(ii) How many colourful things they saw during the day would be a participant variable; for instance if one person saw lots of red things they might dream more about that, rather than the colour they were given in the experiment. Also, some people might dream more vividly.

(c) (i) Conduct: Respecting participants' well-being, Consent: making sure that the participants know what they are letting themselves in for.

(ii) The researchers should be sure that showing people colours before they sleep isn't going to harm them – for example red is an aggressive colour and looking at it before sleep might cause disrupted sleep or nightmares – so they should do a pilot study first before putting lots of people at risk.

(iii) Participants would be told beforehand it was a study on dreams and colour and they would need to look at pictures before they went to sleep and then record only the main colour in their dream and not be asked about anything else about their dreams. They could then give their informed consent but should also be told they could stop if they wanted to so they knew about their right to withdraw.

Examiner commentary on Candidate A's answer

Question 1

(a) (i) Only the first answer is accepted so, even though the second answer is correct, it does not earn marks.

(ii) The advantage described – which relates to the second answer in (a) (i) but is credited here – is worth 1 mark. The candidate could have gone on to say that this raises ecological validity. The disadvantage almost gets 2 marks, one for observing the problem and the second is very close – if the candidate had said what you wouldn't know, this would have been complete.

(b) (i) Good answer; it had to be more informative than just 'smiling'.

(ii) Good answer again; it had to be more than just 'jokes'.

(iii) This answer indicates that the candidate has understood and thought about the situation described. You need to use the information in the source for research methods questions.

(c) This answer is the most plausible.

(d) This is a 'nonsense null'. Beware of writing these! Of course there is a difference between the IV and the DV: you manipulate one and measure the other. What the candidate meant to say was that there was no difference in the DV caused by, or in different levels of, the IV.

(e) This is an appropriately operationalised hypothesis, both 'jokes' and 'smiling' are operationalised.

(f) This answer is right so far but the candidate needs to add why this was important.

(g) (i) This definition gains 2 marks because it provides a basic understanding followed by an appropriate description of an example.

(ii) Again this answer gains full marks by having an explanation elaborated by an example.

Question 2

(a) (i) This is a full answer, though even just 'independent groups' would have been sufficient.

(ii) The first sentence is irrelevant; it is an advantage of field experiments, not an advantage of the design. The disadvantage is correct and well expressed.

(b) (i) This answer begins well and the example helps to indicate that the candidate understands the concept. They could alternatively have gained the second mark for elaborating the answer, such as by making reference to the importance of these variables, i.e. that they could affect the outcome of the study.

(ii) The candidate identifies a suitable participant variable and briefly describes how it could affect the study. To gain the third mark the candidate needed to elaborate this answer. The second point they make (a repetition of the previous answer which, in itself is acceptable) is a different idea and only identifies the issue so would only be worth 1 mark. As a consequence, the first part of the answer is credited instead.

(c) (i) The guidelines only needed to be stated, not described.

(ii) This is a good answer although it would have been better if the candidate restated which guideline they were explaining – and included the phrase describing the guideline from the answer above.

(iii) This answer is sufficient for 3 marks. It is clearly linked to the study and well detailed.

Marks given on page 138

January 2003: Answer from Candidate B

Question 1

(a) (i) A natural experiment.

(ii) A natural experiment is good because it is a real-world situation so is high in ecological validity because the situation isn't artificial. But natural experiments are also bad because the IV isn't manipulated by the researcher so you can't be sure that differences really are due to that factor.

(b) (i) How many times the teachers told jokes.

(ii) Smiling more or less than usual.

(iii) Some people smile more than others anyway.

(c) Nominal (jokes or no jokes).

(d) There will be no difference between the number of jokes told by teachers in a typical lesson when students smile lots or the normal amount.

(e) When students smile teachers tell more jokes.

(f) So that they knew how many jokes each teacher normally told. Then they could see if there was a change during the experiment.

(g) (i) It's where the DV or IV are precisely defined rather than just vaguely.

(ii) Even in really dull classes you smile sometimes.

Question 2

(a) (i) Independent.

(ii) It avoids problems with fatigue and practice effects, which is good, but individual differences might be a problem because there are different participants in each of the conditions and they might not all respond the same way to each colour anyway.

(b) (i) An example would be that some people dream in colour but others dream in black and white.

(ii) If people saw different coloured things during the day this would cause a differences; e.g. if someone worked in a shop where all the wrappers were blue (like Tesco) and someone else worked in a shop where all the wrappers were green (like Asda) then there would be a difference between them.

(c) (i) Confidentiality and debriefing.

(ii) Confidentiality – they need to make sure that the participants know that their results will only be the predominant colour not anything about what was in the dream and will not be made public as dream content is a private thing.

(iii) Give them a thorough briefing telling them about the study, and what it is about, being careful not to tell them too much because that would be a problem too. So they would need to know that it is a psychology experiment on sleep and dreaming and colour.

Examiner commentary on Candidate B's answer

Question 1

(a) (i) This answer is incorrect as the experimenters were clearly manipulating the IV.

(ii) This is a good answer which relates appropriately to the candidate's response to (a) (i) – even though that was incorrect, this answer is therefore described as a 'transferred error'. As a consequence, the answer here gains full credit.

(b) (i) The IV and DV have been 'reversed' between this part and the next so both marks have been missed.

(ii) Had the answers to (b) (i) and (b) (ii) been the other way round, both would have gained marks.

(iii) This is an appropriate answer and does not need to be elaborated to gain 1 mark.

(c) This answer is not acceptable (although any scale would have been accepted – ordinal, interval or ratio). This is because the researchers were counting the number of jokes, not just whether there were any or not.

(d) A good answer, in which both the IV and DV have been operationalised.

(e) This is a experimental hypothesis but has not been operationalised so misses the second mark.

(f) In this answer the second mark has been awarded for appropriate elaboration of the idea.

(g) (i) This answer is sufficient for 1 mark; to gain the second the candidate needed to elaborate their response, for example by giving an example – it would not need to relate to the context of the question providing it was clear.

(ii) Again, this needed more detail, for example saying how this would affect the data collected.

Question 2

(a) (i) Even though this is only one word (it should say 'independent groups') it still gains a mark as it is clear that the candidate knows which design is being used.

(ii) The advantage is correct but not detailed, so the second mark is missed. The disadvantage is correct and successfully elaborated.

(b) (i) This example is appropriate and clarifies the candidate's understanding so earns 1 mark; but there is no definition of the term.

(ii) The example is appropriate and there is sufficient detail for both elaboration marks as it is clear how this factor could affect the outcome of the study.

(c) (i) Note that debriefing is acceptable as an answer here as the question asks for guidelines (not issues).

(ii) A good, clear answer which earns both marks. Note that any guideline could be relevant here – except ones relating to animal research.

(iii) The last sentence of this answer is essential as it links the response to the study and contextualisation is required here. However, more detail was required for full marks.

Marks given on page 138

Marking exercise: June 2003

1. SOURCE MATERIAL

Two researchers investigated whether eyewitness memory would be affected by subsequent discussion of the witnessed events. The researchers arranged a fake crime, where students in a lecture would witness a thief enter the lecture hall, steal a handbag and leave. The students were then told that the theft was a set-up and given the option to withdraw. Those who continued were tested individually on their recall of events, using a 16-item questionnaire.

The participants were then instructed to discuss the witnessed events for a set period of time. During the discussion, one participant (who was really an experimental accomplice) was identified as having a particularly good memory, and deliberately set out to mislead the real participants on eight of the questionnaire items. After the discussion, participants were re-tested on their recall, using the same questionnaire. Results showed that all of the participants changed at least one answer on the second questionnaire to conform with the experimental accomplice and 57% of the participants changed all eight answers.

(a) Identify the experimental design used in this study. [1]
(b) Outline **one** advantage of this design. [2]
(c) Explain how order effects might have affected the results of this study. [2]
(d) Identify the independent variable in this study. [1]
(e) Write a suitable null hypothesis for this study. [2]
(f) Identify the method of sampling used in this study. [1]
(g) Outline **one** disadvantage of using this method of sampling. [2]
(h) Would you consider the ecological validity of this study to be high or low? Explain your answer. [4]
(i) Explain whether you would consider this study to be ethical. [4]
(j) What conclusions about eyewitness testimony could be drawn from this study? [3]

(Total 22 marks)

In your answer to this question you should include relevant information from the whole of your course, where appropriate.

2.
(a) What is meant by the following terms?
   (i) **quantitative** data.
   (ii) **qualitative** data. [2]
(b) Clinical interviews are a common way of generating qualitative data. Name **two** other research methods which can generate qualitative data. [2]
(c) Describe **one** way of analysing qualitative data. [3]
(d) Outline **one** disadvantage of using qualitative data. [3]
(e) Explain why a researcher might prefer to use qualitative, rather than qualitative methods. [4]

(Total 14 marks)

TOTAL FOR SECTION : 36 MARKS

Examiner's tips

Question 1

(a) Must be an acceptable term, not a description.

(b) Accept any advantage of the design offered: it doesn't have to relate to the particular situation described. If the answer to (a) was a wrong design, relevant advantages to the answer given can be credited.

(d) Detail must be sufficient, single word answers would not gain credit because both 'parts' of the IV are required.

(e) For full two marks the null hypothesis must be elaborated and refer to both the IV and DV.

(f) Several plausible answers e.g. opportunity or volunteer.

(g) Accept any correct disadvantage offered, it doesn't have to relate to the particular situation described. Detail must be sufficient, single word answers (e.g. 'biased' would not gain credit).

(h) An argument either way, or an answer that's argued both ways, could gain full credit. Elaborating on reasons gains further marks, do not have to have four separate ideas.

(i) An argument either way, or an answer that's argued both ways, could gain full credit. Issues that do not appear in the text must be explained in order to earn marks.

(j) Conclusions in terms of populations, not participants.

Question 2

(a) Examples that illustrate the terms can be credited though they would not be sufficient for full marks on their own.

(d) Accept any correct disadvantage offered: it doesn't have to relate to the particular situation described. Detail must be sufficient single word answers are unlikely to gain credit.

Exam tip

If a question asks for a definition for 2 marks and you're not sure that your answer is sufficiently detailed, add an example. This can help to illustrate that you understand the concept.

June 2003: Answer from Candidate A

Question 1

(a) Repeated measures. A lab experiment.

(b) It controls for participant variables.

(c) The participants could be affected by fatigue effects.

(d) The effect of a leading or non-leading discussion, i.e. whether the participants had been exposed to the leading effects of a confederate with a good memory in the discussion.

(e) Memory will change when participants are exposed to a leading accomplice in a discussion.

(f) Opportunity sampling.

(g) You can't be sure that the sample contains a good range of the different sorts of people in the population.

(h) It's good because students are used to discussing things in groups; this means it was a real-life task. Also, it took place in their familiar setting when they were engaged in a normal task. Lectures might often be boring so they would be used to paying attention to any interruptions instead. There are lots of students in lectures so they wouldn't have known that the accomplice wasn't one of them so this couldn't have affected their behaviour. Finally, students go to lectures expecting to have to remember things, so although the theft wasn't part of the lecture it was realistic to expect them to remember it.

(i) Yes, because although the participants were deceived, they were told that the theft was staged and were given the chance to withdraw at that point. However, there is no mention of the participants being debriefed at the end, which is wrong because they were deceived again, about the role of the accomplice.

(j) People's recall of events they have witnessed are affected by the opinions of others. There is a lot of variation between individuals, some being affected much more than others.

Question 2

(a) (i) and (ii) Quantitative data is basically numbers, qualitative consists of descriptions.

(b) Case studies, questionnaires.

(c) By looking for repeated themes or items in the data (such as transcripts of television shows) and finding out what else they commonly relate to in the transcript.

(d) It is difficult to compare data from different sources, which makes the findings less useful. For example, you couldn't do stats tests on qualitative data from two conditions in an experiment.

(e) Because they want to find out the reasons behind a particular behaviour. They could do this by exploring deeply through an interview that would provide real-life data including quotes from people. This would give them much more detail than using a quantitative method, which might miss out on important information.

Examiner commentary on Candidate A's answer

Question 1

(a) The candidate will have earned the mark for 'repeated measures', the only correct answer (a research method, even if it is correct, does not answer the question). Anything after this first answer would probably be ignored, so if the answer is written 'A lab experiment. Repeated measures' the candidate may well score zero.

(b) Right so far but the candidate needs to go on to say why this is important, for example 'so that any differences in the DV between the levels of the IV are the result of the manipulation and not extraneous variables'.

(c) There is not enough here for any marks. The answer could be made creditworthy by adding 'they may be bored with the questions so give different responses because they can't be bothered to answer properly' OR the candidate could gain 2 marks by identifying both fatigue and practice effects.

(d) This is a good answer because the candidate has operationalised the IV.

(e) This is an alternative hypothesis, not a null.

(f) This is one possible correct answer – they were the people who happened to be in the lecture at the time.

(g) This is fine so far but the candidate needed to go on to say why this was a problem – because that means the findings can't be generalised or that it doesn't represent everyone.

(h) This is a good answer because the candidate has made several separate points and expanded them. The candidate didn't need the last sentence to get full marks. Note that it would have been possible (and perhaps easier) to get the marks by arguing that the study wasn't ecologically valid!

(i) This is a good answer. The question doesn't say you have to argue in one direction (either that it is, or is not, ethical) so you can present arguments in either direction to gain marks.

(j) The candidate could have finished this by observing that some individuals conform completely to the effect of leading opinions, so some eyewitnesses may be very unreliable.

Question 2

(a) This is a short but effective answer.

(b) Another possible answer would have been surveys, but since they tend to rely on questionnaire or interview techniques, this is a better answer.

(c) This answer is insufficient for full marks. It would have been sensible for the candidate to have identified the method they were describing (content analysis) even though there are no marks for this. They should then have gone on to give more detail, for example that these themes would be the recording units or that the researcher would need to decide how to sample from the transcripts.

(d) Sensible answers could also have been given for different disadvantages.

(e) This answer is good and just sufficient. It could have easily been improved by adding that these aspects make the data highly valid.

Marks given on page 138

January 2003: Answer from Candidate B

Question 1

(a) It is where each participant performs in both levels of the independent variable which avoids problems caused by participant variables.

(b) By controlling for participant variables, the experiment can show that the differences found in the DV, such as on recall, are not due to individual differences but due to the effects of the discussion, the IV.

(c) A practice effect could occur. This is where the participants do better on the second test because they know what to do. In this case the participants will have had a chance to rehearse their memory when they did the first questionnaire. Their answers on the second one might be affected by being able to remember what they had said the first time rather than being affected by the IV.

(d) The IV is whether there is a difference between leading discussions and the recall of the event.

(e) There is no difference between the recall of the event, as measured by the questionnaire, when tested before or after an accomplice expressed a leading view.

(f) Volunteer sample because they were told that it was a set-up and had the chance to withdraw.

(g) Volunteers are likely to be similar people – willing ones. This means that they are all of one type and won't represent the variety in the population.

(h) The study wasn't very ecologically valid because if you were going to steal a handbag you wouldn't do it in front of a lecture hall full of people. You'd do it when you'd be less likely to be seen like in the locker rooms or in the bar so it doesn't represent a real-life situation. Also, when crimes happen, people don't form organised groups to talk about it so that wasn't very real either. When you are asked to recall a crime it isn't usually by questionnaire – it's either face-to-face with the police, in a courtroom or with your friends, so the task lacked ecological validity as well as the situation. Also in real life in a cell you'd feel a lot different from how you would in this study so the emotions would be different too.

(i) No, because they might have been scared by the theft and after the experiment they might be worried that they were going to have their bag stolen and experiments shouldn't have lasting effects on participants because this breaks the ethical guideline about not causing psychological harm. Because it was staged and the participants didn't know what was going on they were deceived which is also wrong and because it was in a public place the participants couldn't say 'no' which means they couldn't give their consent. They were given the option to withdraw but not until they had already participated in the staged theft so they couldn't withdraw from that part.

(j) Discussion affects the memory of eyewitnesses so the police shouldn't listen to witnesses who have talked to each other. This is especially true when someone who might have influence is involved in the discussion.

Question 2

(a) Quantitative data are things like scores on a test, qualitative data are things like answers to open questions that describe how somebody feels.

(b) Experiments and correlations.

(c) In a case study in the psychodynamic approach, the researcher would look for symbols in the participant's comments and try to interpret these according to their understanding of hidden meanings in the unconscious. This could be based on reports of their dreams or their waking experiences such as phobias.

(d) With analysis of symbols there is a problem because one analyst might find different meanings from another – this is because their interpretation is subjective. Because of this generalisation from these analyses might not be valid.

(e) Qualitative data means that you can get really in depth information about the participant so that you can be sure that nothing important has been missed out whereas in quantitative studies, because the focus is on recording just one variable, important details might be overlooked.

Examiner commentary on Candidate B's answer

Question 1

(a) Even though the candidate has described the design (rather than some other aspect of the experiment) they have not *identified* it.

(b) This answer is good, although it has been contextualised unnecessarily – this wasn't asked for but it is clear that the candidate understands the advantage.

(c) The candidate identifies an appropriate order effect but then attempts to define practice effects (which is not required in this answer so would be ignored) and then suggests a sensible problem associated with practice effects and earns full marks.

(d) This is a common mistake but is usually made in the expression of hypotheses. What the candidate has done is observed that the experiment is looking for differences, and that this has to do with leading discussions, but has not correctly distinguished between levels of the IV (before and after the leading discussion) and the difference between the IV and the DV (recall). Be very careful that you do not make this mistake – always think about what you are writing.

(e) This is an appropriate null hypothesis and indicates that the candidate could have scored full marks on the previous question if they had thought about their answer.

(f) This answer is correct and did not need the justification in order to earn the mark.

(g) This is a good answer that demonstrates the candidate's understanding that the sample is biased.

(h) The level of detail on how to steal a handbag is more than is necessary. The first sentence was sufficient to indicate that the candidate was aware of the lack of mundane realism in the situation. They go on to identify two further problems with the method which are both appropriate.

(i) Another long-winded answer but it makes four useful points: psychological harm, deception, lack of consent and lack of opportunity to withdraw. The response could have been much more concise but in this section the only penalty is the time it takes to write an answer this long!

(j) This is a good, concise answer just about making three important points.

Question 2

(a) Even though this answer does not define the terms, it is clear from the examples that the candidate understands them.

(b) The candidate seems to have misread 'qualitative' for 'quantitative' in this question and proved the wrong answer.

(c) This is just enough for three marks. The candidate could have expanded the answer by explaining that the symbols represent unconscious motives or fears and that the purpose of the interpretation is to reveal these.

(d) This is an appropriate answer with good amplification and, although it should not have been set in the context of analysis of symbols, it does apply to qualitative data in general.

(e) The contrast to quantitative studies is valuable here.

Marks given on page 138

Marking exercise: June 2004

1. SOURCE MATERIAL

A group of researchers tested the effectiveness of a programme designed to improve literacy in primary school children (Pro-LIT). Sixty school children were randomly assigned to one of two conditions. In condition A, children were taught using conventional teaching methods. In condition B, children were taught using Pro-LIT instructed classes. Pro-LIT classes used a specially devised curriculum making use of co-operative learning with highly qualified teachers. At the end of the year all children were assessed using standardised tests of reading ability. Results showed the test scores of children allocated to Pro-LIT classes to be higher than those children instructed in ordinary classes. An unrelated t-test was used to analyse the data, producing a calculated value (observed value) of 2.493.

Table 1 Critical Values of t.

$p \leq 0.05$	$p \leq 0.01$	$p \leq 0.005$
1.671	2.390	2.660

(a) Name the experimental design in this study. **[1]**
(b) Outline **one** advantage and **one** disadvantage of using this method. **[4]**
(c) Why did the researchers randomly allocate the children to each condition? **[2]**
(d) Name the **independent** variable in this study. **[1]**
(e) How is the **dependent** variable operationalised in this study? **[1]**
(f) Write a directional (one-tailed) alternative hypothesis for this study. **[2]**
(g) What is the difference between a directional and a non-directional hypothesis? **[2]**
(h) Give **three** reasons why an unrelated t-test was chosen to analyse the data. **[3]**
(i) Which statistical test would be used if the study had generated ordinal data? **[1]**
(j) Explain what is meant by the term '$p \leq 0.05$' in Table 1. **[2]**
(k) Explain whether the null hypothesis should be rejected or accepted in this study. **[3]**

(Total 22 marks)

In your answer to this question you should include relevant information from the whole of your course, where appropriate.

2.
(a) Outline the main features of an observational study. **[3]**
(b) Define the following terms used in relation to ethics in psychological research.
  (i) deception.
  (ii) informed consent. **[4]**
(c) What is the difference between a participant and a non-participant observation study? **[2]**
(d) In a covert observation participants are not aware that they are taking part in a study. Explain the ethical considerations that should be taken into account when planning a covert observation. **[5]**

(Total 14 marks)

TOTAL FOR SECTION : 36 MARKS

Examiner's tips

Question 1

(a) This must be a name, not a description but can be as little as a single word.

(b) If the answer to (a) is incorrect but the responses here are appropriate to the answer in (a) then marks can be awarded for part (b) if part (a) did name a research design. Similarly, if (a) is blank but the answer relates to a clearly identifiable design, credit can still be given. For the advantage and the disadvantage there is 1 mark for a simple answer, 2 if it is complete.

(c) Award 1 mark for a simple answer, 2 if it is elaborated. The question doesn't state 'one', so two reasons could gain 2 marks.

(d) You will not be able to answer this well with a single word.

(e) The answer must do more than just identify the DV: it has to refer to how the variable has been defined in order to gain the mark.

(f) The answer must be an alternative hypothesis (not a null) and, for both marks, must have the IV and the DV operationalised.

(g) The second mark may be gained for elaboration or for a relevant example.

(h) The marks can be gained for points relating to the purpose of the test, the design of the study, the level of measurement of the data or the appropriateness or value of parametric tests.

(i) There is only one correct answer.

(j) A partial or incomplete answer can gain 1 mark.

(k) There are a number of different answers which would gain full marks. For 3 marks a candidate might do some of the following: refer to the critical and observed values, compare them, draw a conclusion in terms of significance, if the null hypothesis is rejected state that the difference is in the predicted direction or justify the significance level. Only some of these points would be required.

Question 2

(a) Examples, as well as amplification, can be used to gain the second mark. For 3 marks the example must give a feature as well. An example of a study would not be enough.

(b) (i) and (ii) 1 mark is available for the basic definition, the second mark is gained for amplification – this could include the use of examples.

(c) The 2 marks can be gained either for one detailed difference or for two differences.

(d) The answer must relate to ethical issues that would be relevant in covert observations and this link must be clear, if it is not, the answer can only gain a maximum of 2 marks.

June 2004: Answer from Candidate A

Question 1

(a) Matched pairs.

(b) This is a good method because you can be more certain than you can with independent groups that any differences are due to the IV not participant variables because you have tried to make the groups similar by pairing participants in the two groups on important characteristics. However, it's very difficult to do because you have to match up the people and you might not know what the important characteristics are so they might be different anyway.

(c) They took a random sample so that it would be representative.

(d) Pro-LIT or not.

(e) The children's literacy.

(f) Children's scores on the literacy test at the end of the year would be better in the conventionally taught group than the Pro-LIT group.

(g) A directional hypothesis says which level of the IV will be best but a non-directional hypothesis only says they will be different.

(h) Matched pairs, interval data, experiment not correlation.

(i) Mann-Whitney U.

(j) '$p \leq 0.05$' means that there is a 5% chance that the results are due to chance.

(k) The null hypothesis should be rejected because the results are not significant.

Question 2

(a) In an observational study the researcher watches behaviour and might either be obvious (overt) or hidden (covert). They might also be participant (involved in the events being observed) or non-participant (not involved in the events being observed).

(b) (i) Deception is where the participants are lied to.

(ii) Informed consent is where the participants are told what will happen to them so that they can decide whether to join in.

(c) In a participant observation the observers participate (they are involved in the events being observed); in non-participant observation the observers are not involved in the events being observed.

(d) They cannot give their informed consent so they need to be debriefed at the end so they know what has been going on. Once they know they should be offered the right to withdraw their results from the study. If they aren't told that might be okay if they have been involved in a covert observation of public behaviour in a public place because then their privacy hasn't been invaded, but even so some people might not like it.

Examiner commentary on Candidate A's answer

Question 1

(a) The only correct answer is 'independent groups' or other terms for this design, e.g. unrelated groups.

(b) This is a good answer in relation to matched pairs, so earns full credit – it is an example of a 'transferred error'.

(c) This answer relates to random *sampling* not random allocation, as required by the question.

(d) Although 'Pro-LIT' alone would not have earned marks, it is clear from this answer that the candidate recognises that there are two conditions, so the mark can be awarded.

(e) This identifies the DV but does not operationalise it, so misses the available mark.

(f) This is both a one-tailed alternative hypothesis and it successfully operationalises the IV and DV.

(g) The second mark is gained for the second phrase, which serves to expand the idea.

(h) Two of the three points are correct but the design is not, so 1 mark is missed.

(i) This is the only possible correct answer.

(j) This answer just gains 1 mark; for the second mark the candidate needed to explain the 'less than or equal to'.

(k) Although the candidate is correct, the null hypothesis should be rejected, this answer is not based on reasoning from the information provided in the question, so the marks cannot be awarded.

Question 2

(a) This answer only describes different types of observation, it doesn't outline what an observational study is. To complete the description, the candidate needed to elaborate on *how* behaviour is observed, e.g. non-experimentally.

(b) (i) Although deception may involve deliberately misleading participants by 'lying' it can also arise from withholding information, so this answer is incomplete.

(ii) Although brief, this is a sufficient answer for 2 marks as it makes the two key points – that participants need information about the procedure and that this enables them to make a reasoned choice.

(c) The first part of this answer is good, but the candidate misses the second mark as the second part of their answer does not add to the idea.

(d) This is a good answer, making a range of different points.

Marks given on page 138

June 2004: Answer from Candidate B

Question 1

(a) Independent groups.

(b) Advantages – no order effects because each participant only does one condition so the order of levels of the IV cannot affect how they perform, unlike in repeated measures where each participant does both so could get practice or get bored. Also there is less risk of demand characteristics.

Disadvantages – there might be lots of bright kids in one group so that would obscure the IV – participant variables.

(c) So that there would be an even representation of different children in the two levels of the IV.

(d) Teaching method – Pro-LIT or traditional.

(e) Scores on standardised test of reading ability at the end of the year.

(f) Children in the Pro-LIT group will score better on the reading test than the traditionally taught group.

(g) A directional hypothesis is one-tailed but a non-directional hypothesis is two-tailed.

(h) For the unrelated t-test to have been the right choice, there must have been an independent groups design and the results would have had to be normally distributed and had equal variance.

(i) Wilcoxon.

(j) Means that there is a probability of less than or equal to 0.05 that the results found could have arisen by chance rather than the IV.

(k) Rejected because the observed value of 2.493 is greater than the critical value at 0.01. You would use 0.01 because it's a new programme so there won't be any research to support it yet.

Question 2

(a) An observation is where the researcher looks at behaviour without manipulating variables and looking for effects like they would in an experiment. Instead, there are set categories of behaviours to record and these are clearly defined. In some observations, naturalistic ones, the researcher does not interfere at all but in others, controlled ones, the researcher can control aspects of the situation such as providing a child with different toys to play with.

(b) (i) Sometimes it is necessary to mislead participants by giving them false information or by omitting to tell them things. This has to be done so that the experiment works; for instance in Milgram's study if they had been told it was about obedience they might not have followed orders.

(ii) Informed consent is important as participants have the right to know what is going on.

(c) Participant observation is where observers are part of the situation that is being observed, such as a social psychologist observing football hooligans by being a supporter. A non-participant observer is generally covert, they hide themselves so that they don't affect the situation by being present but not a part of it as this could make the participants behave differently.

(d) In a covert observation the participants don't know that they are being observed whereas is in an overt observation they do. This might be unethical if they were secretly observed engaging in behaviour they expected to be private, such as in a toilet, or if they were doing something illegal, such as the researcher masquerading as a shopper and observing shoplifting behaviour. The researcher would have to decide whether it was reasonable to publish information like this without the participants' knowledge, so they have to make a judgement about whether a study is important enough to be done even though it invades people's privacy.

Examiner commentary on Candidate B's answer

Question 1

(a) This is the correct design.

(b) The reference to demand characteristics, although correct, would not be credited as it is a second advantage and the question only asks for one (and the first explanation earns both marks, whereas this would not).

(c) This is a simple answer so misses the second mark. This second could have been gained for elaboration, or an example, such as how the children might differ in ways that mattered in this study.

(d) A good answer. It has been operationalised even though this was not expected by the question.

(e) Another correctly operationalised answer – this time operationalisation was requested so it earns 2 marks.

(f) This is correctly an alternative hypothesis and has the IV and DV operationalised so gains both marks.

(g) This answer simply offers different terms; it doesn't explain the difference.

(h) These are acceptable reasons for using a t-test, although more typical answers would suggest testing for differences and stating the level of measurement.

(i) The only correct answer is Mann–Whitney U test.

(j) This answer comfortably earns 2 marks.

(k) A mark could alternatively have been gained for saying that the difference is therefore significant.

Question 2

(a) This is an effective answer which describes a range of features of observations. One mark is gained for the example.

(b) (i) This earns 2 marks, although the second one would have been missed if the elaboration of the example had not been given. Alternatively, the candidate could have explained why it is sometimes necessary to mislead participants.

(ii) This statement is evaluative; it does not define the term.

(c) This is a thorough answer and has more information than is needed.

(d) The first sentence is describing the difference between overt and covert observations. This was not asked for by the question so, although correct, does not earn the candidate marks. The remainder of the answer is good and appropriately detailed.

Marks given on page 138

Marks for candidates' answers to exam questions

	Specimen paper	Specimen paper	January 2003	January 2003	June 2003	June 2003	June 2004	June 2004
	A	B	A	B	A	B	A	B
Question 1								
(a)	1	2	0+2	0+4	1	0	0	1
(b)	1	0	1+1+1	0+0+1	1	2	4	3
(c)	1	1	1	0	0	2	0	1
(d)	3	4	0	2	1	0	1	1
(e)	2	4	2	1	0	2	0	2
(f)	1	2	1	2	1	1	2	2
(g)	1	3	2+2	1+1	1	2	2	0
(h)	2	0			4	4	2	3
(i)	0	0			4	4	1	0
(j)					2	3	1	2
(k)							0	3
Question 2								
(a)	1	2	1+2	1+3	1+1	1+1	2	5
(b)	0	4	2+2	1+3	2	0	0+2	2+0
(c)	5	5	2+2+3	2+2+2	2	3	1	2
(d)	3	3			3	3	5	5
(e)					4	3		
Total for question out of 36	21	30	27	26	28	31	23	33

More exam-style questions

(Question A)

1. SOURCE MATERIAL

A group of psychology students wanted to look at the effect of reinforcement on rats who were being tested on their ability to learn the route through a maze. In the first condition they put carrot in the goal box in the middle of the maze on every trial. They allowed each rat up to twenty sessions in the maze and timed how long it took to find the goal box. In the second condition the students only rewarded the rats every other time they reached the goal box to see if the frequency of reinforcement affected the time the rats took to learn the maze. In this condition they used lettuce because they hoped that a different food would mean that the rats would still be motivated to run to the goal box.

(a) What was the aim of this research? **[2]**

(b) (i) Identify the independent and dependent variables in this study. **[2]**

    (ii) Explain how the dependent variable was operationalised. **[1]**

    (iii) Explain how the independent variable was operationalised. **[2]**

(c) (i) What participant (experimental) design was used in this study? **[1]**

    (ii) Describe **one** advantage and **one** disadvantage of using this experimental design. **[4]**

(d) When the students produced the findings, they described the data using the mean and standard deviation.

    (i) What does the mean tell us about the data? **[1]**

    (ii) What does the standard deviation tell us about the data? **[2]**

    (iii) Describe **one** advantage using the mean as a measure of central tendency. **[2]**

(e) There are several flaws in the design of this experiment.

    (i) Identify **two** of these. **[2]**

    (ii) Explain in detail how and why you would improve the design of the experiment to overcome the flaws you have identified in part (i). **[4]**

(Total 23 marks)

In your answer to this question you should include relevant information from the whole of your course, where appropriate.

2. Psychologists sometimes use non-human animals in their research, as in the study described above. There are ethical guidelines for the use of animals in research.

(a) (i) Outline **two** guidelines that are relevant to this study. **[2]**

    (ii) What steps should the students have taken to ensure that requirements of **one** of these guidelines were met in this instance? **[2]**

(b) Laboratory experiments (on both humans and animals) are a common way to conduct psychological research. Discuss the relative merits of laboratory experiments compared to field experiments. **[9]**

(Total 13 marks)

TOTAL FOR SECTION : 36 MARKS

(Question B)

1. SOURCE MATERIAL

A group of psychology students were interested in non-verbal behaviour and decided to conduct an observation of people's behaviour when chatting up the opposite sex, i.e. 'flirting behaviour'. They decided to observe the body signals of women when they were talking to a man. To do this, each member of the class had the task of locating a target individual in a suitable public place (such as a pub or club) and observing the woman's behaviour for 10 minutes.

(a) (i) Identify the method used to select participants in this study. **[1]**

    (ii) Name **one** other method of selecting participants. **[1]**

    (iii) Describe **one** disadvantage of the method identified in part (ii) in the context of this study. **[2]**

(b) Identify **two** methods of operationalising 'flirting behaviour'. **[2]**

(c) Explain how you would collect the data for this study. **[3]**

(d) (i) What is meant by reliability? **[2]**

    (ii) Identify **one** way in which you could ensure reliability between the different observers, and explain how you might put this into practice. **[3]**

(e) Describe **one** way in which you could minimise the intrusive nature of your observations. **[2]**

(f) Explain **two** features of the study that might affect the validity of the data being collected. **[4]**

(g) (i) Identify **one** way in which the students ensured that this study would be carried out in an ethically acceptable manner. **[1]**

    (ii) Describe **one** limitation to this approach. **[2]**

    (iii) Name **one** other ethical issue that might arise in this study and explain how you would deal with this. **[3]**

(Total 26 marks)

In your answer to this question you should include relevant information from the whole of your course, where appropriate.

2. A group of students decides to conduct an investigation into discovery learning. They intend to measure how focused children become in a classroom task about floating that requires the children to try to get different substances to float on water.

(a) (i) Suggest **two** categories of behaviour that the students could record. **[2]**

    (ii) Suggest **two** items that could form part of a checklist of behaviour in one of these categories. **[2]**

(b) Describe **two** advantages of conducting an observational study. **[2]**

(c) (i) What is a longitudinal study? **[2]**

    (ii) Outline **one** strength of longitudinal studies. **[2]**

(Total 10 marks)

TOTAL FOR SECTION : 36 MARKS

More exam-style questions

(Question C)

1. SOURCE MATERIAL

Sigmund Freud developed a theory of personality. He proposed that children go through various stages of development, in each stage energy being focused on an area of the body. During the first stage of development, the focus is on the mouth (this stage is called the oral stage). Freud suggested that either too much pleasure or too much frustration at this stage would lead a person to develop an oral personality.

One way to test this is to see if adults with a focus on their mouths also have oral personalities. In one study, mouth focus was assessed by observing the number of mouth movements a participant makes in a 20-minute period.

Findings

Oral personality was assessed in an interview, which provided a score for oral personality for each participant. The oral personality scores for 15 participants were:

3, 4, 5, 6, 6, 7, 7, 9, 10, 13, 15, 16, 17, 19, 20

(A highly oral personality would score 20.)

The findings from the study are shown in the graph. The correlation coefficient is 0.74.

(a) (i) One of the variables being assessed in this study was 'mouth focus'. How was 'mouth focus' operationalised? **[2]**

(ii) Identify the second variable being assessed in this study. **[1]**

(b) Write a suitable label for the *y* axis (vertical axis) of the graph of the findings from this study (below). **[1]**

(c) (i) What is meant by a correlation coefficient? **[2]**

(ii) Using the information from the graph and/or correlation coefficient, describe the relationship between the variables. **[2]**

(iii) Give **one** advantage of an investigation using a correlational analysis. **[2]**

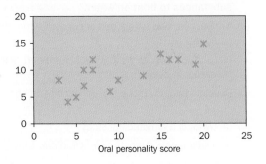

Relationship between mouth focus and oral personality

NB

Oral personality score

(d) A newspaper article reports these findings claiming that 'Mouth focus causes an oral personality'.

(i) Explain why this is not a valid conclusion. **[2]**

(ii) Suggest a more suitable conclusion for this study. **[2]**

(e) The researcher wished to summarise the findings using a measure of central tendency.

(i) Identify a suitable measure of central tendency for the scores for oral personality. **[1]**

(ii) Explain why this would be a suitable measure of central tendency. **[2]**

(f) Explain how the researcher could assess the reliability of the interview that was used. **[2]**

(g) Explain how the researcher could assess the validity of the interview. **[2]**

(h) Identify **one** ethical issue that might arise in this study and explain how you would deal with it. **[3]**

(Total 24 marks)

In your answer to this question you should include relevant information from the whole of your course, where appropriate.

2. A series of observations of parents and children, leads a researcher to believe that there may be a link between parental and child phobias.

(a) This study has the potential to raise ethical issues. Describe **one** issue that is different from the one you identified in question 1(h) and suggest how this issue might be resolved. **[3]**

(b) (i) How could the severity of a phobic response be operationalised? **[2]**

(ii) Write a one-tailed alternative hypothesis for this investigation. **[2]**

(c) (i) Interviews can produce quantitative data. Give one advantage and **one** disadvantage of quantitative data compared to qualitative data. **[4]**

(ii) Name **one** method, other than interviews or questionnaires, that could be used to generate qualitative data. **[1]**

(Total 12 marks)

TOTAL FOR SECTION : 36 MARKS

(Question D)

1. SOURCE MATERIAL

There is a saying that 'hunger is the best cook'. A psychologist decided to test the relationship between hungriness and the tastiness of food. He prepared a dish of scrambled eggs and toast for each participant. Before they started to eat he asked them how long it was since they had last eaten. After they had the meal he asked them to rate the tastiness of the meal on a scale of 1 to 10 where 10 is very tasty.

Findings

He plotted his findings as shown below. The correlation coefficient was 0.15.

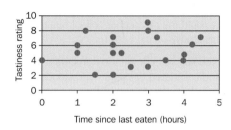

Graph showing the relationship between hungriness and tastiness

(a) Describe the aims of this study.   [1]

(b) How were hungriness and tastiness operationalised?
                                                                         [2]

(c) This study uses a correlational analysis. Describe **one** advantage and **one** disadvantage of a study using this method of analysis.   [4]

(d) (i) Describe **one** possible threat to the validity of this study.
                                                                         [2]

   (ii) Explain how the psychologist could deal with this problem.
                                                                         [2]

(e) (i) Explain what is meant by reliability.   [2]

   (ii) Tastiness was measured using a rating scale. How could you check the reliability of this scale?   [2]

(f) (i) The scores for 'hungriness' were 2, 2, 3, 3, 4, 4, 4, 5, 5, 5, 6, 6, 6, 6, 7, 7, 7, 8, 8, 9 (units of time without food). Suggest **one** suitable method of central tendency to use with this data.   [1]

   (ii) Explain how you would calculate this measure of central tendency.   [2]

   (iii) Describe **one** advantage of this method of central tendency.   [2]

(Total 20 marks)

In your answer to this question you should include relevant information from the whole of your course, where appropriate.

2. A class of students are studying questionnaire design as part of their psychology course. In order to learn about questionnaire design they decide to try to construct their own questionnaire on the value of homework for A level students.

The following is an extract from their questionnaire.

> 3. How many hours of homework do you do on average every week?
>   None 1 hour   2 hours   3 hours   4 hours   5 hours
>   6 hours   More than 6 hours   (Circle your answer)
>
> 4. Do you like doing homework?   Yes No (Circle your answer)
>
> 5. Give one reason in favour of having to do homework.
>   _____
>
> 6. Suggest one reason against doing homework.
>   _____
>
> 7. Write down all your GCSE exam results.
>   _____

(a) Give **one** advantage and **one** disadvantage of using a questionnaire.   [4]

(b) (i) Identify a suitable method of selecting participants and explain how you would do this.   [3]

   (ii) Describe **one** advantage of the method of selecting participants that you used in (i).   [2]

(c) (i) Identify **one** question in the extract that would produce qualitative data.   [2]

   (ii) Outline **one** disadvantage of using a question such as this.   [2]

(d) The students decide to ask about GCSE results to see if there is a correlation between average amount of time spent doing homework and GCSE results. For each student they calculate an average score for GCSE results by allocating 10 points for an A star, 9 points for an A and so on, and then adding these up and dividing by the number of GCSE results.

   (i) State a suitable hypothesis for this part of the study.   [2]

   (ii) Is your hypothesis directional or non-directional?   [1]

(Total 16 marks)

TOTAL FOR SECTION : 36 MARKS

aren't they actually tastiness?

(Question E)

1. SOURCE MATERIAL

A psychology class wishes to investigate the effects of emotional factors on recall. Some research suggests that emotion leads to better recall whereas other research suggests that recall is less good in emotional situations. In order to investigate whether emotion is associated with better or less good recall they decide to test recall under two emotional conditions. Group 1 will be given a list of words to remember. In order to create emotional arousal, the participants in this group will be asked to run on the spot while learning the list (creates physiological arousal).

Group 2 are given the same list to remember but remain seated during the learning period.

An hour after learning the list, all participants are invited back and asked to write down all the words they can remember.

Findings

The graph below shows the mean words recalled for each group.

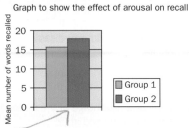

Graph to show the effect of arousal on recall

(a) Identify the independent variable and the dependent variable in this study. **[4]**

(b) (i) State a suitable non-directional hypothesis for this study. **[2]**

(ii) Explain why it would be appropriate to use a non-directional hypothesis in this study. **[1]**

(c) (i) What is an experiment? **[2]**

(ii) Give **one** advantage of laboratory experiments compared with field experiments. **[2]**

(d) (i) What was the experimental design that was used in this study? **[1]**

(ii) Give **one** advantage of using this design. **[2]**

(iii) State an alternative experimental design that could have been used. **[1]**

(iv) Explain how you would re-design this study using this new method of experimental design. **[3]**

(Total marks 18)

In your answer to this question you should include relevant information from the whole of your course, where appropriate.

2. A psychologist was interested in why people sleep, and investigated the effects of extra exercise on the amount of sleep people have.

He asked marathon runners to record the number of hours they slept on two different nights. One of the study nights was after running a race and the other was after a rest day.

(a) Identify the independent and dependent variable in this study. **[2]**

(b) If the psychologist found that each individual slept for about the same length of time on both occasions what might he conclude in terms of his original aims? **[2]**

(c) (i) Explain why it would be a good idea to collect qualitative as well as quantitative data. **[2]**

(ii) How could the researcher collect qualitative data from this study? **[2]**

(f) The psychologist recorded the numbers of hours slept for each night and calculated the mean and standard deviation for these two data sets as shown below:

	Mean number of hours slept	Standard deviation
Night before the race	7.9	1.2
Night after the race	8.2	2.5

(i) Which is a measure of dispersion? **[1]**

(ii) From the table above what can you conclude about the dispersion of the data? **[2]**

(g) Which inferential test would you use to find out if there was a significant difference in time spent sleeping between nights following a race or rest day? Justify your choice. **[3]**

(h) Describe how you would design a study to investigate the effects of exercise on sleep using and alternative research method from the one used here. **[4]**

(Total marks 18)

TOTAL FOR SECTION : 36 MARKS

(Question F)

1. SOURCE MATERIAL

Research has found that familiar things reduce stress. A recent study investigated this further by seeing whether you could lower the stress levels of sheep by exposing isolated sheep to photos of other sheep (Kendrick *et al.*, 2001).

The team took 40 sheep of a Welsh lowland breed called Clun Forest, and isolated them one at a time. For the first 15 minutes, four identical pictures of a white inverted triangle were projected on to the rear wall. For the next 15 minutes, the animals were shown four photos of an unfamiliar sheep face or shown four pictures of an unfamiliar goat.

As soon as the animals were left alone, their heart rates began to soar and stress hormone levels also increased. The animals seemed to ignore the triangle pictures, but after 15 minutes of simulated sheep company, the animals became calmer. Heart rates fell to pre-isolation levels. Stress hormone levels more than halved, and the number of unhappy bleating noises dropped by 20-fold. The goat photos had no effect.

(a) Identify **two** ways in which stress responses were operationalised in this study. **[2]**

(b) (i) Write a suitable hypothesis for this study. **[2]**

(ii) Is your hypothesis a directional or non-directional hypothesis? **[1]**

(iii) Explain why you chose such a hypothesis. **[1]**

(c) (i) Identify the experimental design used in this study. **[1]**

(ii) Describe **one** advantage and **one** disadvantage of this experimental design. **[4]**

(d) Explain why the researchers started with an inverted white triangle and why they showed some participants photos of goats instead of sheep. **[3]**

(g) A subsequent study intends to observe the behaviour of sheep with familiar and unfamiliar sheep. The researchers intend to observe the sheep for signs of stress.

(i) Describe **one** advantage of a naturalistic observation. **[2]**

(ii) Describe how you would conduct this observation. **[6]**

(Total marks 22)

In your answer to this question you should include relevant information from the whole of your course, where appropriate.

2. A group of students decide to conduct some research to find out how homosexuality is presented in the media. They collect a range of different newspapers and magazines by picking them up on the train to and from the university. They identify some key words and phrases to look for. They decide to group these into positive, negative and neutral statements and count how many of each they find per newspaper or magazine.

(a) (i) Identify the research method being used in this study. **[1]**

(ii) Describe **one** advantage and **one** disadvantage of this method in the context of this study. **[4]**

(b) Identify **one** factor that should be controlled in this study and explain why it would be necessary to do so. **[2]**

(c) (i) What is the sampling method being used by the students to obtain the information from newspapers and magazines? **[1]**

(ii) Suggest an alternative sampling method and outline why this may be a better choice. **[3]**

(d) (i) Will the students' method produce qualitative or quantitative data? **[1]**

(ii) Describe **one** advantage of this kind of data. **[2]**

(Total marks 14)

TOTAL FOR SECTION : 36 MARKS

Appendix 1 EDEXCEL specification for research methods

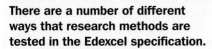

There are a number of different ways that research methods are tested in the Edexcel specification.

- At AS, the written papers for Units 1 and 2 ask for descriptions, evaluations and comparisons of the research methods associated with each approach named in the specification. These are tabulated on the right to remind you. One third of the marks for the AS examination are awarded on the basis of a single piece of coursework. The concepts relating to this coursework are represented by the lighter areas in the table opposite.

- At A2, the research methods from the AS approaches are tested in Unit 5. Half of the Unit 5 exam is devoted to a section of written questions on research methods (see examples in Chapter 7) and the research methods concepts from AS and A2 also appear in the synoptic paper, Unit 6. There are concepts on the A2 specification in addition to those required at AS. These are represented in the lighter areas of the table opposite.

AS Approach	Commonly used research methods
social	• field experiments
	• surveys
cognitive	• experiments
	• case studies of brain-damaged people
cognitive-developmental	• observations
	• longitudinal studies
learning	• laboratory experiments
	• animal learning studies
psychodynamic	• case studies
	• clinical interviews
	• analysis of symbols
physiological	• brain scanning
	• EEGs
	• lesioning
	• correlational techniques (e.g. *twin studies*)

A very shy guy goes into a pub and sees a beautiful woman sitting at the bar. After an hour of gathering up his courage, he finally goes over to her and asks, tentatively, 'Um, would you mind if I chatted with you for a while?'

She responds by yelling, at the top of her voice, 'NO! I won't sleep with you tonight!' Everyone in the bar is now staring at them. Naturally, the guy is hopelessly embarrassed and slinks back to his table.

After a few minutes, the woman walks over to him and apologises. She smiles and says, 'I'm sorry if I embarrassed you. You see, I'm a psychology student, and I'm studying how people respond to embarrassing situations.'

To which he responds, at the top of his voice, 'What do you mean £200?!'

This table shows the AS and A2 research methods concepts that are required for the Edexcel exam. The topics required for the AS unit exams or coursework are shaded in the darker purple, and those for the A2 unit exams are shaded in the lighter purple (see comments on the opposite page).

This is not simply a copy of the research methods specification but has been logically organised to show how the AS and A2 content areas map onto each other.

> Words that are in **BOLD** are key terms. Words in *ITALICS* are only examples and are not mentioned on the specification.

1. Describe the following **research methods:**
- **Experiment**
- **Observation**
- **Questionnaire**
- **Interview**
- **Case study**
- **Content analysis**

Evaluate methods in terms of advantages and disadvantages

You could also be asked about <u>any</u> research methods from AS in <u>Unit 5</u>

2. Analysing data from qualitative studies with data collected by interview, observation or case study
- Describe the difference between **qualitative** and **quantitative** data

3. Define, describe, distinguish and compare **objectivity** and **subjectivity**

4. Describe the BPS **ethical guidelines** used in human psychological research:
- **Consent**
- **Confidentiality**
- **Debriefing**
- **Right to withdraw**

Describe **ethical guidelines** relating to the use of non-human animals in psychological research:

5. **Describe** participant **(experimental) designs:**
- **Repeated measures**
- **Independent groups**
- **Matched pairs**

Describe the **correlational design**

At least **one** advantage and **one** disadvantage of each design

6. Describe **sampling methods:**
- **Random**
- **Systematic**
- **Opportunity**
- **Quota**
- **Volunteer**

Evaluate these sampling methods, know at least **one** advantage and **one** disadvantage of each

7. Describe, identify and operationalise **IV**s and **DV**s

8. Define, produce and use appropriately: **hypotheses:**

- **Alternative (experimental)**
- **Null**

- **One-tailed (directional) / two-tailed**

9. Describe **levels of measurement:**
- **Nominal**
- **Ordinal**
- **Interval**
- **Ratio**

Decide which level of measurement is being used in an example and utilise this information in choosing an inferential test

10. Identify, describe and control:
- **Situational variables**
- **Participant variables**

11. Describe and know when to use **counterbalancing**

12. Describe types of **reliability**
Describe how to test and improve reliability

13. Describe types of **validity**
Suggest how to improve validity

14. Define and discuss **generalisibility**

15. Select and justify suitable materials for research

16. Calculate and justify the choice of:

Measures of central tendency, e.g.:

- *Mean*
- *Median*
- *Mode*

Measures of dispersion:

- **Range**

- **Standard deviation** (don't need to calculate)
- **Variance** (don't need to calculate)

17. Draw and justify when to use **graphs,** e.g.:

- *Bar charts*
- *Histograms*
- *Scattergraphs (scatter plots)*

18. Testing for statistical significance:

- When to use which test:
  - **Chi-square** test of association
  - **Sign** test
  - **Mann–Whitney** U test
  - **Wilcoxon** signed-rank matched pairs test
  - **Spearman's** rank order correlation coefficient
  - **Unrelated** t-test
  - **Related** t-test
  - **Pearson** product-moment correlation coefficient
- Which of these are parametric and which are non-parametric?
- **Levels of significance:**
  - What they mean
  - Which one to choose
- How to look up a **critical value:**
  - The calculated (**observed**) values
  - **N**
  - The significance level
  - **One-or two-tailed**
- Drawing conclusions from inferential tests
- **Normal distribution**
  - What it is
  - Why it matters to inferential tests

Appendix II How exam questions are set and marked

Research methods is assessed in the coursework element of AS exams (Unit 3) and in the A2 exams (Units 5 and 6). Unit 6 is the synoptic paper so can include any elements of the course. The main way in which research methods is examined at A2 is on the Unit 5 paper where it carries half of the available marks (the other half of the marks are for one of the Applied Psychology questions: Health, Environmental or Child psychology). The research methods section usually consists of two questions, each broken down into several parts. Each question typically has a piece of 'stimulus material'. The total marks available for research methods question on this paper are 36.

Assessment Objectives

There are three Assessment Objectives (AO) which are listed in the box on the right. The three assessment objectives are described below, in relation to the way they are tested in coursework and the research methods questions in Unit 5.

AO1: Knowledge and understanding**

This tests your ability to:

- explain terms such as 'two-tailed' or 'qualitative' and concepts such as 'validity' and 'objectivity'
- use such terms and concepts appropriately
- demonstrate your knowledge of research methods by selecting and presenting and discussing them appropriately – for example in response to a question or in your coursework

AO2: Applications of knowledge and understanding, analysis, synthesis and evaluation**

This tests your ability to:

- analyse and evaluate relevant concepts through discussion and appraisal, such as in a consideration of the strengths and weaknesses of a method or design in a particular situation (either in a question or in your coursework)
- appraise psychological methods through the analysis and evaluation of existing research – as you might do in relation to source material in a questions
- apply and evaluate different research methods in relation to psychological data (either generated by your own research in your coursework or presented to you in a research methods question)

AO3: Experiment and investigation

This tests your ability to:

- design and evaluate the plan of a psychological study (including your own coursework and ones presented in questions)
- take into account ethical issues (either in a question or in your coursework)
- collect data (coursework only) and interpret it, with a consideration for reliability and validity
- appraise outcomes of studies in relation to aims, methods and topic of studies

** Note that in Unit 5 the AO1 and AO2 marks are synoptic, that is, the questions will require you to demonstrate that you appreciate when different research methods are appropriate to the investigation of different psychological issues and problems. Questions will expect you to be able to bring together concepts from different areas of psychology and apply them to contexts – such as those given in the source material – and to express your ideas clearly using specialist vocabulary.

The assessment objectives

Assessment objective 1 (AO1)
Description (knowledge and understanding of psychology)

Assessment objective 2 (AO2)
Evaluation (assessment and commentary)

Assessment objective 3 (AO3)
To design, conduct and report research

Assessment Objective	AS coursework (%)	A2 unit 5 (%)*
AO1	20	20
AO2	20	20
AO3	60	60

* Note that this is as a percentage of the research methods question, which is only *half* of Unit 5.

In practice, exam papers don't tell you which questions are AO1, AO2 or AO3 and sometimes it will be hard to tell. For example, and both AO1 and AO3 questions could ask you about hypotheses, both AO2 and AO3 could ask you to appraise different methods. One important thing to remember, however, is that AO3 includes marks for designing and evaluating studies and that this can mean that you have to 'think on your feet' and find a way to test an idea presented in a question or comment on the design of a described study.

How examination questions are marked

Coursework marking:
Your teacher will assist you in the production of your coursework, but it must ultimately be your own work. The final document is sent to an examiner who uses the marking scheme summarised on pages 84–85 to allocate marks for each of the sections.

Unit 5:
Your written papers are marked by examiners who are working from a marking scheme written specifically for that examination paper. Although they follow very similar patterns of mark allocation from year to year, there may be small variations. These marking schemes are similar to the 'advice on marking' given alongside the Edexcel examination questions in Chapter 7, though more detailed. An example of an entire marking scheme can be seen on the Edexcel website (see page 148 for web reference).

Appendix III Where candidates go wrong

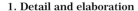

1. Detail and elaboration

If a question is worth 2 marks, your answer needs to contain two creditworthy points. If the question does not specify 'one' you may achieve this by giving two reasons, advantages, etc. Alternatively, the question may be asking for a detailed answer; make sure that the detail you are providing is relevant – is the question asking you to describe, explain or evaluate and is that what you are doing? Finally, if you are describing or explaining, it may help to clarify your answer by including an example.

2. Operationalisation

A common way in which candidates miss marks in questions asking for an IV, DV or hypothesis is by not operationalising when this is required. If in doubt, operationalise!

3. Defining instead of explaining

Very few questions require you to define a term. Most questions require you to use your knowledge. For example, instead of asking you 'What is meant by control?' you would more often be asked to 'Describe how the researcher might have controlled one of the variables in this study.' The focus is on 'how' instead of 'what'.

4. Explaining how instead of why

Questions often ask you to explain *how* a particular problem was dealt with or *how* a procedure could have been conducted. In an attempt to provide elaboration candidates often explain *why* the solution was chosen but such information is irrelevant to the question and thus not creditworthy.

For example:

Question: Explain how qualitative data could be collected about participant's experience.

Answer: The researchers could use open-ended questions. These are better than closed ones for getting qualitative data. [The first sentence is 'how'. The second sentence is 'why' and not creditworthy].

5. Better than what?

An advantage or disadvantage of anything is a comparative statement. If you say that the dinner you had last night was good, it implies it was better *than on other* occasions. When you say a 'questionnaire is easier' you mean that it is easier than, for example, doing an interview.

You need to go even further and explain why it is easier, or why you can collect more data, or why it is less expensive, or why participants are more honest or whatever. Don't just make these bold statements that something is easier, quicker, cheaper, better but say in comparison to what, and explain the basis of your claim.

6. Contextualisation

Many questions use the phrase '... in this study'. Candidates can miss marks if they do not make any reference to the study. Thus, the question 'Describe one disadvantage of using an independent groups design in this study' requires an answer which says 'Participant variables, such as susceptibility to alcohol, are not controlled' (when the study was about alcohol) rather than 'Participant variables are not controlled'.

7. Findings and conclusions

Candidates can be asked to describe conclusion(s) that could be drawn from a table or graph. They mistakenly describe the findings instead of conclusions. Findings are part of conclusions and can be used as a platform for giving the conclusions.

Findings are facts. Conclusions are an interpretation of the facts – making generalisations.

Findings concern participants (samples) and are usually given in the past tense, for example 'The study found that the male participants conformed more than the female participants'.

Conclusions concern people (populations) and are usually stated in the present tense, for example 'The study found that the male participants conformed more than the female participants which suggests that men are less conformist than women'.

8. Not answering all parts of the question

Some questions contain several parts such as 'Identify one ethical issue that the researchers do not appear to have considered and explain how this ethical issue could have been dealt with'. Some candidates fail to identify an ethical issue (just saying that participants were given alcohol which some might have objected to – no ethical issue identified, no marks).

Qs **49**

Explain what's wrong with these student answers and write a fully correct answer.

1. Question: *Describe* **one** *advantage of a correlational design.*

   Student answer: They are easy to do and provide information that can't be obtained in an experiment.

2. Question: *Give an example of a situational variable.*

   Student answer: A situational variable is when the behaviour of participants is affected by something about the setting other than the IV.

3. Question: *Identify* **one** *ethical issue and explain how the researcher might have dealt with it.*

   Student answer: Informed consent should be sought in all experiments because it provides a participant with information to make a decision about whether to participate.

4. Question: *State* **one** *conclusion that could be drawn from Graph X.*

   Student answer: The study found that age and intelligence are positively correlated.

5. Question: *Describe* **one** *advantage of a questionnaire.*

   Student answer: You can collect lots of data.

6. Question: *State an appropriate hypothesis for a study about the effects of noise on memory.*

   Student answer: Participants will do better when it is noisy.

7. Question: *Explain how stress and illness could be operationalised.*

   Student answer: Stress could be operationalised by identifying a set of life events and developing a scale.

8. Question: *Explain how participant variables could be controlled in the context of this study.*

   Student answer: Participant variables need to be controlled so that each individual in the sample has the same experience so that you can be sure that any change in the DV has been caused by the IV.

9. Question: *Give one advantage of using a repeated measures design.*

   Student answer: It means that there are fewer extraneous variables.

Appendix IV Websites

General psychology sites for which include research methods

AQA A sites, both are full of information, quizzes and links to elsewhere.

psYonline http://psyonline.edgehill.ac.uk/

s-cool http://www.s-cool.co.uk/default.asp

An OCR site but has useful material and good links

http://www.holah.karoo.net/links.htm

Another vast collection of psychology material including research methods http://psychology.about.com/

Gerry Kegan's site for Scottish High Psychology, again full of useful materials

http://www.gerardkeegan.co.uk/

Research methods

An interactive site for learning about research methods

http://www.mcli.dist.maricopa.edu/proj/res_meth/index.html

syNAPse, the A-Level psychology website developed by Northampton & District A-Level Psychology Teachers Group (NAP). The site is packed full of resources and activities to help Alevel students learn about psychology and in particular psychological research methods.

http://nap.northampton.ac.uk/

Psychological research on the net

Site full of links to a vast array of psychology experiments to take part in

http://psych.hanover.edu/Research/exponnet.html

Yahoo list of on-line tests and experiments

http://dir.yahoo.com/Social_Science/Psychology/Research/Tests_and_Experiments/)

Ethical guidelines

APA code http://www.apa.org/ethics/code.html

BPS code www.bps.org.uk/documents/Code.pdf

Descriptive statistics

A nicely presented introduction to descriptive statistics

http://www.mste.uiuc.edu/hill/dstat/dstat.html

Sites where you can try out correlation simulations (and other statistics)

http://www.stattucino.com/berrie/dsl/regression/regression.html

http://davidmlane.com/hyperstat/prediction.html

http://www.ruf.rice.edu/~lane/rvls.html

http://www.statsoft.com/textbook/stathome.html

Observation coding systems and checklists

Checklists, observations forms etc.

http://www.umchs.org/umchsresources/administration/forms/umchsforms.html#education

Coding Rules for the Hall/Van de Castle System of Quantitative Dream Content Analysis

http://psych.ucsc.edu/dreams/Coding/

Questionnaires

Claims to be the world's largest testing centre, tests and questionnaires on everything

http://www.queendom.com/

Various health surveys and other scales

http://www.rand.org/health/surveys.html

Site providing access to copywrited psychological tests that can be downloaded and used by student researchers including dieting beliefs scale and self-esteem scales

http://www.atkinson.yourku.ca

Edexcel site

Contains a copy of the specification, specimen papers and mark schemes, report on each exam (check comments on research methods), and a student guide to the A level course

http://www.edexcel.org.uk/quals/

Glossary

Words in CAPITALS are Edexcel KEY WORDS. Words in *italics* are explained elsewhere in the glossary.

An edited version of this glossary can be found in Edexcel supplementary materials on the Nelson Thornes website, www.nelsonthornes.com/researchmethods, so that you can make the definitions into a game – paste the descriptions onto cards and then ask students to identify what terms are being defined.

abba A form of *counterbalancing* to deal with *order effects* in which participants do condition A, then B, then B and finally A, (p. 9).

AIMS A statement of what the researcher(s) intend to find out in a research study, (pp1, 16).

ALTERNATIVE HYPOTHESIS A testable statement about of the relationship between two variables. Sometimes called the 'experimental hypothesis'. See *hypothesis* and *research prediction*, (p. 7).

attrition The loss of participants from a study over time. Those participants who are less interested or who have done less well may not be available for re-assessment in a *longitudinal study* or in the second condition of a *repeated measures design*, which means that the remaining sample is biased in favour of those who are more interested/ motivated/doing well.

availability sampling See *opportunity sample*.

bar chart A graph used to represent the frequency of data; the categories on the *x*-axis have no fixed order, and there is no true zero. See *histogram*, (p. 15).

behaviour checklist A list of the behaviours to be recorded during an observational study. Similar to a *coding system*, (p. 67).

bias A systematic distortion. It is a problem in research studies (e.g. *experimenter bias, interviewer bias, observer bias, sampling bias, social desirability bias, volunteer bias*), (p. 44).

boredom effect A kind of *order effect*. In a repeated measures design, participants may do less well on one condition rather than another because they have not completed it first, and become 'bored'.

CASE STUDY A research investigation that involves a detailed study of a single individual, institution or event. Case studies provide a rich record of human experience but are hard to generalise from, (pp. 72,76).

CLINICAL INTERVIEW (clinical method) A form of semi-structured or *unstructured interview* similar to the kind of interview used by your GP, (p. 48).

closed questions In a questionnaire, questions that have a range of answers from which respondents select one. Produces *quantitative data*. Answers are easier to analyse than those for *open questions*, (p. 46).

coding system A systematic method for recording observations in which individual behaviours are given a code for ease of recording. Similar to a *behaviour checklist*, (pp. 67, 70).

CONCLUSIONS The implications drawn from the findings of a study; what the findings tell us about people in general rather than about the particular participants in a study, (pp. 14, 16).

concurrent validity A form of *external validity* related to questionnaires and interviews. It aims to demonstrate the extent to which performance on the test correlates positively with other tests of the same thing. If the test is a good one, we would expect a high *positive correlation*, (p. 53).

confederate An individual in an experiment who is not a real participant and has been instructed how to behave by the investigator/experimenter. May act as the *independent variable*, (p. 13).

CONFIDENTIALITY An *ethical issue* concerned with a participant's right to have personal information protected, (pp. 33, 35, 49, 69).

confounding variable A variable that is not the independent variable under study but may be found to have an effect on the dependent variable, thus confounding the findings of the study. See *extraneous variable*, (pp. 12, 26, 31).

CONSENT See *informed consent*.

CONTENT ANALYSIS A kind of *observational study* in which behaviour is observed indirectly in written or verbal material. A detailed analysis is made of, for example, books, diaries or TV programmes. It is possible to count the frequency of particular behaviours using categories, (p. 71).

continuous observation Every instance of a behaviour is recorded in as much detail as possible. This is useful if the behaviours you are interested in do not occur very often, (p. 67).

CONTROL Refers to the extent to which any variable is held constant or regulated by a researcher, (pp. 12, 25).

control condition In an experiment, the condition that provides a baseline measure of behaviour without the experimental treatment, so that the effect of the experimental treatment may be assessed. See *experimental condition*, (p. 38).

control group In an experiment, a group of participants who receive no treatment. Their behaviour acts as a baseline against which the effect of the independent variable may be measured. See *experimental group*, (p. 38).

controlled observation A form of investigation in which behaviour is observed but under controlled conditions, in contrast with a *naturalistic observation*, (pp. 66, 68).

CORRELATION (CORRELATIONAL DESIGN OR ANALYSIS) Determining the extent of a relationship between two variables; *co-variables* may not be linked at all (*zero correlation*), they may both increase together (*positive correlation*), or as one co-variable increases, the other decreases (*negative correlation*). Usually a *linear correlation* is predicted, but the relationship can be curvilinear, (pp. 50, 51, 54).

correlation coefficient A number between -1 and $+1$ that tells us how closely the *co-variables* in a correlational analysis are related, (pp. 50, 51).

COUNTERBALANCING An experimental technique designed to overcome *order effects*. Counterbalancing ensures that each condition is tested first or second in equal amounts, (p. 9).

co-variables When one conducts a correlational analysis there is no *independent variable* or *dependent variable* – the two measured variables are called co-variables, (p. 50).

covert observations See *undisclosed observations*.

cross-cultural study A kind of *natural experiment* in which the *IV* is different cultural practices and the *DV* is a behaviour such as attachment. This enables researchers to compare the effects of culture/socialisation.

cross-sectional design One group of participants of a young age are compared with another, older group of participants, with a view to finding out the influence of age on the behaviour in question, (p. 76).

curvilinear correlation A non-linear relationship between *co-variables*. For example, arousal and performance do not have a *linear* (straight line) relationship. Performance on many tasks is depressed when arousal is too high or too low; it is best when arousal is moderate, *(p. 54)*.

DEBRIEFING A post-research interview designed to inform the participants of the true nature of the study and to restore them to the same state they were in at the start of the experiment. It may also be used to gain useful feedback about the procedures in the study. Debriefing is <u>not</u> an *ethical issue*; it is a means of dealing with ethical issues, *(pp. 13, 34, 35)*.

deception An *ethical issue*, most usually where a participant is not told the true aims of a study (e.g. what participation will involve) and thus cannot give truly *informed consent*, *(pp. 32, 35, 49, 69)*.

demand characteristics Features of an experiment that a participant unconsciously responds to when searching for clues about how to behave. These may act as a *confounding variable*, *(pp. 26, 47)*.

DEPENDENT VARIABLE (DV) A measurable outcome of the action of the independent variable in an experiment, *(p. 4)*.

difference studies Studies in which two groups of participants are compared in terms of a DV (such as males versus females, or extraverts versus introverts). This is not a true *experiment* because the apparent *IV* (gender or personality) has not been manipulated, *(p. 31)*.

DIRECTIONAL HYPOTHESIS Predicts the kind of difference (e.g. more or less) or relationship (positive or negative) between two groups of participants or between different conditions. See *non-directional hypothesis*, *(p. 7)*.

disclosed observations See *undisclosed observations*.

double blind A research design in which neither the participant nor the *experimenter* is aware of the condition that an individual participant is receiving, *(pp. 12, 26)*.

DV see *dependent variable*.

ECOLOGICAL VALIDITY A form of *external validity*, concerning the ability to generalise a research effect beyond the particular setting in which it is demonstrated to other settings. Ecological validity is established by *representativeness* (*mundane realism*) and *generalisability* (to other settings), *(pp. 28, 29, 31, 38)*.

ethical committee A group of people within a research institution that must approve a study before it begins, *(pp. 34, 35, 69)*.

ETHICAL GUIDELINES Concrete, quasi-legal documents that help to guide conduct within psychology by establishing principles for standard practice and competence, *(pp. 34, 35, 69)*.

ethical issue Ethical issues arise in research where there are conflicts between the research goals and the participant's rights, *(pp. 13, 32, 33, 34, 35, 49, 69)*.

event sampling An observational technique in which a count is kept of the number of times a certain behaviour (event) occurs. See *time sampling*, *(p. 67)*.

EXPERIMENT A *research method* that involves the direct manipulation of an *independent variable* in order to test its possible causal relationship with a *dependent variable*. See *laboratory experiment, field experiment, natural experiment*, *(pp. 4, 51)*.

experimental condition In a repeated measures design, the condition containing the *independent variable*. See *control condition*, *(p. 38)*.

experimental control The use of techniques designed to eliminate the effects of *extraneous variables* in an experiment. See *control*.

experimental design A set of procedures used to control the influence of participant variables in an experiment *(repeated measures design, independent groups design or matched pairs participants) design*, *(p. 8)*.

experimental group In an independent groups design, a group of participants who receive the experimental treatment (the *independent variable*). See *control group*, *(p. 38)*.

EXPERIMENTAL HYPOTHESIS See *alternative hypothesis*.

experimental realism The extent to which participants take an experiment seriously. If the simulated task environment is sufficiently engaging, the participants pay attention to the task and not to the fact that they are being observed, thus reducing *participant reactivity*, *(p. 26)*.

experimental validity Concerns the legitimacy of an *experiment* – the way in which it is carried out, the conclusion(s) drawn and its implications for understanding related aspects of real life. Includes both *internal* and *external validity*, *(p. 28)*.

experimenter The person who directly interacts with participants when an experiment is carried out. The study may be designed by someone else, the *investigator*, *(pp. 4, 27)*.

experimenter bias The effect that the experimenter's expectations have on the participants and thus on the results of the experiment. See *investigator effect*, *(p. 27)*.

external reliability A calculation of the extent to which a measure varies from another measure of the same thing over time. This can be assessed using the *test-retest* method. See also *reliability*, *(pp. 52, 53)*.

external validity The degree to which an experimental effect can be generalised to other settings (*ecological validity*), other people (*population validity*) and over time (*historical validity*), *(pp. 28, 31, 53, 69)*.

extraneous variable In an experiment, any variable other than the *independent variable* that might potentially affect the *dependent variable* and thereby confound the results. If this happens, it is called a *confounding variable*, *(p. 12)*

face validity A form of *external validity* related to questionnaires and interviews. The extent to which the items look like they measure what the test claims to measure, *(p. 53)*

fatigue effect A kind of *order effect*. In a repeated measures design, participants may do less well on one condition rather than another because they have become tired or bored, *(p. 9)*

FIELD EXPERIMENT This is a controlled experiment that is conducted outside a laboratory. The key features are that the *independent variable* is still manipulated by the experimenter, and therefore causal relationships can be demonstrated; it is conducted in a more natural setting and may therefore have greater *ecological validity*; and participants are usually unaware that they are participating in an experiment, thus reducing *participant reactivity*, *(pp. 24, 25, 28, 29, 31, 51)*

field study Any study that takes place away from the laboratory and within the context in which the behaviour normally occurs, *(pp. 24, 28, 29)*

findings The factual data produced in a study, *quantitative* or *qualitative data*. *Conclusions* may be drawn from findings <u>if</u> the study was *valid* and *reliable*, *(p. 16)*

forced choice question The participant must choose one item or alternative from (usually) the two offered, *(pp. 46, 47)*

GENERALISIBILITY The degree to which the findings of a particular study can be applied to the *target population*, *(pp. 28, 29)*

give voice A technique used when analysing *qualitative data*. The report of the findings uses selective quotations from participants to illustrate points made.

graph A pictorial representation of the relationship between variables, *(pp. 15, 16, 50)*

Greenspoon effect The tendency for an interviewee's responses to be affected by the reaction (e.g. saying 'mm-hmm' or 'uh-huh') of the interviewer (an example of operant conditioning).

grounded theory A technique used when analysing *qualitative data*. It is an emergent research process in which theoretical explanations 'emerge' during the course of the investigation.

Hawthorne effect The tendency for participants to alter their behaviour merely as a result of knowing that they are being observed. It acts as a *confounding variable*, *(pp. 25, 26)*

histogram A type of frequency distribution in which the number of scores in each category of continuous data are represented by vertical columns. In contrast to a bar chart, the data in a histogram have a true zero and a logical sequence, *(p. 15)*

historical validity A form of external validity, concerning the ability to generalise a research effect beyond the particular time period of the study, *(p. 28)*

homage to formal terms (Coolican, 2004b).The problem that technical terms create an illusion that things are 'black and white'. They aren't. You should focus on the 'general drift' and not be fazed when you find that there are slightly different meanings as your understanding increases, *(p. 27)*

HYPOTHESIS A precise and testable statement about the world, specifically of the relationship between data to be measured. It is a statement about *populations* and not *samples*. Usually derived from a theoretical explanation, *(p. 7)*

INDEPENDENT GROUPS DESIGN
An *experimental design* in which participants are allocated to two (or more) groups representing different conditions. Allocation is usually done using *random techniques*. Contrast with *repeated measures design* and *matched participants design* (RIM), *(pp. 8, 9, 76)*

INDEPENDENT VARIABLE (IV) Some event that is directly manipulated by an experimenter in order to test its effect on another variable (the *dependent variable*), *(p. 4)*

informed consent An *ethical issue* and *ethical guideline* in psychological research whereby participants must be given comprehensive information concerning the nature and purpose of the research and their role in it, in order that they can make an informed decision about whether to participate, *(pp. 32, 35, 69)*

inter-interviewer reliability The extent to which two interviewers produce the same outcome from an *interview*, *(p. 49)*

internal reliability A measure of the extent to which something is consistent within itself. For a psychological test to have high internal reliability, all test items should be measuring the same thing. This can be assessed using the

split-half method. See also *reliability, (p. 52)*

internal validity An experiment is internally valid if the observed effect can be attributed to the experimental manipulation rather than some other factor. A questionnaire or observation is internally valid if it is measuring what it was intended to measure (rather than some other behaviour), *(pp. 26, 31, 53, 69)*

inter-observer reliability The extent to which there is agreement between two or more observers involved in observations of a behaviour. This is measured by correlating the observations of two or more observers. A general rule is that if (total number of agreements) / (total number of observations) > 0.80, the data have inter-observer reliability, *(pp. 69, 71)*

inter-rater reliability See *inter-observer reliability.*

INTERVAL DATA Data are measured using units of equal intervals, such as when counting correct answers or using any 'public' unit of measurement. Many psychological studies use *plastic interval scales* in which the intervals are arbitrarily determined so we cannot actually know for certain that there are equal intervals between the numbers. However, for the purposes of analysis, such data may be accepted as interval, *(pp. 15, 90, 102, 103)*

INTERVIEW A *research method* that involves a face-to-face, 'real-time' interaction with another individual and results in the collection of data. See *structured interview* and *unstructured* interview, *(pp.48, 49, 52, 53)*

interviewer bias The effect of an interviewer's expectations, communicated unconsciously, on a respondent's behaviour, *(p. 49)*

investigator The person who designs a research study and <u>may</u> conduct it. In some cases someone else (sometimes referred to as the *experimenter*) is the one who directly interacts with participants. See *investigator effects, (p. 27)*

investigator bias The effect that the investigator's expectations have on the participants and thus on the results of the experiment, *(p. 27)*

investigator effect Anything that the investigator/experimenter does which has an effect on a participant's performance in a study other than what was intended. Note that it is only the person who is interacting directly with the participant (sometimes called the *experimenter*) who creates an investigator effect. The unconscious cues from the investigator/experimenter act as a *confounding variable*. Investigator effects are not the same as *participant effects, (pp. 27, 31)*

IV see *independent variable.*

John Henry effect A *control group* might try extra hard to show that the old way is just as good or better than the new approach. This is a form of *participant effect* and a threat to *internal validity, (p. 38)*

laboratory Any setting (room or other environment) specially fitted out for conducting research. The laboratory is not the only place where scientific experiments can be conducted. It is, however, the ideal place for experiments because it permits maximum control. Laboratories are not used exclusively for experimental research; e.g. *controlled observations* are also conducted in laboratories, *(pp. 24, 37)*

LABORATORY EXPERIMENT An experiment carried out in the controlled setting of a *laboratory* and that enables the experimenter to draw conclusions about the causal relationship between the *independent* and *dependent variable, (pp. 24, 25, 28, 29, 31, 36, 37, 51)*

leading question A question that is phrased in such a way (e.g. 'Don't you agree that…?') that it makes one response more likely than another. The form or content of the question suggests what answer is desired, *(pp. 46, 49)*

LEVEL OF SIGNIFICANCE See *significance level.*

LEVELS OF MEASUREMENT The type of system or scale against which a variable is being assessed (see *nominal, ordinal interval, ratio), (p. 102)*

Likert scale A means of providing an answer to a question where respondents can indicate the extent to which they agree or disagree with a statement. There are usually five levels ranging from 'strongly agree' through 'neutral' to 'strongly disagree', *(p. 46)*

linear correlation A systematic relationship between *co-variables* that is defined by a straight line. See *curvilinear correlation, (p. 54)*

longitudinal design A form of *repeated measures design* in which participants are assessed on two or more occasions as they get older. The *IV* is age. See *longitudinal study, (p. 76)*

LONGITUDINAL STUDY A study conducted over a long period of time to compare the same individual(s) at different ages.

MATCHED PAIRS (PARTICIPANTS) DESIGN
An *experimental design* in which pairs of participants are matched in terms of key variables such as age and IQ. One member of each pair is placed in the *experimental group* and the other member in the *control group*, so that *participant variables* are better controlled than is usually the case in an *independent groups design* experiment, *(p. 9)*

mean A measure of central tendency. The arithmetic average of a group of scores, calculated by dividing the sum of the scores by the number of scores. Takes the values of all the data into account, *(p. 15)*.

MEASURES OF CENTRAL TENDENCY A descriptive statistic that provides information about a 'typical' response for a set of scores. See *mean, median, mode, (p. 15)*.

measures of dispersion A descriptive statistic that provides information about how spread out a set of scores are. See *range, standard deviation, (p. 15)*.

median A *measure of central tendency*. The middle value in a set of scores when they are placed in rank order, *(p. 15)*.

mode A *measure of central tendency*. The most frequently occurring score in a set of data, *(p. 15)*.

mundane realism Refers to how an experiment mirrors the real word. The simulated task environment is realistic to the degree to which experiences encountered in the environment will occur in the real world, *(pp. 25, 29, 31)*.

natural experiment A *research method* in which the experimenter cannot manipulate the *independent variable* directly, but where it varies naturally and the effect can be observed on a *dependent variable*. Strictly speaking, an experiment involves the deliberate manipulation of an IV by the experimenter, so causal conclusions cannot be drawn from a natural experiment. In addition, participants are not randomly allocated to conditions in a natural experiment, which may reduce *external validity*. See also *quasi-experiment, (pp. 30, 31, 70)*.

naturalistic observation A *research method* carried out in a naturalistic setting, in which the investigator does not interfere in any way but merely observes the behaviour in question, *(pp. 66, 67, 68, 70)*.

negative correlation A relationship between two *co-variables* such that as the value of one co-variable increases, that of the other decreases, *(p. 50)*.

NOMINAL DATA The data are in separate categories, such as grouping people according to their favourite football team (e.g. Liverpool, Inverness Caledonian Thistle, etc.), *(pp. 15, 102, 103)*

non-directional hypothesis A form of hypothesis that proposes a difference, correlation or association between two variables but does not specify the direction (e.g. more or less, positive or negative) of such a relationship, *(p. 7)*.

non-participant observations Observations made by someone who is not participating in the activity being observed, *(p. 68)*.

NORMAL DISTRIBUTION A symmetrical bell-shaped frequency distribution. This distribution occurs when certain variables are measured, such as IQ or the life of a light bulb. Such 'events' are distributed in such a way that most of the scores are clustered close to the mean, *(p. 102)*.

NULL HYPOTHESIS An assumption that there is no relationship (difference, association, etc.) in the population from which a sample is taken with respect to the variables being studied, *(p. 7)*.

OBJECTIVITY Being accurate and unbiased, *(pp. 68, 69, 71, 72)*.

OBSERVATION See *naturalistic observation*.

observation techniques The application of systematic methods of observation in an observation, *experiment* or other study, *(p. 67)*.

observational systems Systematic methods for recording observations such as a *coding system* or *behaviour checklist*, *(p. 67)*.

observer bias In observational studies, there is the danger that observers might 'see' what they expect to see. This reduces the *external validity* of the observations, *(pp. 69, 71)*.

ONE-TAILED HYPOTHESIS See *directional hypothesis*.

open questions In an interview or questionnaire, questions that invite the respondents to provide their own answers rather than select one of those provided. Tend to produce *qualitative data*. Answers are more difficult to analyse than those for *closed questions, (p. 46)*.

OPERATIONALISATION Ensuring that variables are in a form that can be easily tested. A concept such as 'educational attainment' or 'social development' needs to be specified more clearly if we are going to investigate it in an experiment or observational study. The researcher lists various behaviours that can be measured, such as breaking 'social development' into the following 'operations: the tendency to seek the company of others, to show enjoyment when with others, to have a number of friends, to display social skills such as negotiating with friends, etc, *(pp. 11, 25, 46, 67)*.

OPPORTUNITY SAMPLE A *sample* of participants produced by selecting people who are most easily available at the time of the study. Sometimes called availability sampling, *(p. 10)*.

order effect In a repeated measures design, a *confounding variable* arising from the order in which conditions are presented, e.g. a *practice effect* or *fatigue effect*. Counteracted by using *counterbalancing, (p. 9)*.

ORDINAL DATA Data are ordered in some way, e.g. asking people to put a list of football teams in order of liking. Liverpool might be first, followed by Inverness, etc. The 'difference' between each item is not the same; i.e. the individual may like the first item a lot more than the second, but there might only be a small difference between the items ranked second and third, *(pp. 15, 102, 103)*.

PARTICIPANT DESIGN See *experimental design*.

participant effects A general term used to acknowledge the fact that participants react to cues in an experimental situation and that this may affect the validity of any conclusions drawn from the investigation. For example, *demand characteristics*. Participant effects are not the same as *investigator effects, (p. 26)*.

participant observations Observations made by someone who is also participating in the activity being observed, which may affect their objectivity, *(p. 68)*.

participant reactivity The bias in responses that occurs because a participant knows they are being studied. See *participant effects, (pp. 26, 31)*.

PARTICIPANT VARIABLES Characteristics of individual participants (such as age, intelligence, etc.) that might influence the outcome of a study, *(pp. 9, 76)*.

pilot study A small-scale trial of a study run to test any aspects of the design, with a view to making improvements, *(p. 6)*.

placebo A condition that should have no effect on the behaviour being studied so can be used to separate out the effects of the IV from any effects caused merely by receiving any treatment, *(p. 75)*.

plastic interval scale See *interval scale*.

POPULATION (*target population*) All the people in the world. In any study, the sample of participants is drawn from a *target population, (p. 10)*.

population validity A form of *external validity*, concerning the extent to which the findings of a study can be *generalised* to other groups of people besides those who took part in the study, *(p. 28)*.

positive correlation A relationship between two *co-variables* such that as the value of one co-variable increases, this is accompanied by a corresponding increase in the other co-variable, *(p. 50)*.

practice effect A kind of *order effect*. In a repeated measures design, participants may do better on one condition rather than another because they have completed it first and are therefore more 'practised', *(p. 9)*.

presumptive consent A method of dealing with lack of *informed consent* or deception, by asking a group of people who are similar to the participants whether they would agree to take part in a study. If this group of people consent to the procedures in the proposed study, it is presumed that the real participants would agree as well, *(pp. 34, 35)*.

privacy An *ethical issue* that refers to a zone of inaccessibility of mind or body and the trust that this will not be 'invaded', *(pp. 33, 35, 49, 69)*.

procedures Can include design decisions as well as all the steps taken when a research study is conducted. See *standardised procedures, (p. 16)*.

protection from psychological harm An *ethical issue*. During a research study, participants should not experience negative psychological effects, such as lowered self-esteem or emabarrassment, *(pp. 32, 35)*.

qualitative analysis Any form of analysis that focuses more on words (i.e. what participants say) than on other forms of numerical data. Qualitative analyses interpret the meaning of an experience to the individual(s) concerned. See *grounded theory* and *thematic analysis, (p. 73)*.

QUALITATIVE DATA Data that express what people think or feel. Qualitative data cannot be counted or quantified. Qualitative data can be turned into quantitative data by placing them in categories, *(pp. 46, 48, 68)*.

quantitative analysis Any form of analysis (e.g. descriptive statistics) that uses numerical data as the basis for investigation and interpretation, *(p. 15)*.

QUANTITATIVE DATA Data that represent how much or how long, or how many, etc. there are of something; i.e. a behaviour is measured in numbers or quantities, *(pp. 46, 48, 68)*.

quasi-experiment Experiments that are not true experiments, either because the *IV* is not directly manipulated and/or because participants are not randomly allocated to conditions. Therefore, we cannot claim to investigate cause and effect relationships.

QUESTIONNAIRE A *research method* in which data are collected through the use of written questions, which may be *open* or *closed questions*. Also called a survey, *(pp. 48, 49)*.

questionnaire fallacy The erroneous belief that a questionnaire actually produces a true picture of what people do and think.

QUOTA SAMPLE See *stratified sample*.

random allocation Allocating participants to experimental groups or conditions using random techniques, *(pp. 9, 10, 31)*.

RANDOM SAMPLE A *sample* of participants produced by using a *random technique* such that every member of the *target population* being tested has an equal chance of being selected, *(p. 10)*.

random technique Any technique in which there is no systematic attempt to influence the selection or distribution of the items or participants that form part of the investigation, *(p. 10)*.

RANGE A *measure of dispersion* that measures the difference between the highest and lowest score in a set of data, *(p. 15)*.

RATIO DATA There is a true zero point, as in most measures of physical quantities, *(pp. 15, 102, 103)*.

RELIABILITY A measure of consistency both within a set of scores or items (*internal reliability*) and also over time such that it is possible to obtain the same results on subsequent occasions when the measure is used (*external reliability*). The reliability of an experiment can be determined through *replication, (pp. 52, 69)*.

REPEATED MEASURES DESIGN A type of *experimental design* in which each participant takes part in every condition under test. Contrast with *independent groups design* and *matched participants design* (RIM), *(pp. 8, 9, 76, 102)*.

replication The opportunity to repeat an investigation under the same conditions in order to test the *reliability* of its findings, *(pp. 28, 29, 52)*.

representative sample A *sample* selected so that it accurately stands for or represents the *population* being studied, *(p. 10)*.

representativeness The extent to which an experiment mirrors the real world. This is *mundane realism, (pp. 28, 29)*.

research The process of gaining knowledge through the systematic examination of data derived empirically or theoretically.

research design The overall plan of action to maximise meaningful results and minimise ambiguity using systematic research techniques, *(p. 1)*.

RESEARCH METHOD A way of conducting research (such as an *experiment* or a *questionnaire*) as distinct from the design of the investigation, *(pp. 1, 47, 66)*.

research prediction A prediction about the outcome of a study based on the *hypothesis*. The research prediction is about *samples*, whereas the hypothesis is about *populations, (p. 11)*.

research technique The specific techniques used in a variety of research methods, such as *control* of variables, *sampling* methods and *coding systems*, *(pp. 47, 66)*.

response set A tendency for interviewees to respond in the same way to all questions, regardless of context. This would bias their answers, *(p. 53)*.

RIGHT TO WITHDRAW An *ethical issue* that participants should have the right to withdraw from participating in an experiment if they are uncomfortable with the study, *(pp. 33, 35)*.

role play A controlled observation in which participants are asked to imagine how they would behave in certain situations, and act out the part. This method has the advantage of permitting one to study certain behaviours that might be unethical or difficult to find in the real world, *(p. 69)*.

sample A selection of participants taken from the *target population* being studied and intended to be *representative* of that population, *(p. 10)*.

sample bias A particular problem with questionnaire studies as certain *types* of people are more likely to complete and return the questionnaire, *(p. 49)*

sampling The process of taking a sample, *(p. 10)*.

SAMPLING TECHNIQUE/procedure The method used to *sample* participants, such as *random, opportunity* and *volunteer sampling*, or to sample behaviours in an observation such as *event* or *time sampling, (pp. 10, 67)*.

scattergraph A graphical representation of the relationship (i.e. the *correlation*) between two sets of scores, *(p. 50)*.

screw you effect A participant who knows the aims of an experiment deliberately behaves in a way to spoil an experiment. This is a form of *participant effect* and a threat to *internal validity, (p. 26)*.

semantic differential technique A method of assessing attitudes by measuring the affective component using bipolar adjectives. This means that an attitude can be evaluated on a number of different dimensions, whereas the *Likert scale* only represents one dimension of an attitude (agreement or disagreement), *(p. 46)*.

SIGNIFICANCE A statistical term indicating that the research findings are sufficiently strong to enable us to reject the *null hypothesis* and accept the research hypothesis under test, *(p. 51)*.

SIGNIFICANCE LEVEL The probability (p) that a research finding is due to the effect of the *IV* rather than chance factors, *(pp. 101, 104)*.

single blind A type of *research design* in which the participant is not aware of the research aims or of which condition of the experiment they are receiving, *(pp. 9, 26)*

SITUATIONAL VARIABLES factors in the environment that could affect the DV, so should be controlled, *(p. 12).*

social desirability bias A tendency for respondents to answer questions in such a way that presents themselves in a better light, *(pp. 26, 46, 49).*

speciesism Human intolerance or discrimination on the basis of an individual's species, *(p. 37).*

split-half method A method of determining the *internal reliability* of a test. Test items are split into two halves and the scores on both halves compared. Scores should be similar if the test is reliable, *(p. 52).*

STANDARD DEVIATION A *measure of dispersion* that shows the amount of variation in a set of scores. It assesses the spread of data around the mean, *(p. 15).*

standardised instructions A set of instructions that are the same for all participants so as to avoid *investigator effects* caused by different instructions, *(p. 12)*

standardised procedures A set of *procedures* that are the same for all participants so as to enable replication of the study to take place, *(p. 12).*

stratified sample A *sampling technique* in which groups of participants are selected in proportion to their frequency in the population in order to obtain a *representative sample*. The aim is to identify sections of the population, or strata, that need to be represented in the study. Individuals from those strata are then *randomly* selected for the study. If the sample is not randomly selected from the stratum, it is then a *quota sample*, *(p. 10).*

structured interview Any *interview* in which the questions are decided in advance, *(p. 48).*

structured observations The researcher uses various 'systems' to organise observations, such as a *sampling technique* and an *observational system*, *(p. 67).*

SUBJECTIVITY being biased e.g. as a result of expectations or theoretical perspective, *(p. 66).*

studies using a correlational analysis See *correlation*.

SURVEY See *questionnaire*.

SYSTEMATIC SAMPLE A method of obtaining a representing sample by selecting every 5th or 10th person. This can be random if the first person is selected using a random method; then you select every 10th person after this, *(p. 10)*

TARGET POPULATION The group of people that the researcher is interested in. The group of people from whom a *sample* is drawn. The group of people about whom *generalisations* can be made, *(p. 10).*

test-retest method A method used to check *reliability*. The same test or interview is given to the same participants on two occasions to see if the same results are obtained, *(p. 52).*

thematic analysis A technique used when analysng *qualitative data*. Themes or concepts are identified before starting a piece of research; then responses from an *interview* or *questionnaire* are organised according to these themes, *(p. 73).*

time sampling An observational technique in which the observer records behaviours in a given time frame, e.g. noting what a target individual is doing every 30 seconds. You may select one or more categories from a checklist. See *event sampling*, *(p. 67).*

TWO-TAILED HYPOTHESIS See *non-directional hypothesis*.

undisclosed observations Observing people without their knowledge, e.g. using one-way mirrors. Knowing that your behaviour is being observed is likely to alter your behaviour, *(p. 69).*

unstructured interview The interview starts out with some general aims and possibly some questions, and lets the interviewee's answers guide subsequent questions, *(p. 48).*

unstructured observation An observer records all relevant behaviour but has no system. The behaviour to be studied is largely unpredictable, *(p. 67).*

VALIDITY Refers to the legitimacy of a study, the extent to which the findings can be applied beyond the research setting as a consequence of the study's *internal* and/or *external validity*, *(pp. 26, 28, 29, 31, 38, 53, 69).*

VARIABLES Anything of relevance in a study that can vary or change (see *independent variable* and *dependent variable, extraneous* and *confounding variable*).

VARIANCE the average variation around the mean (the average difference from the mean of each score), *(p. 15).*

volunteer An individual who, acting on their own volition, applies to take part in an investigation, *(p. 10).*

volunteer bias A form of *sampling bias* because *volunteer* participants are usually more highly motivated than randomly selected participants, *(p. 10).*

VOLUNTEER SAMPLE A *sample* of participants produced by a *sampling technique* that relies solely on volunteers to make up the sample, *(p. 10).*

zero correlation No relationship (*correlation*) between *co-variables*, *(p. 50).*

References

Austin, J.R. (1988) The power of pictional images when ad processing involvement is low and subsequent brand evaluations are memory based. *Dissertation Abstracts International section A: Humanities and social Sciences*, 59, 241, (pp. 87, 88, 92, 93).

Baddeley, A. D. and Longman, D. J. A. (1978) The influence of length and frequency on training sessions on the rate of learning type. *Ergonomics*, 21, 627–635, (p. 29).

Bandura, A., Ross, D. and Ross, S. A. (1961) Transmission of aggression through imitation of aggressive models. *Journal of Abnormal and Social Psychology*, 63, 575–582, (pp. 25, 66).

BEO (2004) Behavioural observation, University of Bern http://www.psy.unibe.ch/beob/proj_ex.htm and http://www.psy.unibe.ch/beob/home_e.htm (accessed September 2004), (p. 29).

Berg, E.M. and Lippman, L.G. (2001) Does humour in advertising affect recognition of novel brand names? *The Journal of general Psychology*, 128, (pp. 87, 88, 92, 93).

Bickman, L. (1974) Clothes make the person. *Psychology Today*, 8(4), 48–51, (p. 24).

Brugger, P., Landis, T. and Regard, M. (1990) A 'sheep–goat effect' in repetition avoidance: extra sensory perception as an effect of subjective probability. *British Journal of Psychology*, 81, 455–468, (p. 54).

Charlton, T., Gunter, B. and Hannan, A. (eds) (2000) *Broadcast television effects in a remote community*. Hillsdale, NJ: Lawrence Erlbaum, (p. 30).

Coolican, H. (1996) *Introduction to research methods and statistics in psychology*. London: Hodder & Stoughton, (p. IV).

Coolican, H. (2004a) Personal communication, (p.30).

Coolican, H. (2004b) *Research methods and statistics in psychology* (3rd edition). London: Hodder & Stoughton, (p. IV).

Crabb, P. B. and Bielawski, D. (1994) The social representation of material culture and gender in children's books. *Sex Roles*, 10(1/2), 69–79, (p. 70).

Craik, F. I. M. and Lockhart, R. S. (1972) Levels of processing: a framework for memory research. *Journal of Verbal Learning and Verbal Behavior*, 11, 671–684, (pp. 87, 88, 93).

Craik, F.I.M. and Tulving, E. (1975) Depth of processing and the retention of words in episodic memory. *Journal of Experimental Psychology*, 104, 268–294, (p. 124).

Dicks, H. V. (1972) *Licensed mass murder: a socio-psychological study of some S.S. killers*. New York: Basic Books, (p. 38).

Ekman, P. and Friesen, W. V. (1978) *Manual for the facial action coding system*. Palo Alto, CA: Consulting Psychology Press, (p. 70).

Festinger, L., Riecken, H. W. and Schachter, S. (1956) *When prophecy fails*. Minneapolis: University of Minnesota Press, (p. 68).

Fick, K. (1993) The influence of an animal on social interactions of nursing home residents in a group setting. *American Journal of Occupational Therapy*, 47, 529–534, (p. 67).

Gilligan, C. and Attanucci, J. (1988) Two moral orientations: gender differences and similarities. *Merrill-Palmer Quarterly*, 34, 223–237, (p. 48).

Gray, J. A. (1991) On the morality of speceisism.

The Psychologist, 14, 196–198, (p. 37).

Hofling, K. C., Brontzman, E., Dalrymple, S., Graves, N. and Pierce, C. M. (1966) An experimental study in the nurse–physician relationship. *Journal of Mental and Nervous Disorders*. 43, 171–178, (pp. 29, 38).

House of Lords (2002) Select Committee on Animals in Scientific Procedures. http://www.parliament.the-stationery-office.co.uk/pa/ld200102/ldselect/ldanimal/150/15003.htm accessed December 2004, (p. 36).

Jones, W. H., Russell, D. W., and Nickel T. W. (1977) Belief in the Paranormal Scale: an instrument to measure beliefs in magical phenomena and causes. *JSAS Catalogue of Selected Documents in Psychology, 7:100* (Ms. no. 1577), (p. 62).

Jost, A. (1897) Die assoziationsfestigkeit in iher abhängigkeit von der verteilung der wiederholungen. *Zeitschrift für Psychologie*, 14, 436–472, (p. 29).

Kendrick K. M., da Costa, A. P., Leigh A. E., Hinton, M. R. and Pierce, J. W. (2001) Sheep don't forget a face. *Nature*, 414, 165–166, (p. 143).

Kohlberg, L. (1978) Revisions in the theory and practice of moral development. *Directions for Child Development*, 2, 83–88, (p. 48).

Harlow H.F. (1959) Love in infant monkeys. *Scientific American*, 200 (6), 68–74, (p. 36).

Lamb, M. E. and Roopnarine, J. L. (1979) Peer influences on sex-role development in preschoolers. *Child Development*, 50, 1219–1222, (p. 66).

Lewis, M. K. and Hill, A. J. (1998). Food advertising on British children's television: a content analysis and experimental study with nine year olds. *International Journal of Obesity*, 22, 206–214, (p. 71).

Mandel, D. R. (1998) The obedience alibi: Milgram's account of the Holocaust reconsidered. *Analyse und Krtik: Zeitschrift für Sozialwissenschaften*, 20, 74–94, (p. 38).

Middlemist, D. R., Knowles, E. S. and Matter, C. F. (1976) Personal space invasions in the lavatory: suggestive evidence for arousal. *Journal of Personality and Social Psychology*, 33, 541–546, (p. 31).

Milgram, S. (1963) Behavioural study of obedience. *Journal of Abnormal and Social Psychology*, 67, 371–378, (pp. 29, 38).

Morgan, E. (1995) Measuring time with a biological clock. *Biological Sciences Review*, 7, 25, (p. 36).

Morris, R. G. M., Garrud, P., Rawlins, J. N. P., & O'Keefe, J. (1982). Place navigation impaired in rats with hippocampal lesions. *Nature*, 297, 681–683, (p. 36).

Peterson, L. R. and Peterson, M.J. (1959) Short-term retention of individual verbal items. *Journal of Experimental Psychology*, 58, 193–198, (p. 25).

Pieter, R, Warlop, L. and Wedel, M. (2002) Breaking through the clutter: Benefits of advertisement originality and familiarity for brand attention and memory. *Management Science*, 48 (6), 765–781, (pp. 87, 92, 93).

Piliavin, I. M., Rodin, J. and Piliavin, J. A. (1969) Good Samaritanism: an underground phenomenon. *Journal of Personality and Social*

Psychology, 13, 1200–1213, (p. 25).

Rank, S. G. and Jacobsen, C. K. (1977) Hospital nurses' compliance with medication overdose orders: a failure to replicate. *Journal of Health and Social Behaviour*, 18, 188–193, (p. 29).

Regan, T. (1984) The Case for Animal Rights. New York: Routledge, (p. 37).

Roethlisberger, F. J., and Dickson, W. J. (1939) *Management and the worker: an account of a research program conducted by the Western Electric Company, Chicago*. Cambridge, MA: Harvard University Press, (p. 25).

Rosenthal, R. and Fode, K. L. (1963) The effect of experimenter bias on the performance of the albino rat. *Behavioural Science*, 8(3), 183–189, (p. 19).

Ryback, R. S. (1969) The use of the goldfish as a model for alcohol amnesia in man. *Quarterly Journal of Studies on Alcohol*, 30, 877–882, (p. 4).

Schellenberg, E.G. (2004) Music lessons enhance IQ. *Psychological Science*, 15, 511–514, (p. 30).

Schultheiss, O.C., Wirth, M.M. and Stanton, S. (2004) Effects of affilaton and power motivation arousal on salivary progesterone and testosterone. Hormones and Behavior, 46 (5), 592–599, (p. 40).

Schunk, D. H. (1983) Reward contingencies and the development of children's skills and self-efficacy. *Journal of Educational Psychology*, 75, 511–518, (p. 25).

Singer, P. (1975) Animal Liberation, New York: Avon.

Sneddon, L. U., Braithwaite, V. A., Gentle, M. J., Broughton, B. and Knight, P (2003) 'Trout trauma puts anglers on the hook', Proceedings from the Royal Society, April 30, (p. 37).

Stroop, J. R. (1935) Studies of interference in serial verbal reactions. *Journal of Experimental Psychology*, 18, 643–662, (p. 6).

Veitch, R. and Griffitt, W. (1976) Good news, bad news: affective and interpersonal effects. *Journal of Applied Social Psychology*, 6, 69–75, (p. 25).

Waynforth, D. and Dunbar, R. I. M. 1995. Conditional mate choice strategies in humans – evidence from lonely-hearts advertisements. *Behaviour*, 132, 755 779, (p. 71).

Weick, K. E., Gilfillian, D. P. and Keith, T. A. (1973) The effect of composer credibility on orchestra performance. *Sociometry*, 36, 435–462, (p. 4).

White, G. L., Fishbein, S. and Rutstein, J. (1981) Passionate love and the misattribution of arousal. *Journal of Personality and Social Psychology*, 41, 56–62, (p. 14).

Widdowson, E. M. (1951) Mental contentment and physical growth. *Lancet*, 1, 1316–1318, (p. 30).

Williams, T. M. (1985) Implications of a natural experiment in the developed world for research on television in the developing world. *Journal of Cross Cultrual Psychology* 16(3) Special issue, 263–287, (p. 30).

Zuckerman, M. (1994) *Behavioral experssions and biosocial bases of sensation seeking*. New York: Cambridge University Press, (p. 53).